A Dictionary of Diplomacy
Second edition

Also by G. R. Berridge

*DIPLOMACY AT THE UN (*co-editor with A. Jennings*)

*DIPLOMACY: Theory and Practice (*second edition*)

*DIPLOMATIC THEORY FROM MACHIAVELLI TO KISSINGER (with Maurice Keens-Soper and T. G. Otte)

*ECONOMIC POWER IN ANGLO-SOUTH AFRICAN DIPLOMACY: Simonstown, Sharpeville and After

INTERNATIONAL POLITICS: States, Power and Conflict since 1945 (*third edition*)

THE POLITICS OF THE SOUTH AFRICA RUN: European Shipping and Pretoria

*RETURN TO THE UN: United Nations Diplomacy in Regional Conflicts

*SOUTH AFRICA, THE COLONIAL POWERS AND 'AFRICAN DEFENCE': The Rise and Fall of the White Entente, 1948–60

*TALKING TO THE ENEMY: How States without 'Diplomatic Relations' Communicate

Also by Alan James

THE BASES OF INTERNATIONAL ORDER (*editor*)

*BRITAIN AND THE CONGO CRISIS, 1960–63

*KEEPING THE PEACE IN THE CYPRUS CRISIS OF 1963–64

*PEACEKEEPING IN INTERNATIONAL POLITICS

THE POLITICS OF PEACEKEEPING

SOVEREIGN STATEHOOD: The Basis of International Society

STATES IN A CHANGING WORLD (*co-editor with Robert H. Jackson*)

*from the same publishers

A Dictionary of Diplomacy

Second Edition

G. R. Berridge
Emeritus Professor of International Politics
University of Leicester

Alan James
Emeritus Professor of International Relations
Keele University

Editorial consultant

Sir Brian Barder
Formerly British High Commissioner in
Australia and Nigeria and British Ambassador to Bénin, Poland and Ethiopia

First edition published by Palgrave Macmillan 2001

Second edition published 2003 by
PALGRAVE MACMILLAN
Houndmills, Basingstoke, Hampshire RG21 6XS and
175 Fifth Avenue, New York, N. Y. 10010
Companies and representatives throughout the world

PALGRAVE MACMILLAN is the global academic imprint of the Palgrave Macmillan division of St. Martin's Press, LLC and of Palgrave Macmillan Ltd. Macmillan® is a registered trademark in the United States, United Kingdom and other countries. Palgrave is a registered trademark in the European Union and other countries.

ISBN 1 4039 15350 hardback
ISBN 1 4039 15369 paperback

This book is printed on paper suitable for recycling and made from fully managed and sustained forest sources.

A catalogue record for this book is available from the British Library.

A catalogue record for this book is available from the Library of Congress.

10   9   8   7   6   5   4   3   2   1
12 11 10 09 08 07 06 05 04 03

Printed and bound in Great Britain by
Antony Rowe Ltd, Chippenham and Eastbourne

To GRB's children:
Catherine and William

and AJ's grandchildren:
Elizabeth, David, and Thomas
Violet, Jada, Jem, and Jasper
Reniece and Taija
Joshua, Daniel, and Timothy

Contents

Preface to the First Edition

Peaceful contacts between independent groups have always, since the start of human time, required the kind of representational activity which has come to be known as diplomacy. In its modern form – that is, throughout the last half-millennium or so – diplomacy has retained a broadly constant character and given rise to a burgeoning diplomatic profession. Like all professions, it has spawned its own terminology and categories; and inasmuch as its activity concerned relations between proud and jealous sovereigns, later replaced by no less proud and jealous sovereign states, diplomatic language has been finely honed and carries very precise meanings. It also bears the marks of having found expression in the languages of civilizations beyond those of the West. Furthermore – and again accentuated by the very sensitive nature of this particular representational task – issues of protocol and precedence have been of considerable significance, and have made their distinctive contribution to diplomatic terms. Thus it occasions no surprise at all that diplomacy has, over the centuries, developed a lexicon of specialized words and of other technical usages which it necessarily employs. And as diplomats routinely deal not just with matters of policy but also with the many legal issues which arise between states, these aspects of their work have also made their marks in the diplomatic vocabulary.

During the last half-century, however, the day-to-day language of diplomacy has been enormously augmented as a result of the quantitative revolution which the activity has undergone. The agenda of diplomacy has widened hugely, as almost everything (it seems) has become a legitimate subject of international discussion. The economic connections of states, in particular, have become much more extensive and elaborate. The development of common bilateral and multilateral standards in a variety of fields has meant that the legal framework within which international relations take place has greatly expanded, and the lengthened jurisdictional reach of states, made possible by technological advance, has also added markedly to the growth of international law. International organizations have multiplied, often being the venue for the extra diplomatic business which the just-mentioned changes have generated. And each of them, as is to be expected, has contributed its own layer to the terminology in which diplomatic intercourse is customarily carried on. The essence of diplomacy is unchanged: as always, it has to do with promoting and justifying states' interests. But in content and expression, as in busyness and complexity, it has grown way beyond its condition earlier in the century.

It is hoped that this *Dictionary* will be a valuable tool of reference for anyone who has dealings with the diplomatic maze. Historians of diplomacy, their close cousins the diplomatic historians, and all students of international relations can turn to this book for assistance in understanding the technicalities of diplomatic and related language which crop up in their subject matters. More especially, an attempt has been made to cater for the needs of the increasing number of graduate students of diplomacy. The terms they commonly come across in their reading often require elucidation; and references to the 'great names' in diplomacy sometimes lack the biographical material which helps to bring such figures to life. Such information is, we trust, supplied within. Most immediately, however, the authors have in mind the less senior members of the now-very-numerous diplomatic establishments. We have aimed to answer their queries about the ways and preoccupations of what can easily seem a somewhat arcane profession; and to provide explanations for key terms concerning the legal and political contexts within which diplomacy takes place. With this help, they may even become more successful at their tasks. Certainly, we believe, they will thereby obtain a better understanding of what the diplomatic life entails.

We should like to pay tribute to Maurice Keens-Soper, who originally suggested the idea of a *Dictionary of Diplomacy*, and to the many people who have provided us with ideas for entries, details for inclusion, and criticism of first drafts. In particular, we must thank Peter Bursey, Jane Crellin, Maurice Dalton, David Dunlop (for the introduction to whom we thank Mark Brady), Saikat Dutta, Robin Gorham, Nevil Hagon, Lt Col. John Kimmins, Jane Loeffler, Anton Loubser, Alexandra McLeod, Simon Malpas, Stanley Martin, Jörg Monar, Marcia Morris, Syed Sharfuddin, and Sue Smith; additionally we would like to thank the staffs of the national archives of Britain, Canada, Ireland, South Africa, and the United States, and also of the Lyndon Baines Johnson Library and the *Service Culturel* of the French Embassy in London. We both wish to recognize, too, the excellent work done on this manuscript by our copy editor, Anne Rafique. G. R. Berridge also wishes to acknowledge that the Study Leave granted to him by the University of Leicester in the first half of 1999 was of great assistance in the completion of this project.

The authors must give special thanks for the efforts on their behalf of their Editorial Consultant, Sir Brian Barder, not least for the speed with which – in trying circumstances – he turned round the first draft of the manuscript of this book. It came as no surprise to us to learn (from another source) that during his distinguished diplomatic career he was himself the cause of the introduction of at least one new diplomatic term: the 'bardergram'. Although we have never seen one, we have benefited hugely from his many e-mails and on this basis deduce the following definition as our token of appreciation to him:

> **bardergram**. An ambassadorial *telegram which is at once robust and graceful. The bardergram, which may be pithy in expression and passionate in tone, is not always short and is usually fired in salvos. It ends typically with the following statement: 'I await your homicidal riposte.'

We must add that we have often used lower case, for example 'note' rather than 'Note', in spite of his strenuous protests.

Finally, we would both like to thank our wives most warmly for contributions they have made to the *Dictionary*. Sheila Berridge has advised on French and German terms, while Lorna Lloyd has supplied much material discovered during her own archival research, suggested a number of subjects for inclusion, answered questions, and made comments on certain entries. Lorna Lloyd has also kindly let us use her Guide to the Key Articles of the Vienna Convention on Diplomatic Relations (1961), which precedes the text of the Convention at the end of the book. We are both very lucky.

G. R. BERRIDGE and ALAN JAMES

Preface to the Second Edition

In this second edition of *A Dictionary of Diplomacy* we have added a considerable number of entries, excluded some which no longer seemed significant,
reworked others in the light of further reflection, and corrected a few errors.
We would like to thank all of those who offered criticisms of the first edition
and suggested new entries for inclusion in this one, notably Lorna Lloyd
(who also gave much valuable advice) and Kishan Rana. For most helpful
advice on particular points, we would like to thank John Duncan, Malcolm
Shaw, and the Treaty Section of the FCO. For her sharp but ever tactful copy-
editing, we are again in debt to Anne Rafique. Last but not least we must
record our warm thanks to our editorial consultant, Sir Brian Barder, for
bringing once more to bear on our drafts his great wisdom, long professional
experience, good humour, and effortless mastery of Outlook Express.

The authors are aware that, despite the best efforts of their various helpers,
sins of commission as well as omission will have been made in this book.
Since in due time they would like to produce a further edition, they would
be grateful to any reader who would care to identify mistakes or propose new
entries. If so moved, please write to Professor G. R. Berridge at the
Department of Politics, University of Leicester, Leicester LE1 7RH, England or
e-mail gb@grberridge.co.uk

G. R. BERRIDGE and ALAN JAMES
FEBRUARY 2003

Notes on Using the Dictionary

In using the *Dictionary* the following points should be noted:

- Each entry consists of a title or catchword, and such material as seems appropriate. An *asterisk preceding a word in an entry signifies that there is a separate entry on the term – or one of its close derivatives – beginning with this word in the *Dictionary*. However, a term is only asterisked if it seems that reference to it might help the reader to understand the entry in which the asterisk appears. Any other useful cross references are indicated by an italicized instruction at the end of the entry concerned.

- Where there is more than one usage or 'sense' of the term, this is indicated by insertion of the numbers '(1)', '(2)' and so on before each separate definition. When there is an asterisked reference to another entry which has more than one sense, the one to which the cross reference is directed is numerically indicated by the use of such terms as '(sense 1)'.

- As a rule, the English version of technical diplomatic terms has been employed in preference to the French ones, except where it remains conventional to employ French.

- The style of entries is *ex cathedra* and, as a result, we only rarely cite authorities to support our definitions. Nevertheless, our debt to certain works is considerable and the ones on which we have placed greatest reliance are listed in the Bibliography at the end of the *Dictionary*.

- We have followed the convention of using the words 'diplomacy', 'diplomat' and 'diplomatic' in references to the years before the late eighteenth century, though we are aware that this is anachronistic since it was only at that time that these words entered the English language.

- References to the 'early modern period' signify that time between the end of the middle ages (mid-fifteenth century) and the French revolution (1789), and to the 'late modern period' that extending from that fateful event to the end of the Second World War in 1945. The period since 1945 is described as the 'contemporary period'.

- In accordance with wide practice, and notwithstanding the fact that in formal (and also geographical) terms Northern Ireland is not part of Britain, the term 'Britain' is generally used when referring to the state whose official name is 'the United Kingdom of Great Britain and Northern Ireland'.

- The use of acronyms has been minimized, and only in the cases of certain ones which are exceptionally well known, such as 'NATO' and 'CIA', are they used as entry titles on their subjects. When acronyms are used in the body of an entry the names which they represent are generally spelled out on first use.

- The *Dictionary* is not conceived as a handbook of protocol, and has sought to avoid the minutiae of that area. Nonetheless, points relating to protocol have from time to time necessarily been touched upon.

A

abrogation. Often used to describe a *unilateral act which brings or purports to bring an unwelcome international obligation to an end. Unless the legal arrangement in question provides for abrogation, such an act has no legal effect. It is a synonym for denunciation.

abstention. The decision, in a multilateral forum, to refrain from voting either for or against a proposed *resolution. *See also* constructive abstention.

acceptance and approval. *See* ratification.

accession. Sometimes employed in the same sense as *ratification; but also used more specifically to mean adhesion to a *treaty by a state which is not an original signatory to that treaty.

accord. *See* agreement.

accredited diplomatic representative. Another way of describing a *head of mission or, more generally, a *diplomatic agent. Occasionally, however, it may be given as a formal title to a representative to whom the *receiving state accords *diplomatic privileges and immunities, but who is not eligible for *diplomatic status because the sending entity does not enjoy *sovereignty (sense 1), or because its sovereignty is widely denied by other states. During the 1960s and 1970s this title was given to the representative in South Africa of the non-sovereign Federation of Rhodesia and Nyasaland and then of the controversially-independent entity of Rhodesia.

accredited representative. Yet another way of describing a *head of mission or, more generally, a *diplomatic agent. Occasionally, however, it may be given as a formal title to: (1) a representative of an entity which is thought, probably by the *receiving state, to lack the entitlement to appoint agents with *diplomatic status. In 1939 South Africa's representative to

Canada was given this title, reflecting South Africa's wish to avoid the non-sovereign-sounding title of *high commissioner, and Canada's refusal to give diplomatic status to the representative of a *dominion. This title had also been used by South Africa for the head of her *permanent delegation to the *League of Nations. During the Second World War the term was used to designate the Australian and New Zealand members of the British War Cabinet. *See also* polred, representative. (2) A representative of a *sovereign state with which the receiving state is not in *diplomatic relations (sense 1), and to whom the latter does not therefore accord the normal range of *diplomatic privileges and immunities. Such an individual may head a *representative office.

accreditation. (1) Furnishing a *head of mission with *credentials. In most cases these consist of *letters of credence, but *high commissioners are given either *letters of commission or a *letter of introduction. (2) More generally, the appointment of an individual as a head of mission or as a member of a diplomatic mission.

acquis communautaire. The accumulated legislation (including judgments of the Court of Justice) and political practice which has developed within the *European Union. Any new member must accept the *acquis* in full.

acte de présence. An appearance made by a *head of mission or post at a diplomatic function chiefly as a sign of respect and in order to be observed in attendance. *See also* national day; representation (sense 2).

acte finale. *See* final act.

acting head of mission. *See* acting high commissioner; acting permanent representative; chargé d'affaires *ad interim*.

acting high commissioner. (1) The diplomat who acts as the head of a *high commission during the *high commissioner's temporary absence or pending the arrival of a new high commissioner. The *receiving state's foreign ministry must be informed of the appointment of an acting high commissioner by the high commissioner or, if that is not possible, by the *sending state's foreign ministry. As is implied, the term *chargé d'affaires *ad interim* is not used in high commissions. (2) Where a high commissioner is non-resident in a particular capital, but an office of the high commission is maintained there, its head (if not of a very junior capacity) is likely to be designated acting high commissioner.

acting permanent representative. The member of a *permanent mission who, during the temporary absence of the *permanent representative, acts as such. As is therefore implied, the term *chargé d'affaires *ad interim* is not used in permanent missions.

Act of Anne. The name by which the (British) Diplomatic Privileges Act of 1708 is often known. It was passed in response to the embarrassment of Queen Anne at the inability of her courts to punish under the common law those responsible for the arrest and detention of M. de Matveev, the Russian ambassador in London, to enforce payment of debts. She immediately procured his release and expressed her regret, but he left the country in high dudgeon and without presenting the *letters of recall which he had been carrying when bundled out of his coach. Further measures were called for: amidst much pomp, the British envoy to Russia presented the Queen's apologies to the Tsar; and as an indication of Britain's determination to prevent such a thing happening again, the Act was passed. Besides declaring the proceedings against the ambassador null and void, it stated that all such civil proceedings which might in future be instituted against ambassadors, their *families, and their domestic servants would also be null and void – and that those who instituted them would be deemed 'violators of the law of nations' and would suffer such 'pains, penalties, and corporal punishment' as might be imposed. Certainly in its giving domestic servants complete protection against civil proceedings, the Act went beyond the then *customary international law on diplomacy, but

this was another aspect of the Queen's endeavour to mollify the Tsar. The Act remained in force for the next two-and-a-half centuries. *See also* service staff; Sheriffs' List.

act of formal confirmation. *See* ratification.

adhesion. A synonym for *accession.

ad hoc diplomacy. A term which is sometimes used to refer to diplomacy conducted by intermittent or sporadic means, such as a *roving ambassador or a *special mission. It is therefore to be distinguished from the conduct of diplomacy through *resident and *permanent missions.

ad hoc diplomat. This phrase does not have a specialized meaning. It is sometimes used: (1) as a way of describing the role played by the holders of political office – the head of government, for example, or the minister for foreign affairs – when they are engaged in diplomatic activity. Such activity might take place at a *summit meeting, an *international organization, or at an international conference; and (2) to designate the members of a *special mission.

***ad interim*.** A way of indicating that an office or arrangement is held or made temporarily, as in *chargé d'affaires *ad interim*.

adjudication. A process for settling disputes, possibly **ex aequo et bono* but almost always on the basis of *international law. It may take the form of resort to *arbitration or to *judicial settlement. In the former case, adjudication involves the establishment by the parties of an ad hoc tribunal, and their determination of the law which the arbitral tribunal is to apply (such matters being dealt with in a *compromis*). In the latter case, the dispute is taken to an already-existing judicial body, the statute of which sets out the manner in which it is to operate, including the law that it is to apply. States may agree in advance that a certain class of dispute shall be taken to *compulsory adjudication.

administrative and technical staff. A category identified by the Vienna Convention on *Diplomatic Relations (1961) within what used to be called the 'ambassador's suite', these are the members of the staff of a diplomatic mission who carry out, for example, interpreting, secretarial, clerical, financial, and communications tasks. They are distinguished from the *diplomatic staff on the one hand and the *service or domestic staff on the other. Controversially, however, the Vienna Convention gave them (and their immediate families) almost the same range of *privileges and immunities as diplomats, and certainly all the important ones. See *also* family of a diplomatic agent.

adoption. The formal act by which a *treaty is agreed by the states involved in a negotiation or by the *international organization within which the negotiation has taken place. The *signature of a treaty is also said to mark its adoption by the state concerned.

ad referendum. This phrase indicates that a decision or an informal agreement by a diplomat has been made without specific instructions, and is therefore conditional on the action being approved.

adviser. A designation sometimes used for the less senior members of a member state's *permanent mission to an international organization. The United States is a notable follower of this practice in respect of its mission to the United Nations. *See also* service adviser.

advisory opinion. The answer to a question on a point of law put to the *International Court of Justice by organs of the United Nations or the *specialized agencies authorized to make such a request. In such proceedings there are neither parties nor a dispute which the Court has to decide – or at least, not in a formal sense. Nor is the opinion *binding on the organ which has sought it, although it is unlikely to be disregarded. The *Permanent Court of International Justice was also empowered to give advisory opinions.

advisory treaty. A *treaty between a colonial power and a tribal ruler under which, in return for patronage and other favours (typically money and weapons), the latter undertook to accept political advice only from the former.

affirmative vote. A 'yes' vote. Affirmative votes do not include *'abstentions'.

African Union (AU). The AU was founded in 2002 as the successor to the Organization of African Unity, which was established in 1963 to foster African unity and solidarity. Modelled loosely on the *European Union, the AU's principal policy-making organ is the Assembly of heads of state and government. There is in addition an Executive Council composed of ministers of foreign affairs or other ministers; a Permanent Representative Committee; a Commission based at headquarters and directed by the Chairperson of the AU; and a set of Specialized Technical Committees established within the secretariat and headed by Commissioners. It is also hoped that there will be more *'civil society' participation in the AU than in the old OAU. The headquarters remains in Addis Ababa.

agency system. *See* agent (sense 4).

agenda. (1) The list of topics to be discussed in a negotiation. This is itself an important subject in *prenegotiations, when the order in which topics are to be taken as well as the nature of the topics themselves should be agreed. (2) In the phrase 'hidden agenda', the term has the related meaning of 'aims'; hence hidden or secret aims.

agent. (1) In the early modern period and for some time afterwards, the lowest of *diplomatic ranks (sense 1). Agents were maintained at courts where commercial advantages might be obtained by their presence but political interests were marginal. George III, the eighteenth century British king forced to grant independence to his American colonies, thought that this was the most appropriate level at which to establish relations with the new United States. (2) In conjunction with 'diplomatic', the term is used to refer to a *diplomat. (3) A representative of a state or territory who lacks *diplomatic status. In some circumstances such an agent may be termed an 'agent-general' or 'delegate-general'. *See* non-diplomatic agent. (4) A clerk in the eighteenth and early nineteenth century *Foreign Office employed by a British diplomat as his private banker. Attempts to abolish the 'agency system', as it was known, had been made since the latter decades of the eighteenth century. However, in the face of strong resistance in the Foreign Office, where it was regarded as providing useful supplementary income to official salaries, it did not finally come to an end until 1870. (5) An abbreviated way of referring to a *secret agent. *See also* agent in place.

agent-general. The title generally given to the representative in London of a constituent State of the *federal state of Australia, and of a constituent Province of the federal state of Canada. Most Australian states but only a minority of Canadian provinces have such representation. Such representatives do not enjoy *diplomatic status. But Britain accords them privileges and immunities at the level specified in the Vienna Convention on *Consular Relations (1963). *See also* agent (sense 3).

agent in place. A person with access to highly sensitive information (for example in a ministry, intelligence agency or weapons research establishment) who delivers this, usually on a regular basis, to an intelligence agency of another state. Agents in place are not persons 'planted' in such positions but are nationals of the state in which they live and are usually long-serving and trusted employees. It is for these reasons that they are regarded as priceless *'humint assets' by agencies charged with gathering *foreign intelligence (sense 1).

aggression. An attack by one state on another that is unwarranted in any one or more of three respects: politics, law, and morality. At all these levels there is often disagreement as to whether an attack is warranted or not. The UN has tried to clarify the matter by seeking a definition of aggression and in 1974 its *General Assembly managed to agree on one by *consensus. But the eight-article definition still left much scope for argument, in any particular case, about its proper interpretation and application.

agréation. See *agrément.*

agreed minutes. *See* minutes.

agreement. Whenever the term is used with a degree of formality, a name often given to certain international legal *instruments. It is generally employed with regard to those which are relatively informal in expression, limited in scope, and do not have many *parties. *See also* executive agreement.

agrément. Earlier described as '*agréation*', the formal agreement by a *receiving state to accept a named individual as *head of a diplomatic mission. Obtaining such agreement before an individual is despatched (in practice, before a name is publicly announced) is a firm requirement under the Vienna Convention on *Diplomatic Relations (1961) – although when addressing such requests to *Commonwealth states, Britain does not use the term '*agrément*'. A refusal of *agrément* may be prompted by objections either to the personal character or past record of the proposed new head of mission. This does not require justification but often comes out. In 1997 the Turkish government refused *agrément* to Ehud Toledano, who had been nominated by the Israeli government as its new ambassador to Ankara. Turkish officials stated that Toledano, an academic specializing in Ottoman history, had given a pro-Armenian account of the massacre of 1.5million Armenians by Turkish troops in the First World War in an Israeli radio interview in 1981. The Vienna Convention on Diplomatic Relations also states that a receiving state 'may' require the names of *service attachés to be submitted beforehand for its approval as well. It appears to be customary for all members of *interests sections to require *agrément.*

aide-mémoire. A written statement of a government's attitude on a particular question which is left by a diplomatic agent with the *interlocutor, typically a ministry official, to whom an oral presentation has just been made. Occasionally known as a *pro-memoria* or simply as a 'memorandum', it is usually handed over in person by the diplomat at the end of the interview, or if necessary delivered shortly afterwards with a covering *note attached. As a result, the *aide-mémoire* has no need for marks of provenance or courtesy and bears little resemblance to a note. It has no address or embassy stamp, contains no salutations, and is unsigned. Instead, the classic *aide-mémoire* is simply headed *Aide-Mémoire* and dated at the end. Its

purpose is to reinforce the representations made by the diplomat and – in case he or she should have forgotten to mention some important point, made a mess of a second, or given insufficient or too much emphasis to a third – leave no room for ambiguity about the attitude of his or her government. Since it will only be in exceptional circumstances that its text is not also the main part of the diplomat's own script, the *aide-mémoire* is well named: it is an aid to everyone's memory. The more junior the official to whom a statement has been made, the more important it is that its contents be confirmed by an *aide-mémoire.*

air adviser. *See* air attaché.

air attaché. An air force officer temporarily attached to a diplomatic mission. As between member states of the *Commonwealth, the equivalent individual is designated as an 'air adviser'. *See also* service attaché.

Air Force One. The radio call-sign of any US Air Force aircraft carrying the president of the United States. (If he flies on an Army plane this becomes Army One; if on a Navy aircraft Navy One.) Dedicated presidential air transport began in 1944, though this call-sign was not used until the 1950s and first applied popularly to the Boeing 707 introduced for President Kennedy at the beginning of the following decade. In current practice, Air Force One is the name and call-sign given to one or other of the two extensively modified Boeing 747-200Bs which, since the beginning of the 1990s, have been maintained for use by the President. They have conference facilities, aerial refuelling capability, sophisticated defences (including shielded wiring to counter the effects of nuclear blast, as well as anti-radar and missile protection), and encrypted communications. As a result, Air Force One is an adjunct to US *summit diplomacy (as well as presidential travel within the United States) of great symbolic as well as practical significance.

airgram. A *State Department term for a formal diplomatic communication sent in the *diplomatic bag by air when a *telegram was considered too laborious (if encoding was needed), or (because of its length) too expensive. The airgram fell into disuse when telegrams became a more cost-effective means of communication.

air space. The area lying immediately above the land and the sea of a state's territory. Each state enjoys *sovereignty (sense 2) over the air space above its territory and its *territorial sea at least up to the height at which the density of the air is sufficient for conventional aircraft to fly. How far state sovereignty extends beyond that is unclear, but state practice suggests that the flight through the higher air space of objects launched for peaceful or scientific purposes is in any event permissible. The passage through airspace of all types of foreign aircraft – scheduled services, military planes and private ones – requires the consent of the subjacent state. It was the First World War (1914–18) which precipitated general acceptance of the doctrine of state sovereignty over air space. Previously, its status had been contentious.

Aix-la-Chapelle,   Congress   of (1818). *See* Regulation of Vienna; resident.

alliance. A *treaty entered into by two or more states to engage in cooperative military action in specified circumstances. With the advent of nuclear weapons in the second half of the twentieth century, alliances were increasingly concluded in the hope of deterring the outbreak of war rather than with a ready willingness to fight in one. Accordingly (and also for strategic reasons), these recent alliances have often, from the time of their making, involved detailed contingency planning and complex organizational arrangements. The hallmark of an alliance, compared to an *entente, is the precision of its commitments. *See also* NATO; Warsaw Pact.

Alliance Française. The chief vehicle of French *cultural diplomacy. Founded in 1880, the *Alliance Française* was an influential model for other states, not least Britain.

alliance of convenience. In French an *alliance à rebours*, an *alliance between opposites inspired by a common peril. In English the phrase 'marriage of convenience' is sometimes employed.

all necessary means. A euphemistic (some might say diplomatic!) way of referring to armed force.

all-source analysis. An *intelligence community term for the analysis of information on foreign targets gathered from all sources, including reports from all the different collection agencies and diplomatic and consular missions abroad. This work is conducted by some central agency such as the *CIA in the United States or the *Joint Intelligence Committee in Britain. It is often referred to as 'intelligence assessment'.

alphabetical seating. When *seating arrangements at a *multilateral conference or *international organization are arranged alphabetically, each participating or member state is placed on the basis of its own rendering of its name in the language to be used at the conference or organization in question. The choice of language, however, could turn on political expediency. At a meeting in November 2002 of the Euro-Atlantic Partnership Council (which is linked with *NATO), members' names were rendered in French rather than the usual English, so as to ensure that Britain's prime minister did not have to sit next to the president of Ukraine, relations between the two states then being particularly fraught. *See also* Commonwealth; name of a state; precedence (c).

alternat. The procedure whereby as many original copies of a *treaty or other document are drawn up as there are signatories. By this means each state is able to have its own copy and – more importantly – its own *head of state and *plenipotentiaries named first in the preamble of this copy. These plenipotentiaries are also able to sign this copy before the plenipotentiaries of the other *parties. Thus the signatories alternate in occupying the place of honour in the treaty.

One of a number of devices designed to alleviate the rancour aroused by arguments between states over *precedence, the alternat appears first to have come into vogue in Europe in the sixteenth century. The flaw in this system of treaty signature, of course, was that it assumed universal acceptance of the principle that each state was *entitled* to participate in a 'rotation in precedence'. It assumed, in other words, precisely that equality between states the perceived absence of which had led to arguments over precedence in the first place. Not surprisingly, it was not universally accepted and disputes over whether or not one state 'had the alternat' with another became just another vehicle of *power politics. France, for example, did not grant the alternat to Russia until

1779. Nevertheless, the idea of equality within classes of states (especially the class of *great powers), coupled with the force of established precedents, gave currency to the system and it remains the usual practice in signing bilateral treaties today. (Where there are language differences between the parties each state's own copy also displays the version in its own language first, that is, on the left-hand page or column.) In light of the great growth in the number of states in the twentieth century, however, it is not surprising that the alternat has been abandoned for multilateral treaties, where it is regarded as much more convenient to sign just one original in the agreed *alphabetical order of the names of the participating states.

alternate representative. A member of a *permanent mission to an *international organization who has been nominated and accepted as an alternate to a member state's representative on an organ of the organization which (as is customary) limits the number of permissible representatives.

Amarna letters. An archive of diplomatic correspondence exchanged in the fourteenth century BC between the Egyptian king and neighbouring courts, some of which were his *vassals while others were also 'great kings'. The archive, which consists of 382 cuneiform tablets, was written chiefly in Akkadian, the *diplomatic language (sense 3) of the time. It takes its name from the place of its discovery in 1887: El Amarna, a plain on the east bank of the Nile about 190 miles south of Cairo which was the site of the capital of Egypt for a short period in the fourteenth century BC. The correspondence is unique in the extent of the insights that it provides into the diplomatic system of the Ancient Near East. An authoritative English translation, resting on the steady advance in understanding of the letters during the twentieth century, was published by William L. Moran in 1992. *See also* cuneiform diplomacy.

ambassador. A *diplomatic agent of the highest *rank. More particularly the title is used:

(1) In most cases, to designate the *head of a diplomatic mission to a foreign state where that head, as among heads of mission, falls into the first *diplomatic class. By derivation, the mission in question is then called an *embassy. An embassy has just one ambassador. Usually such agents are formally described as the ambassador of [the *sending state] to [the *receiving state]. When at their posts, Britain refers to her ambassadors as 'Her Majesty's Ambassador'; but if this usage could give rise to ambiguity (because of the presence of other ambassadors from states with a female head of state), they are referred to as 'Her Britannic Majesty's Ambassador'.

(2) Almost invariably, to designate a member state's *permanent

representative to the UN and some other international organizations. An exception may (but will by no means necessarily) occur if that individual is not a regular member of his or her state's *diplomatic service; thus, when Lord Caradon, Minister of State in Britain's government, was her permanent representative to the UN (1964–70), he was not called ambassador. A state's permanent mission to an international organization may include more than one individual with this title – but only one of them can be the state's permanent representative, who is also the head of mission.

(3) In some states, as a courtesy title given to those who have served as an ambassador in either of the above two senses. Britain does not follow this practice; the United States does.

Ambassadors in senses 1 and 2 are always called His or Her *Excellency; and their full title is Ambassador *Extraordinary and *Plenipotentiary.

Ambassadors in sense 1 require the *agrément of the receiving state before they can be appointed. Inasmuch as an ambassador is, in form, the personal representative of the *head of state, he or she will probably be received by the head of the sending state before (or soon after) taking up the appointment. This is certainly the practice in Britain.

The heads of diplomatic missions exchanged between members of the *Commonwealth are called *high commissioners, not ambassadors. But in point of status and function there are no differences whatsoever between ambassadors and high commissioners (although in London some small differences of treatment continue to exist).

See also envoy; full powers; resident; Rosier, Bernard du; roving ambassador.

ambassador-at-large. See roving ambassador.

ambassador's suite. See family of a diplomatic agent.

Amcits. American citizens who are members of a US *expatriate community. This is a *State Department abbreviation.

American Foreign Service Association (AFSA). The professional association of active and retired members of the US *Foreign Service, established in 1924.

annexation. The formal act by which a state incorporates conquered foreign territory within its own jurisdiction. It is now almost universally regarded as a violation of *international law. Annexation must be distinguished from the acquisition of foreign territory with the willing agreement of the foreign state concerned, and also from what used sometimes to be called peaceful annexation – that is, the acquisition by way of proclamation and settlement of territory not under the authority of any other state.

annexe. A detailed appendix to a *treaty, which sometimes contains its most important provisions and is of equal validity with the provisions of the preceding, more general part of the document. Sir Percy Cradock, who as British Ambassador in Peking and then as Foreign Policy Adviser to his *head of government played such an important role in the negotiations between Britain and China over Hong Kong, said of the Joint Declaration on the colony signed in 1984: the 'annexes would be vital: the main agreement would be generalized; the meat would be in the fine print'.

annual review. The end of year report which the ambassadors in some diplomatic services are expected to submit on recent and anticipated developments in the country to which they are posted. In British practice, where the annual review is cast in the form of a *despatch, it is also usual for it to contain a quantified account of the degree of success achieved during the year in meeting the mission's formal 'objectives' and give recommendations for future policy.

anti-localitis. *See* localitis.

apostolic delegate. The Pope's representative to a branch of the Roman Catholic Church outside Italy. Normally, therefore, the apostolic delegate does not enjoy *diplomatic status but in the past he has sometimes functioned as a *de facto* envoy to a state. This was especially true of Protestant ones such as Britain and the United States, where until the early 1980s the political risk of openly accepting a papal diplomat was considered too high. Not surprisingly, it is not unknown for apostolic delegates to have previous diplomatic experience. The apostolic delegate sent to London in 1954 had before this been papal *nuncio in Dublin. *See also* Holy See; pro-nuncio; Vatican City State.

apostolic nunciature. *See* nunciature.

apostolic nuncio. *See* nuncio.

apostille. Another term for a *legalization certificate.

apostolic pro-nuncio. *See* pro-nuncio.

appeasement. The policy of trying to satisfy another state by agreeing to some of its demands. Since the unfortunate experience of the British Prime Minister, Neville Chamberlain, at the hands of Hitler in the late 1930s, it has come to mean the dishonourable course of seeking peace at any price. Being charged with appeasement is an occupational hazard of diplomacy.

appel. The salutation used in a formal personal letter sent by a diplomat.

Arab League. *See* League of Arab States.

arbitration. The settlement of a dispute through reference to an arbitral tribunal established ad hoc, the members of which may possibly be selected from the (misleadingly called) *Permanent Court of Arbitration. An arbitral tribunal may also be established to deal with a class of disputes that have arisen or may be expected to arise out of a particular situation. Except to the extent to which two or more states have agreed in advance that a specified class of disputes shall be taken to *compulsory arbitration, this device for *pacific settlement can only be used when the parties agree to it. The agreement by which this is done is called a *compromis.

International arbitration is generally conducted on the basis of *international law, in which case it is in substance akin to *adjudication or *judicial settlement. But if they wish, states resorting to arbitration may provide that it proceed somewhat in the manner of *mediation or *ex aequo et bono.

Arbitration is an arrangement of great antiquity. Internationally, it was most notably used between the late eighteenth century and about 1930. Since then, established arrangements for judicial settlement have been widely regarded as the most appropriate means for the settlement of international disputes on the basis of law. But for reasons of expedition, cost, and the technical-

ity of some disputes, arbitration continues to be used by states.

See also conciliation.

archives and documents. *See* diplomatic archives.

archivist. *See chancelier.*

armed conflict. (1) International armed conflict occurring between states which was not begun by one of them making a formal declaration of intent to wage *war. Since the outbreak of the Second World War in 1939 such declarations have gone entirely out of fashion. However, in the popular sense of the term wars continue. Moreover, the laws of war (now known as *international humanitarian law) continue to be applicable to such armed conflicts. (2) Non-international armed conflict within the territory of a state between its armed forces and other armed and well-organized groups; that is, an internal conflict (or civil war) which takes on many of the military characteristics of international armed conflict. In such conflicts the relevant parts of the laws of war are applicable.

armed forces attaché. *See* service attaché.

armistice. An agreement for the suspension of hostilities. Historically, the suspension offered by an armistice was intended to be temporary (and could be local as well as general). But since 1918 the term has increasingly connoted an intention to terminate hostilities completely. In that event, an armistice may be followed by an agreement on an armistice demarcation line and, later, by a *peace treaty. Nowadays, a temporary suspension of hostilities is more likely to be called a *truce or a *ceasefire than an armistice. But the use of all such terms became rather imprecise during the second half of the twentieth century.

army attaché. *See* military attaché; service attaché.

Arria formula. An extremely informal procedure of the UN *Security Council enabling its members to engage in discussion with non-members, including non-state parties. Under this formula meetings are held in private, away from the Council chamber, usually under the chairmanship of a Council member other than the current Council president, and without the attendance of officials or the keeping of any official records. The formula takes its name from Diego Arria, the Venezuelan ambassador who presided over the first meeting of this nature during his country's tenure of a seat on the Security Council during the period 1992–93.

Arthashastra. *See* Kautilya.

ask for passports. An expression sometimes used when a *head of mission is *recalled, temporarily or permanently, from the *receiving state in protest at some aspect of its behaviour. The phrase derives from the fact that at one time the receipt of a passport, in effect an exit *visa, was necessary for a foreigner to leave his country of residence.

assemblies. *See* parliamentary assemblies.

assistant attaché. *See* attaché.

assistant under-secretary of state. Until recently, a senior position in Britain's *Foreign and Commonwealth Office, coming beneath that of *deputy under-secretary of state and above that of *head of department. (Such a person is now known as a *'director'.) It is also a senior position in the US State Department.

associated state. A status which for most practical purposes is similar to that of a *protected state, but in which the entity in question lacks *sovereignty (sense 1). Thus an associated state will, more or less, enjoy internal self-government, but its defence and external affairs will be in the hands of the state with which it is associated.

The concept of association is much more in accord with contemporary orthodoxy than that of protection, but even so most experiments with it – notably in the West Indies – have been wound up. However, the Cook Islands and

Niue remain as associated states of New Zealand.

It should be noted that the three Pacific states in 'free association' with the United States – the Marshall Islands, Micronesia, and Palau – are not associated states in the sense here discussed. However, in respect of their defence (for which the United States has accepted responsibility) they have assumed one of the key characteristics of *protected states.

Association of South East Asian Nations (ASEAN). This international organization was established in 1967 to promote economic cooperation and development and, more generally, collaboration in all matters of common interest. Since Cambodia's admission in 1999, its members encompass all ten south-east Asian states: Brunei, Cambodia, Indonesia, Laos, Malaysia, Myanmar, the Philippines, Singapore, Thailand, and Vietnam. Papua New Guinea has *observer status. Its headquarters and central secretariat are in Jakarta, Indonesia. The *secretary-generalship rotates among the member states every three years in the alphabetical order of their names. ASEAN's supreme organ is the meeting of Heads of Government, which gathers in formal session every three years, and informally in the intervening years. Each year there is a policy-making Meeting of Foreign Ministers, popularly known as AMM, the ASEAN Ministerial Meeting. It rotates among the member states on an alphabetical basis. There is also an annual meeting to arrange economic cooperation, the ASEAN Economic Meeting (AEM). In 1992 it was decided to set up an ASEAN Free Trade Area with a view to establishing a *common market within 15 years. However, all progress within ASEAN has to overcome the problems presented by the geographical size and diversity of its area, and the political and economic divisions that exist among its member states.

asylum. *See* diplomatic asylum.

attaché. This is a recognized way of designating certain members of a *diplomatic mission and of a *permanent mission. There is no exact uniformity in its use, but principally it is employed in two ways (with a third usage now seemingly out of fashion):

(1) In some *diplomatic services, junior members – usually those ranking beneath *third secretary – are called attachés (or assistant attachés) when they serve in diplomatic missions, or at certain diplomatic missions.

(2) In the overwhelming majority of diplomatic and permanent missions there are specialist staff enjoying *diplomatic status who are not members of their state's diplomatic service. They come from government departments other than the foreign ministry, such as Defence, Finance, Trade, and Agriculture, or may perhaps be temporary members of the foreign ministry who have been

hired for a specific overseas assignment. (The US State Department used to class such people as 'Foreign Service Reserves'.) Some states give at least some of these officials a *diplomatic rank (sense 1), usually indicating their expertise in brackets. Thus Mr X (a member of the Department of Trade who has been seconded to the mission) may be designated First Secretary (Trade). But other states give some or all such officials the title of attaché, indicating that they are attached to its mission from a department with a predominantly domestic focus rather than from the foreign ministry. In such circumstances Mr X would be called a Trade Attaché, or an Attaché (Trade). Other types of attaché include Administrative, Agricultural, Coffee and Cocoa Affairs, Commercial, Cultural, Economic, Education, Financial, Labour, Press, Scientific, Sugar Affairs, Tourism, and Welfare Attachés, and even Medical and Meteorological Attachés.

Depending on the extent to which their work is distinguishable from the general representational and reporting work of the diplomatic or permanent mission, some attachés in sense 2 will report directly to their home departments as well as to the foreign ministry. This will always be true of *service attachés and the subsets of this genre: Army (or Military), Naval, and Air attachés (and assistant attachés) – who also in some other respects are in a different position from that of most other members of a diplomatic mission. (Accordingly, they attract a separate entry.) Armed service personnel attached to diplomatic missions sent by one *Commonwealth state to another are called advisers, not attachés.

(3) The title of honorary attaché used sometimes to be given to certain members of a diplomatic mission. In British practice they were usually well-connected and affluent young men who found attachment to an embassy – preferably at an intriguing place, like Istanbul – an ideal means of widening their knowledge of the world while sampling a possible career. What they actually did depended on their abilities and the attitude of their head of mission; some did valuable diplomatic work; others did not. The custom of appointing such attachés appears to have died out in the middle of the twentieth century.

audience. A formal interview granted by one official personage to another. A notable instance is the audience given to a *head of mission by a *head of state, typically for the *presentation of credentials, and perhaps also to mark the termination of a *tour of duty. In the latter case it has been generally known as the *farewell call and is a more private occasion.

Initial audiences are now rather routine affairs but this was not always the case. Ambassadors newly appointed to the court of the Sultan of the Ottoman Empire could sometimes wait months for their initial audience, and thus be in official limbo. They might then be subjected to varying degrees of humiliation at the ceremony itself. One of the most legendary audiences in the history of diplomacy, however, was that granted in September 1793 by Qianlong, Manchu Emperor of China, to the experienced British envoy, Lord Macartney, who hoped to establish the first resident embassy on Chinese soil. Macartney, however, refused to *kowtow and in consequence it was to be the middle of the next century before a British embassy was opened in Peking. The scene which the caricaturist James Gillray envisaged as Lord Macartney's audience was immortalized in his cartoon entitled 'The Reception of the Diplomatique & his Suite, at the Court of Pekin' (it was actually held at the cooler summer retreat of the emperor at Jehol). Less well known is Gillray's equally if not more remarkable cartoon of the audience granted early in the following year by King George III to Jusuf Aga Efendi, the first permanent Ottoman ambassador ever sent abroad by the Sultan. This is called 'Presentation of the Mahometan Credentials – or – The final resource of French Atheists'. *See also* orator; tribute.

audience de congé. See farewell call.

Auswärtiges Amt (AA). Styled 'Foreign Office' in imitation of the British ministry, the German ministry of foreign affairs created by *Bismarck in 1870. It was housed in the Wilhelmstrasse in Berlin until its destruction in 1943.

autonomy. The enjoyment, by a territorial and often ethnically distinct subdivision of a *sovereign state, of a far-reaching but less-than-full measure of self rule.

award. *See* judgment.

B

back channel. A line of diplomatic communication which bypasses the normal or 'front channel', usually to maximize secrecy and avoid opposition to a new line of policy. This does not necessarily entail sidelining all professional diplomats, just most of them. Two well-documented cases may be mentioned. The first occurred during the arms control talks between the Soviet Union and the United States in the early 1970s. These were formally conducted in Vienna (the front channel) but Henry *Kissinger used the back channel of secret meetings with Soviet Ambassador in Washington, Anatoly Dobrynin, to tackle key difficulties in the talks while the arms control negotiators themselves remained in complete ignorance of what was going on. The second case was provided by the 'Oslo channel', which played the key role in producing the Israel–Palestine Liberation Organization settlement of September 1993. This consisted of elaborately disguised direct talks beginning in 1992 between PLO officials and Israeli academics at discreet Norwegian locations while formal Middle East talks were being held, unproductively, in Washington.

backtracking. In *negotiations, reopening a question on which agreement has already been reached. This is usually most serious if it is an issue of principle.

bailiwick. The territory under the authority of a bailiff or bailie – a sovereign's official. Now largely historical, though the British *'Crown dependencies' of Jersey and Guernsey (the chief Channel Islands), which do not come under the authority of Britain's parliament, are still formally described as bailiwicks. *See also* dependent territory.

bailo. The Venetian representative at Constantinople. The bailo (from *baiulus*, tutor or protector) was part *ambassador, part *consul, and part governor of the large Venetian trading colony in the city; he held the most important post in the *Venetian diplomatic service. In 1453, when Constantinople fell to the sultan of the *Ottoman Empire, Mehmed II, the bailo actually fought alongside his co-religionists on the walls of the city and was beheaded (along with his son) for his pains. Nevertheless, within a year the conqueror had permitted a new appointment to the bailage of Constantinople.

balance of power. (1) The distribution of power between states at any given time. (2) An international distribution of power favouring the supporters of the *status quo* and thereby likely to deter any revisionist state or *alliance of states from attacking them. In reality a preponderance of power in favour of the former, this is described as an 'equilibrium' to avoid provoking the latter. (3) The means by which this equilibrium is achieved, in other words, the main *international institution (sense 2), other than *diplomacy and *international law, by which states preserves themselves against threats from their hegemonial or imperialist (sense 2) fellows. (In practice, this may mean preserving the major ones at the expense of the lesser.) The balance of power in this sense consists of a configuration of alliances shaped, among other things, by broad acceptance of certain practical rules or precepts: for example, that the most effective bulwark against a revisionist power is a coalition of *status quo* powers, and that squeamishness about the domestic policies of potential allies is an expensive luxury. Many hoped that this traditional approach of the European states-system to the problem of international order would be replaced, or at least modified, by the *collective security procedures introduced in the twentieth century; however, these proved disappointing. As 'equilibrium' or as the means of achieving it, the balance of power is the jewel in the crown of the approach to international politics known as *realism (sense 3). *See also* Kissinger; Metternich.

Ballhausplatz. A common way of referring to the foreign ministry in Vienna of the Austro-Hungarian Empire, which was situated at Ballhausplatz 2. Today, the Austrian foreign ministry occupies the building. *See also* Kaunitz, Count Wenzel Anton von.

ballon d'essai. In negotiation, a proposition floated tentatively to test the reaction of the other side, from the French *envoyer un ballon d'essai* (to send up a pilot balloon). *See also* flying a kite.

Barbaro, Emolao (1454–1493). A Venetian scholar-diplomat who in 1490 was sent as resident ambassador to Rome, a key post in the *Venetian diplomatic service. *De Officio Legati*, the short book which he wrote while here, is notable for being the first literary account of the *resident, as opposed to the *special, envoy. It is also remarkable for being the first book on diplomacy to announce, albeit not in this phrase, the doctrine of *raison d'état.

bargaining. (1) The exchange of offers and counter-offers, sometimes known as 'haggling'. In this sense, bargaining is a tactic employed within a *negotiation. (2) A synonym for negotiation. See also concession; quid pro quo.

base, foreign military. That part of the territory of a *sovereign state which is made available for use by the military forces of a foreign state, and is sufficiently extensive and distinguishable to be termed a base. The terms and conditions on which it may be so used will have been agreed by the host and the foreign state. It should be noted that Britain's two bases on the island of Cyprus are not part of the state of Cyprus, as the areas in question are under British sovereignty: hence the phrase, British Sovereign Base Areas. See also status of forces agreement.

belligerency. A status which, under the traditional law of *war, may be accorded by *third parties to an insurgent group within a *sovereign state which as a matter of fact exercises such governmental authority over part of that state and wields such power as to suggest that the conflict has moved beyond the stage of a mere *insurgency. Thus it is a formal recognition of a new situation – one where a new de facto political authority has appeared, with which the recognizing state may need to communicate. However, it does not amount to a *recognition of the insurgent group as a legitimate government. Having recognized a group as belligerents, the recognizing state is obliged to conform to the law of *neutrality in its dealings with both the group and the government against which it is rebelling. It must also allow both of the latter to exercise against itself the legal rights which belligerents in interstate wars customarily enjoy. The recognition of belligerency implies an agnosticism about the conflict's outcome. Such an approach is, at the start of the twenty-first century, deeply out of fashion. Instead, there is general hostility to anything that might facilitate the break-up of states. In this context there is little disposition to consider granting an insurgent group the status of belligerency.

belligerent. (1) A state engaged in *war. (2) An *insurgent group which has been granted the status of *belligerency.

Benelux. An abbreviated way of referring, collectively, to Belgium, the Netherlands, and Luxembourg.

benevolent neutrality. See neutrality.

berāt. *See* letter of protection.

Berlaymont. The building in Brussels which houses the headquarters of the *European Commission.

bid list. The list of postings abroad for which an American *Foreign Service officer would like to be considered. This must be submitted if the officer is eligible for, and desires, a transfer. The list will usually be expected to include bids for positions in *hardship posts and in more than one geographical region.

bilateral diplomacy. (1) The conduct of *diplomatic relations (sense 1) between two states through formally accredited missions, though one or even both of these missions may be physically located in a neighbouring state. In this sense, bilateral diplomacy is identical to 'traditional diplomacy', and has a strong emphasis on written communications. The principle of *reciprocity has a powerful influence on the conduct of bilateral diplomacy and, at least in more recent times, has generated considerable pressure for equivalent levels of *representation in each state. *See also* diplomatic representation; multiple accreditation. (2) Any form of direct diplomatic contact between two states beyond the formal confines of a *multilateral conference, including contacts in the wings of such gatherings when the subject of discussion is different from that of the conference and only of concern to the two states themselves.

binding. The condition of having an obligation, either in terms of morality or of law, to follow or desist from a certain path, or to use a certain procedure if one wishes to achieve a valid legal result. All jural law is, by its nature, binding on those to whom it applies. Much philosophical speculation has taken place, over millennia, as to the means whereby bindingness is conferred on law. But this is a false question, as all societies have worked on the assumption that that which they designate as law is, by virtue of it being law, binding. If, for example, rules or laws are promulgated for a game, those playing it do not ask if those rules are binding on them. It is inherent in the concept of laws or rules that they bind those who come within their aegis. Hence, *international law is no less, and no more, binding on its subjects than any other law is within its area of jurisdiction. It should be noted that, as with all non-scientific law, the word binding in this context refers to the existence of an obligation to follow a rule, and not necessarily to its actual observance. Indeed, in logic an action can only be termed a breach of a rule on the assumption that the entity in question is under an obligation to observe it. *See also* customary international law; international law; *pacta sunt servanda*.

bipartisan foreign policy. In a representative democracy with a two-party system, a foreign policy supported by both major parties.

Bismarck, Prince Otto von (1815–98). A Prussian diplomat and statesman. After a decade serving as a professional diplomat, Bismarck was appointed chief minister of Prussia in September 1862 (and only weeks later foreign minister as well), and is remembered chiefly for orchestrating the unification of Germany in 1871 and then, as Imperial Chancellor until 1890, for his role in holding the *balance of power (sense 2) in Europe. He believed that foreign policy should be based on interest rather than sentiment, that war should never be fought to a point where enemies were permanently alienated, and that all options should be preserved by practising diplomacy (sense 1) with any state with which Germany was at peace.

black box hot line. *See* hot line.

black chamber. The room, often in a central post office, where letters, including diplomatic *despatches sent by ordinary post, were opened and (where necessary) decrypted before being re-sealed and sent on their way. Most European states had a black chamber by the eighteenth century and the introduction of the electric *telegraph gave them more work in the nineteenth. In France it was known as the *cabinet noir*.

bloc. A grouping of states for the purposes of concerting their policies in one or more areas, whether they are bound together by a *treaty or not, and whether they constitute an *alliance or not. The most notable bloc of the post-1945 period was the 'Soviet bloc'. *See also* Cold War.

blockade. The announcement by a *belligerent that part or all of the enemy coast is closed to the ingress or egress of the vessels (and aircraft) of all states. It has legal status only if it is made effective. Ships (and aircraft) attempting to run the blockade may be seized. A prize court established by the belligerent then decides whether their seizure was lawful. If it is so judged, they and their cargoes are designated as *contraband, and confiscated. In contemporary conditions blockade has little relevance.

blue berets. The name by which the military members of a UN *peacekeeping operation are often described, after the colour of their headgear. They are also called blue helmets.

Blue Book. The popular name for a British government paper which, because of its bulk, was given a cover of stronger quality than the inside pages; the colour of this cover happened to be blue. Blue Books, typically long official reports covering matters of domestic as well as foreign policy, were published by the government and formally presented to

Parliament – and thus by one means or another to the public at large. They were introduced at the beginning of the nineteenth century, the chief architect of the new system being George Canning (1770–1827), the brilliant and driven Tory foreign secretary who, in his last period, was also leader of the House of Commons and briefly prime minister.

The Diplomatic Blue Books, which reached foreign governments as well as influential groups within Britain, were, of course, sometimes employed by foreign secretaries as instruments of *propaganda. Documents such as exchanges of telegrams were presented selectively and often edited to be consistent with current policy. *Bismarck disapproved of the British practice of publishing diplomatic correspondence, observing (rather carelessly) that if he were to follow suit his work would be doubled, since for every confidential *despatch he wrote he would need to write another for publication. An excellent guide to the nineteenth-century Blue Books, which contain reports on the British *Diplomatic Service, was written by Harold Temperley and Lillian M. Penson (published in 1938, and reprinted in 1966). The term 'Blue Book' fell into disuse during the twentieth century.

bomber diplomacy. A term which would seem appropriate to describe the process of bombing an adversary in the hope of inducing sub-mission. The contemporary equivalent, perhaps, of nineteenth-century *gunboat diplomacy. *See also* coercive diplomacy.

bottom line. The least for which a party to a *negotiation will settle; as far down as one can be pushed. *See also* sticking point.

boudoir **diplomacy.** A manner of conducting business aspired to by certain ambassadors at courts where one or more women were influential, or where a queen or empress ruled, as for example in St Petersburg during the reign of Catherine II of Russia in the late eighteenth century. Modelling themselves no doubt on Castiglione's courtier, their object was, by flirtatiousness and skill in what Lord Chesterfield described to his son as 'the art of pleasing', to contrive admission to the room where only intimate friends were admitted – the *boudoir*. Here they had unrivalled opportunities for influence. *See also* Harris, Sir James.

bout de papier. A paper with nothing on it but text which may be passed to a foreign representative. Anonymous and completely informal, it typically contains notes to assist an oral presentation or, in a negotiation, a proposed formula. In the first case it fulfils essentially the same functions as an *aide-mémoire* but with even less risk of attribution where this could be damaging; in the second it has the object of trying to break an *impasse where identification of authorship in the outside world could be equally perilous. Sometimes the English-language term 'piece of paper' is used for this device. *See also* non-paper.

boycott. The refusal to have dealings with, for example, a particular state, or to buy some or all of its products. Such acts are intended as a protest against certain of the state's policies, and/or as a means of inducing it to change certain of its ways. The concept is now firmly embedded in the practices of the international society; but the term receives relatively little international use, notwithstanding the impeccable political correctitude of its origin – a nineteenth-century protest by Irish people against the refusal of one Captain Boycott to reduce rents. Instead, the same concept is expressed through the use of the term *sanctions. *See also* embargo.

breach of the peace. As understood in the United Nations, an outbreak of fighting between states or – if deemed to represent a threat to international peace and security – within one. *See also* aggression.

Bretton Woods. The resort in New Hampshire, USA, at which a 1944 conference agreed to establish an International Monetary Fund and an International Bank for Reconstruction and Development (the World Bank). The resultant arrangements are often referred to as the Bretton Woods system.

Brezhnev Doctrine. The name given in the West to the justification offered by the Soviet Union for its invasion of Czechoslovakia in August 1968 (Brezhnev being the Soviet leader). The invasion, in which contingents from some other members of the *Warsaw Pact were attached to Soviet forces, was a response to the desire of Czechoslovakia to follow a more independent line than the Soviet Union was willing to allow its *satellites. The Doctrine was also frequently referred to in the West as one of 'limited sovereignty'. *See also* sphere of influence.

Briand–Kellogg Pact. The name by which the General Treaty of 1928 for the Renunciation of War is generally known (after the French and American foreign ministers who instigated it). It provided for the renunciation of recourse to *war for the solution of international controversies, and as an instrument of national policy. It was seen as largely closing the 'gaps' in the *Covenant of the *League of Nations which, in certain limited circumstances, permitted aggressive war (as distinct from war in *self-defence). The Treaty was widely adhered to, but had little immediate effect. However, at the level of ideas it was of considerable significance, in that it indicated the changing attitude to the propriety of war as a positive instrument of national policy.

brinkmanship. The art of getting to the brink of war without precipitating one. It is associated with the American *secretary of state during much of the 1950s, John Foster Dulles (1888–1959). The most serious case of twentieth-century brinkmanship was the *Cuban Missile Crisis of 1962, in which the parties came *eyeball-to-eyeball. *See also* crisis management.

British Council. Founded in 1934, the British Council is Britain's principal vehicle of *cultural diplomacy. It has always been permitted a degree of autonomy from government to maximize its credibility abroad, and is described officially as 'an independent Non-Departmental Public Body'. Nevertheless, no secret is made of the fact that it receives a substantial 'grant-in-aid' from the *Foreign and Commonwealth Office and that its priorities and objectives are set in close consultation with it.

broker. *See* mediation.

bubble. A US Foreign Service term for an unusual room within a room in a diplomatic mission. It has transparent plastic walls specially coated in an attempt to make *bugging of conversations inside it impossible. At the time of the Reagan–Gorbachev *summit in Reykjavik in 1986 the US embassy in Iceland's capital contained the smallest bubble that had yet been built, with capacity for only eight people. However, this did not prevent its being employed by the American team – including President Reagan – during the summit. Kenneth L. Adelman, who was inside it himself, says that they were 'crammed in like 1950s teenagers in a telephone booth'. *See also* freedom of communication; listening device.

buffer state. This phrase generally referred to a small state lying more or less between two much larger and antagonistic states. It could thus take on the role of a buffer, not because of its own strength but because each of its larger neighbours was reluctant to attempt its *annexation for fear of the reaction of the large rival state on the smaller state's other side. However, such a situation was by no means a guarantee of the small state's territorial integrity: one of the larger states might chance its arm; or they might both agree to divide the intervening state between them. Thus the concept of a buffer state implied the acceptance of the use of armed force and of territorial annexation as instruments of national policy. As, in the second half of the twentieth century, those instruments largely went out of fashion (in both political and legal respects), little is now heard of buffer states. In consequence, small states are much more physically secure than they used to be. But they are no less subject to non-physical pressures from larger states than hitherto.

buffer zone. An area lying between two hostile (and often recently-belligerent) states or groups in which neither of them maintains armed forces. There is thus a dividing zone of territory between their forces, which reduces the likelihood of accidental conflict and may contribute to a calmer disposition on one or both sides. However, to provide a form of guarantee that neither will take advantage of the buffer zone by suddenly introducing its forces into it, a neutral body – such as the UN – may be asked to establish a small and lightly armed *peacekeeping force into the zone. *See also* peacekeeping.

bugging. *See* listening device.

Bunker, Ellsworth (1894–1984). An American businessman with no experience in diplomacy until 1951, when (already aged 56) he was appointed US ambassador to Argentina. Success in this post led to three other postings as head of a major mission, culminating in South Vietnam (1967–73). Bunker's chief renown arose from his skill as a practical negotiator. In 1962, at the request of the UN, he successfully mediated a solution to the dangerous dispute between the Netherlands and Indonesia over West New Guinea/West Irian. Subsequently he mediated between Saudia Arabia and Egypt over

Yemen (1963) and in the Dominican crisis (1965). Not long after his return from Vietnam at the age of 79, with the rank of *ambassador-at-large and the reputation as the greatest American negotiator of his generation, he led the US delegation to the Geneva Conference on the Middle East (December 1973) which followed the *Yom Kippur War. He then headed the US team in the sensitive Panama Canal negotiations, which concluded successfully in 1977. Henry *Kissinger, who chose Bunker for both of these tasks, described him as 'one of the great men of American diplomacy'. He retired finally in 1978.

Bynkershoek, Cornelius van (1673–1743). A Dutch jurist who was appointed a member of the Supreme Court of Holland in 1703 and its President in 1721. It was also in 1721 that he wrote in some haste and published *De Foro Legatorum tam in causa civili quam criminali* (The Jurisdiction over Ambassadors in both Civil and Criminal Cases). Sparked by recent controversies, one of which was the imprisonment of *Wicquefort, the overwhelming majority of the principles of *De Foro Legatorum* – despite certain oddities – were soon firmly rooted in *international law and practice. The book has been authoritatively described as 'undoubtedly the greatest of the classical works on diplomatic law'.

Byzantine diplomacy. The *statecraft of the Eastern Roman Empire, especially during the period of its weakness and decline in the period from the beginning of the thirteenth to the middle of the fifteenth century. In foreign policy this gave emphasis to dividing enemies and solidifying friends among its threatening neighbours; in *diplomacy (sense 1) to enhancing the *prestige of the Emperor by *protocol and extravagant ceremonial at the reception of ambassadors in Constantinople, and to acquiring accurate intelligence.

Despite its meretricious aspect, fraudulent inspiration and manipulative technique, there is a well-established view that Byzantine diplomacy is of great importance in the origins of diplomacy. This is because, according to Harold Nicolson, it was 'the first to organise a special department of government for dealing with external affairs'. Byzantine diplomacy also marked the generalized expansion in the duties of the diplomat from mere *orator to trained negotiator and observer as well. Additionally, it was the school of diplomacy by which the *Venetians – also important in the subsequent development of diplomacy – were substantially influenced.

C

calendar. In diplomatic and archival usage, a list of documents arranged chronologically together with either a brief summary of their contents or complete transcripts – or some combination of the two. A good calendar was indexed and each entry gave the location of the originals. Calendars were first developed in the embryonic bureaucracies of the medieval period to facilitate access to the contents of otherwise scattered original documents such as *treaties, *despatches, and letters. A well-known example of this kind of calendar is the Gascon Calendar of 1322. Subsequently they were produced in some countries to make the contents of the originals known to historians who were unable to inspect them at first hand. The multi-volume *Calendar of State Papers, Venetian*, is a notable example of a calendar designed for this purpose. This was officially published in Britain between the middle of the nineteenth and the middle of the twentieth century and contains summaries in English of *Venetian diplomatic papers bearing on English affairs from the thirteenth to the seventeenth century.

Callières, François de (1645–1717). A man of letters and French diplomat in the age of Louis XIV. Although he had worked as a diplomat from 1670 until 1676, first in the service of the Duke of Longueville and then the Duke of Turin, he did not join that of the king until 1693. Callières had a relatively short but successful career in the French diplomatic service. Specializing in negotiations with the Dutch, he played a key role at the Congress of Ryswick in 1697. In the following year he was recalled to France and became a senior member of the king's circle of foreign policy advisers. Though not published until March 1716, it was probably at about this time that he wrote the book for which he is remembered by students of diplomacy: *De la manière de négocier avec les souverains* (The Art of

Negotiating with Sovereign Princes). More elegant and much shorter than *Wicquefort's great manual, Callières' book is generally regarded as the definitive theoretical exposition of the French system of diplomacy – an elaboration of the practice of *Richelieu. Among other things, he emphasizes the importance of honesty in diplomacy and the need to make it a profession. *See also* Torcy.

calls (on appointment to new post). *See* courtesy calls.

Cambon, Jules (1845–1935). A French colonial governor and diplomat. Younger brother of Paul *Cambon, Jules was governor-general of Algeria (1891–97), and then ambassador at three important embassies. He was then *secretary-general of the *Quai d'Orsay, a delegate to the Paris Peace Conference in 1919, and chairman of the extremely important standing Ambassadors' Conference created in January 1920 to arrange for the execution of certain aspects of the peace treaties. Harold *Nicolson described him as 'witty, wise, conciliatory, high-minded, disillusioned. Perhaps the most intelligent of all French pre-war diplomatists'. In 1926 he published a short book on diplomacy called Le *diplomate*, which was highly praised by practitioners of the *old diplomacy. It appeared in an English translation in 1931 under the title, *The Diplomatist*.

Cambon, Paul (1843–1924). A French diplomat. Elder brother of Jules *Cambon, Paul is known above all for his role in cementing the Anglo-French *entente of 1904 and remaining in London as ambassador throughout the First World War. Paul Cambon is described by Harold *Nicolson as 'one of the most successful diplomatists in modern history'. The fact that he could not speak English is striking evidence of the extent to which French remained the language of diplomacy until well into the twentieth century.

Camp David. A US presidential *retreat 70 miles and half-an-hour by helicopter from the White House in the Catoctin Mountains of Maryland. For security reasons it is marked on no American map. It was established by President Roosevelt in 1942 for the sake of his health (it is almost ten degrees Fahrenheit cooler than Washington) as well as his safety. Initially called 'Shangri-La', in 1953 it was renamed 'Camp David' by President Eisenhower after his grandson. Since the visit of the British prime minister, Winston Churchill, in May 1943, most presidents have used Camp David for *summit meetings.

cancellaria. See chancery.

cancellier. See *chancelier*.

Canning, George. *See* Blue Books.

Canning, Stratford (1786–1880). A British diplomat, known after 1852 as Viscount Stratford de Redcliffe. Stratford was one of the greatest British diplomats of the nineteenth century and a perfect illustration of the influence which, in the pre-telegraphic age, could be wielded by an ambassador who was at once exceptionally able and well connected in governing circles at home. Enjoying the patronage of the Foreign Secretary George Canning, who was his cousin, he went to Istanbul as *first secretary in 1808 and within two years (at the age of only twenty-four) was given temporary charge of this important embassy with the rank of *minister plenipotentiary. Peace between Turkey and Russia was vital to British interests in the war with Napoleon and this was achieved with the assistance of Stratford's *mediation in the Treaty of Bucharest of 28 May 1812. This established his diplomatic reputation and laid the foundation of the immense influence that he was to acquire in Istanbul when he returned there later in his career. He was minister to Switzerland from 1814 until 1818 and attended the *Congress of Vienna to represent the British position on Swiss affairs. He served as minister to the USA from 1820 until 1824 and afterwards went on a special mission to Russia. In 1825 he was sent once more to Turkey, now with the rank of ambassador, and remained there until the end of 1827.

The years following Stratford's return from his second tour in Turkey saw a long period of parliamentary politics leavened with special diplomatic missions to Turkey (again) and Portugal. In 1833 Palmerston wanted to send him as ambassador to Russia but *agrément was refused by the Tsar. However, his full-time diplomatic career was resumed in 1841 when he was sent on his third and final mission to Istanbul, which lasted until 1858. It was especially during this period that Stratford's influence was at its height, both in fostering reform within the Ottoman Empire and stiffening the resolve of its government to resist Russian pressure. Though historians now believe that the Turks would have adopted the posture which contributed to the outbreak of the Crimean War in 1853 without Stratford's encouragement, there is little doubt that he deserved the title which they gave to him: 'the Great *Elchi*'. Technically this meant simply ambassador rather than minister (*elchi*) but when applied to Stratford had the connotation of 'ambassador *par excellence*'.

capital. The city which is a state's seat of government. It is, however, possible for the seat of government to be in a city other than the capital (as in the Netherlands); or the government may be divided between two or even three cities (as in South Africa) – in which case the capital may assume a peripatetic nature.

*Diplomatic missions are almost always based in the capital city, and only in that city. (In the South African case, missions move for some months each year from Pretoria, the administrative capital, to Cape Town, the legislative capital, so that they may have ready access to members of the government during the period when the South African parliament is sitting. In respect of the Netherlands, the *receiving state insists that diplomatic missions be at the seat of government rather than in the capital.) Very occasionally, however, it may not be possible for a *sending state to establish its mission in the capital, as when it does not recognize the legitimacy of the receiving state's occupancy of that city. This occurs in the case of Israel, with the result that almost all diplomatic missions are based not in the capital, Jerusalem, but in Tel Aviv.

capitulations. Privileges extended by the sultan of the Ottoman Empire to foreign states for the benefit of their locally resident subjects. There were earlier examples, but the capitulations negotiated with France in the middle of the sixteenth century were the model for those subsequently granted to the other European powers. The capitulations were prompted chiefly by a mutual interest in the expansion of commerce between Europe and the Levant and the anxiety of the sultan and his household to be absolved of responsibility for administering the affairs of useful but perplexing strangers. They granted to the European states rights to trade and travel freely, pay low customs duties, no domestic taxes, and to have civil and criminal cases arising among and between their own subjects resident in the Ottoman Empire tried in their own consular courts.

From the point of view of diplomatic privileges and procedure the capitulations were important for three main reasons. In the first place, they tended to give a degree of protection to foreign envoys in Istanbul – provided their governments remained at peace with the 'Grand Turk' – before the *customary international law of diplomacy began to be accepted in the Ottoman Empire in the course of the eighteenth century. In the second, since they were not regarded by the Turks as *treaties between equals but personal acts of grace by the reigning sultan, until 1740 the capitulations had to be renegotiated when one sultan was succeeded by another. In the third place, since they were regarded as assuming friendship, any act of hostility by the beneficiary rendered them void; this feature of the capitulations was not surrendered by the Turks until 1774. With the continued weakening of the empire, by the end of the nineteenth century the capitulations gave such a degree of communal autonomy to foreigners that Sir Charles Elliot was able to observe that all of them had 'almost the same immunities as diplomatists in other countries'. Not surprisingly, they became a major target of Turkish nationalism and were finally abolished by the Treaty of Lausanne in 1923.

Capitulations regimes were also established in Egypt, Muscat (Oman), Persia, the Trucial States of the (Persian) Gulf, China, and Japan. That in Muscat continued until 1958, while those of the seven Trucial States were ended only in 1971. *See also* letter of protection; unequal treaty.

career ambassador. A personal rank which the president, with the advice and consent of the Senate, can confer on a career member of the *senior US *Foreign Service in recognition of especially distinguished service over a sustained period. This power was given to the president under the Foreign Service Act (1980). This repealed the 1946 Foreign Service Act, together with the amendment to it made in the Act of Congress of 5 August 1955 that first introduced the class of 'career ambassador'. Under the earlier scheme, an officer had to have served for at least 15 years in a position of responsibility in a government agency, including at least three of these as a *career minister; rendered exceptionally distinguished service to the government; and met other requirements prescribed by the secretary of state. Since the first appointments to this coveted class in 1956, only 37 foreign service officers

have achieved the rank of career ambassador.

career consular officer. A full-time consular officer, as opposed to an *honorary consular officer. A somewhat ambiguous term, it does *not* imply that the person bearing the title is also a member of a separate *consular service and thus likely to spend his or her entire career engaged in the performance of *consular functions. This was the lot of full-time consular officers until about the middle of the twentieth century but since then states have incorporated their consular services within their *diplomatic services. As a result, from time to time many *career diplomats now serve at a *consular post or in the *consular section of an embassy. *See also* consular rank.

career diplomat. A permanent member of a *diplomatic service. A career diplomat is thus different from an *ad hoc diplomat, a *temporary diplomat, or a *political appointee.

career minister. A personal rank in the US *Foreign Service which is second only to that of *career ambassador. Career ministers have often been ambassadors before promotion to this rank.

career officer. A US *Foreign Service officer occupying the broad intermediate stage between a junior officer and a *senior foreign service officer.

care-of-pilot. *See* diplomatic bag.

casual courier. An officer of the British *Diplomatic Service who is temporarily co-opted to carry diplomatic mail on a particular journey; this mail can on occasions be classified 'secret' or above. In addition to a private passport, the courier carries a special 'Casual Courier's Passport'. This confers immunity on the *diplomatic bag being carried. *See also* diplomatic courier; Queen's Messenger.

casus belli. An event or act which precipitates or is used to justify resort to *war.

casus foederis. An event or act which is deemed to justify calling on an ally to fulfil the undertakings of a *treaty of *alliance.

caucus. An informal group that meets in private to forge a common approach to matters brought for decision in a larger, formal group. Not surprisingly this is a most important feature of *multilateral diplomatic gatherings, whether permanent or ad hoc. On the UN *Security Council, for example, the most important caucuses are those of the permanent five (*P5), the Western permanent members (P3), the *non-aligned, and the *European Union. Even the 'non-non-aligned' sometimes meet in caucus.

CAZAB. The acronym for the conferences of senior *counter-intelligence officers (both senses) from Canada, America, New Zealand, Australia and Britain, which began in 1967 and continued at roughly 18-month intervals throughout the *Cold War. Since the end of this conflict, such cooperation has taken a different form, being (according to a former head of *MI5) 'less discreet, broader, more inclusive and above all more immediate'. *See also* Echelon.

ceasefire. An agreement to this effect, which may relate to a specific area where fighting has erupted or to the whole armed front. It is usually implicit in such agreements that the cessation of firing is accompanied by no forward movement of positions or armament. This may be made explicit by the description of the agreement as, for example, a 'ceasefire-in-place' or a 'standstill ceasefire' . A further way of trying to stabilize a ceasefire is through an additional agreement to *delimit and *demarcate the lines beyond which each side may not move. Such a line, like a single line indicating the limits of the ground held by each at the time of the ceasefire, constitutes a 'ceasefire line (CFL)'. It is sometimes known as a *green line. A ceasefire may, perhaps via a *truce, lead to an *armistice and hence, possibly, to a *peace treaty.

ceasefire-in-place. *See* ceasefire.

ceasefire line. *See* ceasefire.

Central Intelligence Agency. *See* CIA.

chancelier. Earlier known as a *cancellier*, an administrator or clerk in a diplomatic mission trusted with the keeping and handling of confidential documents. Conceived as the institutional memory, such persons have generally been expected to have an easy familiarity with local languages and customs and be a permanent fixture in their embassy. Sometimes but by no means frequently they are members of the *diplomatic staff. Most diplomatic services now employ such people, whether they go by this name (as in the French Diplomatic Service) or not, but their introduction was fiercely resisted by the British Diplomatic Service in the second half of the nineteenth century on the grounds that the lower social class origins of such people made them in fact *un*trustworthy. (However, one had for long been employed in the British embassy in Istanbul.) The result was that junior entrants to the diplomatic profession had to spend too much time on routine clerical work, including copying of *despatches, and at best suffered a poor apprenticeship for their craft and at worst got bored and left. Under mounting pressure of routine *chancery work, a version of the *chancelier* was finally introduced into the British Diplomatic Service in the first decade of the twentieth century, though styled an 'archivist'. *See also* diplomatic archives; registry.

chancellery. (1) A ministry of *foreign affairs of a *major power. This was the meaning of this word when it was used before the First World War in the phrase 'the Chancelleries of Europe'. (2) The political section of a *diplomatic mission. This was the sense in which it was sometimes used in the US Foreign Service until the 1960s, though the British usually insisted that this was wrong, not least because it caused confusion with the first meaning of 'chancellery'. The proper term here, they felt, was *chancery. This was a fair point. In their defence, however, the Americans, who tended to use 'chancellery' and 'chancery' interchangeably, could have called in the *Oxford English Dictionary*, which points out that 'chancery' is simply a 'worn down version' of 'chancellery'.

chancery. (1) The political section of a *diplomatic mission. (2) The premises where chancery staff work, and thus a synonym for *embassy or *high commission. *See also* chancellery.

channel of communication. The means whereby a state communicates with another. In this matter there are established usages, the breach of which is likely to be inefficient and also lead to ruffled feathers.

Where one state's foreign ministry wishes to communicate with its counterpart in another state, the message (whether oral or written) is ordinarily passed to the state's diplomatic mission in the capital concerned for onward personal transmission by a *diplomatic agent to the relevant official in the other state's ministry. In this way the message can be delivered at the appropriate level and with exactly the emphasis and tone that is calculated to be most likely to achieve the desired result.

An alternative but usually much less satisfactory channel is to give the message to the recipient state's diplomatic mission which is resident in the capital of the state sending the message. The disadvantage of this channel is the lack of personal delivery to the official responsible for the issue on which the message-sending state seeks a satisfactory response. However, when one state wishes to protest strongly to another, the preferred channel is to use the resident mission of the state to which the protest is addressed. The *head of mission can be summoned to meet a senior figure – a *minister (sense 3) or a very high official – who can register the state's displeasure in no uncertain terms, and with greater weight than would be available to the protesting state's head of mission in the foreign state's capital.

In the event of the message-sending state having no diplomatic representation in the capital of the recipient state, the appropriate channel for the more normal type of message is also through the recipient state's diplomatic mission in the capital of the message-sending state. If there is no such mission (but assuming that the two states are in *diplomatic relations (sense 1)), the message-sending state will select a place where both states have diplomatic representation and send the message to its mission there for passage to the recipient state's mission with the request that it be transmitted to that state's foreign ministry.

A further possibility where neither state has a diplomatic mission in the other's capital but where at least one of them has a *consular post, is for that post to be used. However, in a high diplomatic matter, it might be thought inappropriate to involve a *consular officer. And for the message-sending state to use its consular post in the *receiving state for diplomatic purposes, the consent of the receiving state would need to be secured.

What all this reflects is that in the normal way the foreign ministry is far and away the leading agency responsible for the conduct of a state's *international relations (sense 1); and that its diplomatic agents are the medium through which it makes external representations. Thus *diplomats act as the voice box of the state *vis-à-vis* other states.

Accordingly, when a government department other than the foreign ministry wishes to communicate with a foreign state, the proper channel of communication is for it to use its own foreign ministry. Unless special circumstances obtain (as, for example, in the case of the states of the *European Union), such a department is not entitled to communicate directly with its foreign counterpart, nor with its diplomats resident in the capital of the state concerned, nor with the diplomats of that state resident in its own capital. However, an exception to this rule may be permitted by a foreign ministry in respect of technical or routine matters, where there may well be obvious advantage in the relevant government department – for example, that responsible for transport or for civil aviation – contacting its counterpart directly. Such 'exceptions' are now by no means as exceptional as they used to be.

However, a foreign ministry will always be sensitive about the possibility of such dealings going beyond the permitted ambit, and keen to emphasize its prime responsibility for communications which have the least bearing on principle or policy, or which entail representations to foreign authorities. *See also* diplomacy (sense 1); direct dial diplomacy.

chargé d'affaires (c.d.a.). A generic term for the following three entries. *See also* acting high commissioner, secretary of embassy/legation.

chargé d'affaires *ad interim* (a.i.). The member of a *diplomatic mission who takes charge of an *embassy or a *legation during the temporary absence of its *head, or pending the appointment of a new head. *Sending states generally like a c.d.a. to be a member of their *diplomatic service rather than a high-ranking specialist who is serving as a *temporary diplomat. To achieve that end such an officer's *diplomatic rank may be upgraded to place him or her as number two in the mission's internal order of *precedence. The *receiving state's foreign ministry must be informed of the appointment of a c.d.a (a.i.) by the ambassador or *minister (sense 1) or, if that is not possible, by the sending state's foreign ministry.

In recent times the concept of *ad interim* has been greatly stretched, perhaps as a device to avoid having to call a diplomatic mission something other than an embassy. Thus from 1977 to 1980, due to their deteriorating relations over the Falkland Islands/Las Malvinas, Argentina and Britain reduced their diplomatic missions in each other's capitals to ones headed by a chargé d'affaires – but each officer was designated as acting *ad interim*. Likewise, the Argentinian head of mission in South Africa from 1974 to 1984 was a chargé d'affaires *ad interim*. And throughout the 1990s tension in the relations between Britain and Iran led to a situation in which the missions they exchanged were each headed by a chargé d'affaires (a.i.). *See also* acting high commissioner; secretary of embassy/legation.

chargé d'affaires *en pied*. An alternative name for *chargé d'affaires *en titre*.

chargé d'affaires *en titre*. The diplomat who acts as *head of a mission which is neither an *embassy nor a *legation, and which is thus in the lowest of the three classes into which heads of mission are divided. Unlike other *letters of credence, those of a chargé d'affaires *en titre* are sent by the foreign minister of the *sending state to his or her counterpart in the *receiving state. During the latter part of the twentieth century such missions became very rare, if not extinct. *See also* chargé d'affaires *ad interim*.

Charter of the United Nations. The 1945 *treaty which established the *United Nations and set out what is, in effect, its constitution.

Chatham House. The home of the Royal Institute of International Affairs in St James's Square, London.

Chatham House Rule. This rule states that: 'When a meeting, or part thereof, is held under the Chatham House Rule, participants are free to use the information received, but neither the identity nor the affiliation of the speaker(s), nor that of any other participant, may be revealed.' The Rule originated at *Chatham House in 1927 and was amended in 1992. Designed to promote free discussion, it is now used widely through-out the English-speaking world. Although it is common to speak of 'Chatham House Rules', in fact there is only one Rule.

chief clerk. The title given to the senior official (a *deputy under-secretary of state) in Britain's *Foreign and Commonwealth Office who is responsible for the administration of the *Diplomatic Service.

chief military observer. The title often given to the head of a *peace-keeping operation which consists of *military observers. However, the head of the military observer group on the Arab–Israeli borders – founded in 1948 and still in being – has always been called chief of staff.

chiffreur. A cipher or communications officer on the *diplomatic staff of a French mission.

China Watchers. The staff of the United States *consulate-general in Hong Kong who specialized in gathering information and reporting on the People's Republic of China. This work was of special value to Washington before it was allowed to open a *representative office in Beijing in 1973.

Chinese secretary. *See* oriental secretary.

CHOGM. Commonwealth Heads of Government Meeting. *See* Commonwealth; summitry.

C3I. An acronym from the military and intelligence worlds meaning 'command, control, communication, and intelligence/information'.

C4I. An update on C3I to include 'computers'.

CIA. Created by the National Security Act of 1947, the Central Intelligence Agency was soon the dominant element in the American *intelligence community, as it remains today. It both collects and analyses *foreign intelligence obtained from all sources; it has also acquired a reputation for semi-military *covert action in foreign countries as well as for black *propaganda. Perhaps its real hallmark, however, apart from its size, is the centralization of *intelligence which its name suggests and its independence of any one department which is the corollary of this. (Intelligence gathering developed historically as a fringe activity of ministries of foreign affairs and the different branches of the armed services.) As noted by Michael Herman, a senior figure in British intelligence, 'it was the first specialist, non-departmental *all-source analysis organization which evolved in peacetime to study foreign targets in full and serve any part of government'. If the CIA has remained to any degree dependent on any department, however, it is probably the *State Department, since it relies on it to such a great extent to provide cover for its agents in US embassies and consulates abroad. Since exposure of many of its activities (especially its covert operations) in the first half of the 1970s, the CIA has been subjected to considerably more congressional oversight. *See also* Director of Central Intelligence; humint.

cipher. (1) A symbol, whether letter or number, which represents a single letter or number, as opposed to a *code where plurals are employed. A message written in cipher is said to have been 'encrypted'. The distinction between a cipher and code is a purely technical one and though it is still common to see references to 'codes *and* ciphers', the terms are often used today as synonyms. Consistently with this, messages are said to be 'deciphered' when a government agency translates into plain text one of its own encrypted messages, whether a cipher or a code had been employed. Broken ciphers are said to have been 'decrypted'. (2) The key to a system of symbols used in this manner.

circular note. One which goes to a number of recipients, e.g. all diplomatic missions in a particular capital.

citizen diplomacy. *See* track two diplomacy.

civilian police. Police personnel employed in a *peacekeeping operation.

civil society. *See* non-governmental organization.

claim. A formal demand made by one state on another for the rectification of or compensation for a legal wrong that allegedly has been done to it by the second state.

class. *See* diplomatic classes.

clausula rebus sic stantibus. The doctrine that there is an implied term or clause in a *treaty – the *clausula rebus sic stantibus* – to the effect that the treaty is *binding only for as long as there is no fundamental change in the circumstances which were assumed by the parties at the time of its conclusion. The doctrine finds expression – but not in its Latin form – in the 1969 Vienna Convention on the *Law of Treaties. The mere invocation of the doctrine does not serve to invalidate a treaty. Only if no objection is raised by any other party within three months of having received notice of its invocation is the state in question entitled to regard itself as free from the obligations of the treaty. In the event of an objection, procedures for *pacific settlement must be instituted.

clientitis. *See* localitis.

Clingendael. The Netherlands Institute of International Relations, so called because it is housed in a building of the same name in Clingendael Park in The Hague. Providing eloquent evidence of the desirability of the location, during the Second World War the house was seized and occupied by Seyss-Inquart, the Nazi Commissioner for the Netherlands. The Clingendael Institute, established in 1983 and enjoying 40 per cent budget support from the Dutch ministries of foreign affairs and defence, is, among other things, one of Europe's leading diplomatic academies.

code. (1) A word, symbol or group of symbols representing a whole word or even a group of words. (2) The key to a system of words or symbols used in this manner. As with *ciphers, messages put into code are said to have been 'encrypted' and broken codes 'decrypted'. *See also* cryptanalysis; cryptography.

codecision procedure. A procedure of the EU giving the *European Parliament the power to adopt *instruments jointly with the *Council of Ministers. Introduced by the Treaty of *Maastricht, it has strengthened the parliament's legislative powers in a number of important fields. *See also* qualified majority voting.

Codel. An abbreviation for one of the most feared categories of visitor to an American embassy: a congressional delegation. *See also* visiting fireman.

codification. The systematic presentation of rules of *international law in a *multilateral treaty. In principle, codification is distinct from the *progressive development of the law. But in practice it is hard to codify law without at the same time introducing at least some changes to resolve uncertainties and inconsistencies. The General Assembly is charged by the UN *Charter with both tasks, the detailed preparatory work on which is delegated to the *International Law Commission. The Vienna Conventions on *Diplomatic Relations and on *Consular Relations are successful instances of international codification.

coercive diplomacy. A euphemism for the threat or use of force against an opponent to foster a more cooperative cast of mind. In the shape of *bomber diplomacy, this was a tactic adopted by *NATO against the Federal Republic of Yugoslavia during the Kosovo crisis in 1999. In many international relationships force needs to be either a spoken or unspoken accompaniment to diplomacy. *Machiavelli found this to his cost when he was a representative of the virtually unarmed Florentine government at the court of Louis XII in 1500. 'They call you Mr Nothing', the exasperated envoy was obliged to inform his employers.

Cold War. The conflict which developed shortly after the Second World War between the Soviet Union and the United States, together with their respective allies. It is generally regarded as having been brought to an end at the *summit meeting in Paris in November 1990. It was distinguished by the absence of direct military engagement or 'hot war' and, after the *Cuban Missile Crisis in 1962, agreement on certain ground rules. Its real flavour was provided by *propaganda, subversion, surrogate wars, and the use of foreign aid in the attempt to win adherents in the *non-aligned world. The term was invented in 1947 by the US financier and presidential adviser Bernard Baruch, and popularized in the press. The most evocative symbol of the Cold War was the Berlin Wall (which was erected by East Germany in 1961 and remained in place until late 1989), dividing East from West Berlin.

*Diplomatic relations (sense 1) between the Soviet Union and the United States were never severed during the Cold War and large *embassies were maintained by each in the capital of the other. However, as well as being used for traditional diplomatic purposes, these missions were more than usually important as covers for *intelligence-gathering activities. Furthermore, American and Soviet embassies in many states, not least in the *Third World, were used to direct military assistance programmes and, sometimes, *covert operations. American diplomats sometimes described this as the 'militarization of diplomacy'.

collective note. A single *note addressed to one state by two or more others. Designed to give maximum force to a joint representation, it may nevertheless both be difficult to agree and be seen as an attempt at bullying. As a result, it has always been a rare form of diplomatic communication. *See also* identic notes.

collective security. The principle that all members of the collectivity of states are jointly responsible for the physical security of each of them. The principle emerged in the twentieth century because of dissatisfaction with the individualism of the nineteenth century, and with its associated principle of the *balance of power (sense 3). Thus collective security found (imperfect) expression after the First World War in the *Covenant of the League of Nations, and further (again imperfect) expression in 1945 in the UN *Charter. Its implementation in the practice of both international organizations has also been far from perfect, as states are understandably reluctant to endanger their individual *national interests by acting on the basis of such a broad and demanding principle as that of collective security. Nonetheless, the deference now paid to the principle indicates the far-reaching change in ideas about proper international behaviour that took place during the twentieth century.

The principle of collective security reflected the assumption that the chief threat to a state's physical integrity was an armed attack by a state or states bent on territorial gain. Perhaps in part due to the general theoretical rejection of that activity, this type of threat appears in practice to have substantially diminished, which may explain why the concept of collective security is now not often expressed in those words. However, much is heard about *peace enforcement – which, broadly speaking, is its contemporary semantic equivalent.

See also aggression; Gulf War (sense 2); self-defence.

colonialism. The acquisition and holding of *colonies, and the belief in the propriety of so doing.

colony. A territory possessed or administered by a *sovereign state which is both physically separate from it and not integrated into the governmental arrangements of the metropolitan state. A colony's constitution will thus be subordinate to that of the metropolitan state. But beyond that, a colony's constitutional position can vary enormously, from almost complete control by the colonial power to virtually unhindered internal self-government. Except for some very small or special instances, colonies have largely disappeared, reflecting the anti-colonial ethos of the age. There has also been a corresponding change in terminology. In British practice, 'colony' was first changed to 'dependent territory', but in 1998 that was judged by the new Labour Government to be demeaning, and the term was altered to 'overseas territory'. Correspondingly, whereas the territories in question had been known as 'British Dependent Territories', they were now to be called 'United Kingdom Overseas Territories'. *See also* Committee of 24; Declaration on the Granting of Independence to Colonial Countries and Peoples; dependent territory; non-self-governing territory.

comitology. In the EU, the procedures governing the dialogue which must take place between the *European Commission and various committees consisting of representatives of member states before it adopts any measures to implement legislation at Community level.

comity. Rules of international conduct which are based not in *international law but on considerations of courtesy.

command. A term employed by the British *Foreign and Commonwealth Office for a broad area of geographical, functional or administrative responsibility falling under a *director (formerly assistant under-secretary of state) and usually comprising a number of *departments.

commercial attaché. *See* attaché.

commercial counsellor. Sometimes 'counsellor (commercial)', a diplomatic officer of *counsellor rank responsible for the commercial work of a mission, usually as head

of its *commercial section. *See also* trade commissioner; Commercial Diplomatic Service.

commercial diplomacy. The work of *diplomatic missions in support of the home country's business and finance sectors. Distinct from although obviously closely related to *economic diplomacy, it is now common for commercial diplomacy to include the promotion of inward and outward investment, as well as trade. Important features of this work are the supply to the sending state's trade ministry and businessmen (especially those from small businesses) of information about export and investment opportunities, maintaining contact with the businessmen and chambers of commerce of the receiving state, and organizing and supporting *trade missions from home. In American diplomatic missions this work is currently undertaken largely by officers of the foreign commercial service of the Department of Commerce, assisted by the mission's *economic officer and possibly others.

Commercial Diplomatic Service. The British service created at the end of the First World War and jointly administered by the *Foreign Office and the newly created Department of Overseas Trade. It developed from the growing corps of commercial *attachés and soon saw the appointment to diplomatic missions of its own staff with its own ranks: *commercial counsellors and commercial secretaries. In 1943 it was absorbed by the new, unified *Foreign Service, though until 1965 trade commissioners were still posted abroad by the Board of Trade as part of the Trade Commissioner Service. *See also* Diplomatic Service, British.

commercial office. This post is virtually the same as a *trade office. It is not to be confused with a *commercial section.

commercial officer. A rather loose term which generally signifies a *diplomatic agent who is a member of the *commercial section of a diplomatic mission. In the US *Foreign Service such an individual, if not a member of the Department of Commerce, is known as an *economic officer. *See also* trade officer.

commercial secretary. A *commercial section officer below *counsellor rank. *See also* trade commissioner; Commercial Diplomatic Service.

commercial section. The section within a British *diplomatic mission responsible for all its commercial and financial work, though larger ones now tend to have a separate one for *economic diplomacy (sense 1). Sometimes also known as the 'commercial department' or 'commercial secretariat', a commercial section is to be distinguished from a *commercial office. *See also* economic section.

commission. A document supplied by the *sending state to the head of a *consular post and to the *receiving state which certifies the officer's name, consular rank (also called class), the *consular district he or she is to head, and the seat of the post. However, the officer can only act in that capacity after the receiving state has issued the necessary authorization in the form of an *exequatur*. *See also* letters of commission.

commission of appointment. The document given by the *sending state to a new *head of mission appointing him or her to the position in question. Historically, it sometimes detailed his duties or gave him *instructions. It is to be distinguished from *letters of credence or *letters of commission, both of which accredit the appointee to the *receiving state's *head of state. British *high commissioners, for historical reasons, do not receive commissions of appointment.

commission rogatoire. *See* rogatory letter.

Committee of 24. The usual way of referring to the UN Committee with a much longer name which, from the early 1960s, was the spearhead of the UN *General Assembly's anti-colonial campaign. *See also* Declaration on the Granting of Independence to Colonial Countries and Peoples.

common but differentiated responsibility, principle of. The assertion that while all states bear responsibility for damage to the environment, the extent to which they should seek to remedy such damage depends on their differing circumstances. It appears in some environmental instruments, but is not (yet) a principle of *customary international law – and were it to become so its imprecision might lessen its utility. *See also* precautionary principle.

Common Foreign and Security Policy (CFSP). The term employed in the *European Union which signifies: (a) Union policy on foreign political and security issues where cooperation or joint action is agreed by the *Council of Ministers, and (b) the machinery for generating and implementing it. CFSP grew out of the largely extra-Community, intergovernmental scheme for member state concertation in this area which was known as 'European Political Co-operation (EPC)' and prevailed over the period from the early 1970s until CFSP was introduced by the *Maastricht Treaty in 1993.

Common Market. A popular term for the European Economic Community (EEC) (established by the Treaty of Rome of 1957), and also for the European Communities created in 1967 by the merger of the administrative network of the EEC with those of the European Atomic Energy Community and the European Coal and Steel Community. *See also* customs union; European Union.

common system. The system of salaries, allowances, and benefits applied by the UN, its *specialized agencies, and some other *international organizations. *See also* international civil service.

Commonwealth. An association of 54 *sovereign states which has grown out of the constitutional development and subsequent disintegration of the British Empire. It has no formal constitution, save the acceptance by all members of Queen Elizabeth II (and before her King George VI) as the symbol of their association and as the Head of the Commonwealth. (It should be noted, however, that since the London Declaration of 1949 this is a personal appointment and so does not necessarily pass to the succeeding British monarch.) Of the members, 16 have the monarch as their *head of state, five have their own monarchical arrangements, and the remaining 33 are republics. Until the admission of Mozambique furnished an exception (in 1995), it had been assumed, and is still assumed, that the (normal) prerequisite for membership was for the state in question (or part of it) to have been, in one way or another, under British jurisdiction. Members are expected to behave in accord with certain broad principles, which endorse (for example) democracy, human rights, and the rule of law.

The Commonwealth proceeds on the basis of consultation, and engages in such cooperative action and extends such intra-Commonwealth assistance as can be agreed by all members. Commonwealth Heads of Government Meetings (CHOGMs) are held every two years, and meetings of other *ministers (sense 3) take place periodically. The Commonwealth's central coordinating body is the Commonwealth Secretariat, based in London, which was established in 1965 (Britain having previously undertaken such tasks). Additionally, there are numerous unofficial Commonwealth bodies and agencies.

At CHOGMs and other official Commonwealth meetings, the representative of the *host state (sense 2) is in the chair, with the other members being seated around the table on a clockwise alphabetical basis, the member highest in the alphabet taking the place immediately to the chairperson's left. Thus, at such meetings, the present membership of the Commonwealth results in the representative of Antigua and Barbuda always being to the chairperson's left, with the Zimbabwean representative being next but one on the chairperson's right – the Commonwealth Secretary-General being between the two of them.

See also dominions; high commissioner; Queen's Realms; trade commissioner.

Commonwealth Relations Office (CRO). The British department of state which existed between 1947 and 1966 (when it briefly became the Commonwealth Office) to conduct Britain's relations with the members of the *Commonwealth. Before 1947 these relations were the responsibility of the *Dominions Office. The civil servants who served in these Offices were members of Britain's home civil service, and not of her *foreign service. *See also* Foreign and Commonwealth Office.

communiqué. An agreed statement issued at the end of a *summit meeting or other high-level visit or *multilateral conference. Occasionally described as *declarations, to which they certainly bear a family resemblance, communiqués are designed to give the public some sense of what has been discussed under each head on the agenda and also suggest the substance of any *consensus achieved on future policy. However, they usually have to be drafted very quickly and, while it is fair to describe them as statements which prudence dictates should be honoured, they rarely have the status of *treaties; to emphasize this they are sometimes described as 'press communiqués'. Nevertheless, they can be of huge importance, as in the case of the Shanghai Communiqué, which was issued at the end of US President Richard Nixon's historic visit to the People's Republic of China in February 1972.

Commynes, Philippe de (c. 1447–1511). A French diplomat and historian. Commynes wrote the best-known political and diplomatic memoirs of the late fifteenth century and is chiefly remembered today by students of diplomacy for his hostility to *summitry: 'Two great princes who wish to establish good personal relations', remarked Commynes, 'should never meet each other face to face but ought to communicate through good and wise ambassadors'. Though he had other good reasons for arriving at this conclusion, his attitude may also have been influenced by the fact that when Louis XI and Edward IV met on a bridge over the Somme at Picquigny to discuss the peaceful retreat of the English invasion force of 1475, the king instructed Commynes to wear identical clothes to his own as a precaution against assassination. The *Mémoires* of Commynes, though written only to provide material for a life of Louis XI that was to be undertaken by the archbishop of Vienne, are themselves highly regarded. The first part covers the period 1464–83 and was published in 1524; the second narrated the Italian expeditions of Charles VIII and appeared in 1528. A realist, though a firm believer in the power of the divine in human affairs, there are certain clear parallels between Commynes's thought and that of *Machiavelli.

compellance. *See* coercive diplomacy.

compound. The protected area sometimes constructed to enclose both the *residence and the *embassy of a *sending state. At least where the United States is concerned, this may have so many additional buildings (including staff apartments, recreational facilities, a shopping concourse and school) as to resemble a walled town in microcosm. Diplomatic compounds are a common feature of diplomatic life in parts of the world where security is a serious problem. They have increased in number as fear at the extent and savagery of attacks on diplomatic premises since the 1970s has weakened the earlier feeling that the segregation from the host community which compounds entail was inconsistent with their *diplomatic functions. *See also* emergency room; Inman standards.

compromis. An agreement by which a dispute is submitted to *arbitration or *judicial settlement. In the former case, the *compromis* will have to determine the identity of the arbitrators, the subject of the dispute, the procedures that are to be followed, and the rules on the basis of which the decision is to be given. If the parties are resorting to the so-called *Permanent Court of Arbitration, the arbitrators will be selected from the members of the Court. When two states agree that a dispute be submitted to judicial settlement, the document by which this is done is nowadays more usually known as a 'special agreement' than as a *compromis*.

compromise. An agreement reached by *negotiation in which each party surrenders a portion of its preferred outcome. *See also* endgame; fall-back position.

compulsory adjudication. The situation which exists when two or more states have agreed in advance that disputes between them (possibly only those of a certain type or arising after a certain date) may be taken to *adjudication at the instance of any one of them. It is thus a departure from the normal international principle that the settlement of a dispute by adjudication requires the specific consent of all the parties. *See also compromis*; compulsory arbitration; compulsory jurisdiction.

compulsory arbitration. A scheme for *compulsory adjudication which provides that the disputes in question shall be taken to *arbitration. Accordingly, the parties have also to agree on a *compromis*.

compulsory jurisdiction. The jurisdiction enjoyed by an international judicial body in respect of cases falling within agreements for *compulsory adjudication. Compulsory jurisdiction is bestowed on the *International Court of Justice

through declarations by states under what is known as the *Optional Clause procedure.

Concert of Europe. The term used to describe the main historical model of *great power management of a *states-system, that of nineteenth century Europe. It initially operated through *congresses. However, with the exception of the peace congresses of 1856 (Paris) and 1878 (Berlin), after 1822 the Concert found expression through conferences of ambassadors.

concession. (1) A point surrendered by one party to another in a *negotiation. (2) In the late nineteenth to early twentieth century term 'foreign concession', an area of land in China leased to a foreign power by the government under one or other of the *unequal treaties. The most famous was the International Settlement at Shanghai. The unequal treaties were finally abolished in 1943. *See also* capitulations.

Conciliar Movement. A series of ecumenical Councils held during the first half of the fifteenth century in an endeavour to reform the papacy-led international system of Christendom. The failure of the Movement led directly to the breakdown of the medieval system and to the emergence of a secular international system made up of *sovereign states.

conciliation. (1) The attempt to resolve a dispute by having it examined in depth by an independent commission of inquiry or 'conciliation commission'; this then offers its recommendation for a settlement, which, in contrast to a decision arrived at by *arbitration, is non-binding. Following elaboration of the procedures involved in conciliation by the General Act on the Pacific Settlement of International Disputes in 1928, a normal conciliation commission would have five members, one from each side and the rest (by agreement) from third states. The commission would meet in private and report within six months. Inspired by a somewhat sanguine doctrine concerning the force of an 'objective' analysis of the causes of international conflict, the technique of conciliation had a relatively short heyday in the interwar period. Nevertheless, there are circumstances where it has proved to be of value, and some treaties still provide for it, as in the case of the Convention on the Law of the Sea (1982). (2) In the *European Union, the use since 1975 of negotiation in a joint 'conciliation committee' to resolve legislative disagreements between the *European Parliament and the *Council of Ministers. *See also* good offices; mediation.

conclusions. *See* minutes.

concordat. An *agreement concerning the affairs of the Roman Catholic Church in a particular state made between the Pope and the head of the state in question. The nomination of bishops is a sensitive matter that is typically the subject of such agreements. There has in the past been controversy over whether or not concordats could actually be classed as *treaties since the Pope signs them in his capacity as head of the Roman Catholic Church rather than head of the *Vatican state. In any event, *Satow's Guide* notes that already by the 1970s the concordat was gradually being dropped in favour of the agreement or *modus vivendi*.

concurrent accreditation. *See* multiple accreditation.

conditionality. The principle that, in a negotiation, concession of a point by one party is conditional on receiving one from the other in return. It is therefore, often in a well understood but somewhat imprecisely expressed form, of the essence of very many diplomatic exchanges. But in a form that *is* precisely expressed, it has become closely associated with the International Monetary Fund and with offers of development aid. It refers to the IMF's requirement, before lending a state any money to meet a balance of payments problem, that a convincing explanation be supplied as to how the state intends to solve the problem, and so be in a position to repay the loan within the stipulated period. The IMF may make its own recommendations towards this end. Offers of development aid may similarly be made conditional on the recipient state agreeing to adopt economic, financial and development policies which, in the opinion of the donor state or institution, will ensure that the aid will not be wasted but will make the maximum contribution to development.

condominium. The joint exercise of jurisdiction over a territory by two or more states. The territory is thus in the nature of a joint *colony. This arrangement presents difficult political and administrative issues. Hence it occurs only rarely, with no current instances. The last one was the Anglo-French condominium over the Pacific island territory of New Hebrides, which in 1980 became the *sovereign state of Vanuatu.

confederation. A union of sovereign states in which the member states retain their *sovereignty (sense 1), and hence their international status; but in which the establishment of comprehensive quasi-governmental organs distinguishes the union from a typical *international organization. However, the participant states are unlikely to permit any direct contact between the organs of the union and their citizens. A famous historical instance of a confederation is the United States between 1776 and 1787. Switzerland calls itself a confederation (and was one

before 1848), and Canada is often referred to as a confederation, but in fact both are *federal states. Within its spheres of competence, the *European Union displays many confederal characteristics; but its lack of comprehensiveness means that it is not a confederation. The Turkish Republic of Northern Cyprus favours a confederal constitution as the solution for the Cyprus problem.

conference. Usually involving large *delegations and having ambitious goals (even if beforehand such conferences pretend the opposite), the similarities between international conferences end here. They may be *bilateral or *multilateral, ad hoc or permanent, held on *neutral ground or not, conducted at the *summit or below, and concerned with any subject imaginable. *See also* congress.

conference diplomacy. A synonym for *multilateral diplomacy.

Conference on Security and Cooperation in Europe (CSCE). *See* Organisation for Security and Cooperation in Europe (OSCE).

confessional. In the terminology of the European Union, a secret bilateral meeting conducted at an EU *summit by the leaders of individual member states with the leader of the state holding the presidency. At these private meetings, each leader is supposed to reveal his hopes and fears and *bottom-line negotiating position. The term came into vogue at the Nice summit in December 2000.

confidence-building measure. A joint activity engaged in by parties to a serious dispute with a view to lowering its temperature, demonstrating the advantages of cooperation, and generally preparing the ground for a diplomatic approach to the more difficult issues dividing them. Measures of this kind are very varied but include the regular exchange of military missions and the monitoring of regional arms agreements. Often promoted by a *mediator, 'CBMs' are sometimes seen as an aspect of *preventive diplomacy. *See also* step-by-step diplomacy.

conflict resolution. *See* mediation.

congress. An international *conference of unusual importance and thus often attended by foreign ministers and sometimes monarchs, though this usage passed away with the nineteenth century. Thus the Crimean War was ended by the Congress of Paris in 1856 but the First World War was terminated by the Paris Peace Conference in 1919. *See also* Concert of Europe; Vienna, Congress of (1815); Westphalia, Congress of (1644–48).

consensus decision-making. In discussion of a subject in a *multilateral forum where majority voting would otherwise be used, the attempt to achieve the agreement of all participants without the need for a vote, thereby avoiding the risk of alienating weak majorities if the voting is *weighted and powerful minorities if it is not. A consensus exists when all parties are in agreement, which on the face of it is another way of saying that they are unanimous. However, a consensus may include some members whose support has been given only grudgingly and have simply registered no *formal* objection, whereas *unanimity implies broader enthusiasm; hence the view that in fact they are not the same. It might be more accurate to say that a weak consensus is not the same as unanimity but that a strong one is.

Notice began to be taken of a growing trend away from *majority voting and towards consensus decision-making following its successful employment at the Third UN Conference on the Law of the Sea in the period 1973–82. However, this was not so much a new development as a return to an older one, that is to say, *negotiation, and it may be thought, therefore, that this is a further instance of the regrettable rule that it is inadvisable to use one word when three will do. Having said this, multilateral conferences have certainly seen the advent of novel procedural devices designed to foster consensus, notably in the area of chairmen's powers. Furthermore, under the charter of some international bodies voting is still required, even if it now does little more than ratify a consensus already negotiated. As a result, objection to use of the term 'consensus decision-making' instead of 'negotiation' in multilateral diplomacy should perhaps not be too strenuous. *See also* Council of Ministers (European); silence procedure; straw vote.

consent. A basic principle of *international law, in that it must be given by a *state before that state can be bound by a *treaty; and in that any change in an existing legal arrangement requires the consent of all the parties. *See also* ratification; signature.

constituent assembly. A body convened for the purpose of agreeing a constitution for a new state.

constructive   abstention.   An *abstention in a vote, where *unanimity is required for a decision, which does not have the effect of blocking it; in this situation, an ordinary abstention would be tantamount to a *veto. In the UN *Security Council, and contrary to the UN *Charter, abstentions on non-procedural matters have always been treated as 'constructive', although they have never been so described. The term itself was introduced into the EU's *Common Foreign and Security Policy by the *Treaty of Amsterdam (1997). In the event that a constructive abstention permits a decision in CFSP, the abstaining state is obliged not to impede any action flowing from it and – except in the case of 'operations having military or defence implications' – bear its share of any consequent costs. Nevertheless, it is not required to take any part in this action.

constructive ambiguity. The deliberate use of imprecise language in the drafting of an *agreement on a sensitive issue. The aim is to secure its approval in the hope (perhaps purported and often in vain) that its actual approval will encourage further and more substantive steps towards an agreement. Perhaps the best known instance of this phenomenon is the *Security Council's Resolution 242 of November 1967. Referring to the *Six-Day Arab–Israeli War of the previous June, this required the '[w]ithdrawal of Israeli armed forces from territories occupied in the recent conflict' – not from *the* territories occupied in the recent conflict. It thereby left unclear the question of whether Israel was obliged to engage in a complete or only partial withdrawal. This proved unconstructive. Other terms for constructive ambiguity are 'fudging', and 'glossing' or 'papering over' disagreements.

consul. In general usage, any *consular officer; in more specific terms, one of the four *consular ranks.

The office of consul is of great antiquity, and precedes *resident diplomatic missions. It was instituted by states to protect their commercial interests in a foreign country and those of their nationals who were trading or travelling there. Professionally speaking, consuls were in their prime from about 1850 to 1950. This period saw a huge expansion in international commerce, and a good deal of it occurred in territories that were part of the large overseas and overland empires which then held sway. As *diplomatic missions are sent only to *capital cities, states wishing to provide on-the-spot advice and assistance to their traders had to establish *consular posts.

The ending of colonialism was accompanied by a great increase in the size of *diplomatic services and the number of diplomatic missions. And it happened that in capital cities it quickly became customary for consular matters to be dealt with not by separate consular posts but by newly established *consular sections within diplomatic missions, or by members of the mission's staff who were authorized to perform consular functions – with the individuals concerned enjoying *diplomatic rather than *consular status. Thus consular posts tend nowadays to be found only in large commercial cities or seaports which are not the capital of the state concerned. In some *Commonwealth states, notably India and Pakistan, *consular functions exercised by other Commonwealth states outside the capital city are performed not by

consular posts but by *offices of the deputy high commissioner.

However, consular functions remain of considerable importance, not least in geographically large and economically powerful states. The exponential growth in leisure travel has also created a need for consuls in highly popular holiday areas. Thus consular functions continue to be valuably exercised across much of the international scene, albeit no longer by members of a *consular service, and not always by individuals with a consular rank. *See also* consular relations; factory; honorary consular officer; *proxenos*.

consulage. Historically, a tax on goods passing through their hands paid to a diplomat or consul by the merchants of his own state resident at his posting. Understood to be paid for the benefits of protection received, it was supposed to be employed for the upkeep of his mission.

consular agency. *See* consular post.

consular agent. *See* consular post; honorary consular officer.

consular archives. *See* diplomatic archives.

consular bag. The consular equivalent of the *diplomatic bag. However, unlike the latter, it may be returned to its place of origin if a request by the authorities of the *receiving state that the bag be opened in their presence is refused.

consular commission. Sometimes, to make local enquiries on a matter of international concern in a non-sovereign territory, states have established a consular commission consisting of the heads of their *consular posts in a particular city.

consular corps. The body of *consular officers resident in a particular city. When *trade commissioners were distinguished from consular officers, and resident in a city with a consular corps, they were sometimes, as a matter of courtesy, treated as members of the corps.

consular district. The area assigned by the *receiving state to a *consular post, or the *consular section of a *diplomatic mission, for the exercise of *consular functions. The need for the designation of such districts arises when, by agreement between the *sending and the receiving states, the former establishes more than one consular body within the latter's territory.

consular flag. The flag used by a state on its consular premises and as the personal flag of the consular mission's head. It need not be identical with the national flag, nor with its *diplomatic flag. Britain's consular flag is the national flag with, in the centre, the St Edward's Crown on a white disc.

consular functions. The chief functions of *consular officers are to protect and advance their state's commercial interests; to check that their state's ships and aircraft are observing its laws and regulations; and (the area for which consuls are probably best known) to perform a large variety of duties relating to the well-being of their nationals – such as issuing passports, solemnizing marriages, visiting nationals in prison, and even making small loans. Consular officers serving outside the *receiving state's *capital city may also report to their state on local conditions – an activity of the sort normally associated with *diplomatic missions. And if the *sending state does not have a diplomatic mission in the capital, and is not represented there by a third state, consular officers may, with the consent of the receiving state, perform characteristically-diplomatic acts, principally the transmission of communications between the two states.

consular list. The list maintained, and perhaps periodically published by, a *receiving state which gives the names of those who, being officers of *consular posts in a particular city or cities, enjoy *consular status within the receiving state. In respect of any one city or *consular district, the local authority or the consular corps itself may publish a consular list – although it would not be authoritative so far as the enjoyment of consular status is concerned. *See also* honorary consular officer.

consular officer. Any member of a *consular post who is entrusted with the exercise of *consular functions. Such an officer may be declared *persona non grata*. Consular officers are to be distinguished from non-consular members of the post's staff, such as those engaged on administrative, technical, and service tasks. *See also* honorary consular officer.

consular post. A post which, either throughout the *receiving state or within a designated *consular district, exercises *consular functions only. Thus, when consular functions are exercised by a *diplomatic mission, that does not make the latter a consular post. The intended head of a consular post is supplied with a *commission by the *sending state which must be submitted in advance to the receiving state; if that state has no objection to the appointment, it supplies the officer with an *exequatur*, thereby authorizing this officer to assume the responsibilities of head of post. In accordance with the head of post's rank, a consular post will be called one of the following: consulate-general, consulate, vice-consulate, and (although this category now appears to be rarely used) consular agency. *See also* consular rank; consular relations; consular section; honorary consular officer.

consular privileges and immunities. These are set out in the Vienna Convention on *Consular Relations (1963), which has been widely accepted. In general, this provides *career consular officers with immunity from the jurisdiction of the *receiving state in respect of their official acts but (unlike *diplomatic agents) not in respect of their private acts. Consular premises and documents are inviolable, as are consular communications. It is always open to states to extend these arrangements by way of a bilateral *treaty, and a number of such treaties have been concluded. *Honorary consular officers enjoy a severely restricted version of the immunities granted to career officers. Members of the *consular section of a *diplomatic mission receive the full range of *diplomatic immunities and privileges, as do members of the office of a *deputy high commissioner.

consular rank. *Consular officers are customarily given one of four ranks. In order of seniority they are: consul-general, consul, vice-consul, and consular agent. The head of a *consular post must be given one of these ranks. Members of a *diplomatic mission engaged on consular tasks may be similarly designated. But they are also commonly given such titles as minister (consular affairs), counsellor and consul-general, second secretary (consular), or third secretary and vice-consul.

consular relations. A state must be in consular relations with another state before it can establish *consular posts in that state's territory. Such relations are established by mutual consent. They may, however, be broken unilaterally, requiring the closing of all consular posts in both the states concerned.

Consular relations are distinct from *diplomatic relations (sense 1). Thus two states may be in consular relations but not in diplomatic relations, and vice versa – although normally the establishment of diplomatic relations implies an agreement to the establishment also of consular relations. Two states whose political relations have been poor, and (probably for that reason) are not in diplomatic or consular relations, sometimes make a preliminary move towards the establishment or re-establishment of diplomatic relations by first establishing or resuming consular relations. This procedure is in the nature of a testing of the political water. Nowadays, however, it is rarely adopted.

Consular Relations, Vienna Convention on. The outcome of a conference held in Vienna in 1963 with the object of *codifying and clarifying the existing *customary international law on consular matters, notably the facilities, privileges and immunities relating to *consular posts and officers. The Convention *entered into force in 1967, and the vast majority of states have become parties to it. However, with a view to greater precision, and sometimes also to extending the privileges and immunities set out in the Convention, a number of states have concluded bilateral treaties on the subject.

consular section. That part of an *embassy which executes *consular functions. Alternatively, where a consular section is not formally designated, members of the embassy's *diplomatic staff may be authorized to perform such functions. In either case, as the persons performing these functions are *diplomatic agents, they enjoy *diplomatic and not *consular privileges and immunities. *See also* consul; consular post; consular rank.

consular service. A state service consisting solely of *consular officers, and hence distinct from a *diplomatic or *foreign service. In the past, the larger states even had consular services specializing in a particular region of the world. However, the rigid distinction between the consular and the diplomatic career tended to reflect social class divisions in recruitment which sat ill with the political climate of the twentieth century, as did the corresponding distinction, also now abolished, between separate *commercial diplomatic and diplomatic or foreign services. It also impaired the mobility of personnel and hindered cooperation between the two branches. And it rested on distinctions in tasks which began to grow thin as *diplomats (sense 1), traditionally preoccupied with high politics, were charged increasingly with consular, commercial, and economic duties as well. Accordingly, consular services were steadily incorporated into diplomatic services, and diplomats have become routinely liable to engage from time to time in consular as in commercial work. *See also* career consular officer; Commercial Diplomatic Service; consul; consular section; Levant Consular Service.

consular status. The status held by a member of the staff of a *consular post who is classed as a *consular officer. Those enjoying it are thereby entitled to *consular privileges and immunities.

consulate. *See* consular post.

consulate-general. *See* consular post.

consul-general. *See* consular post; honorary consular officer.

Consulta. The colloquial term for the Italian ministry of foreign affairs following its transfer in 1871 from Florence to Rome, where it began business in the *Palazzo della Consulta* on 1 July. The ministry remained here until the end of 1922, when it was moved to the *Palazzo Chigi. See also Farnesina*.

consultations. Discussions at home with a *head of mission following an unexpected recall. In fact, a summons to return home for 'consultations' is often a means of expressing displeasure at some act of the *receiving state; or, sometimes, a way of enabling the head of mission to make a quick but dignified exit in circumstances where it is anticipated that he or she will shortly be declared *persona non grata*.

consultations of the whole. *See* informal consultations (sense 1).

consultative status. (1) A status which may be granted by an *international organization to a private organization (and sometimes to a state) with a view to establishing a measure of coordination and cooperation between them. The privileges of the status may be non-uniform, as in the best-known instance of the arrangement: that between the UN *Economic and Social Council and approximately 2000 *non-governmental organizations, where the latter are divided into several categories on the basis of their degree of interest in the Council's work. Entities enjoying consultative status usually have privileges exceeding the ones possessed by those with only *observer status, including the right to suggest agenda items and make oral presentations at meetings. (2) More rarely, the status of a state with full rights to participate in meetings of a treaty regime, as notably in meetings under the Antarctic Treaty.

contact group. An ad hoc group of senior diplomats and/or foreign ministers from three or more states created to coordinate their *mediation of a conflict, typically by providing 'contact' between the adversaries in *proximity talks. The first to put the new terminology in the lexicon was the Western Contact Group on Namibia, which was created in 1977 and consisted of representatives of Britain, Canada, France, the USA, and West Germany, which happened to be the Western states on the UN *Security Council at the time – 'The Five'. The Western Contact Group operated in a variety of theatres and with a variety of personnel, including Geneva, the capitals of The Five, the many black African capitals whose governments participated in the negotiations, and South Africa itself, where the ambassadors of the five states were its members. However, its original and chief focus was UN Headquarters in New York, where the *permanent representatives of The Five, or more usually their deputies, constituted the original 'Contact Group'. More recent examples include the Contadora Group and the Bosnia/Kosovo Contact Group, established in 1983 and 1994 respectively.

contraband. Goods considered by a *belligerent (sense 1) to be of assistance to the enemy in the conduct of *war. Under the *laws of war such goods being carried to a belligerent from a *neutral state or by its shipping may be seized and confiscated by an opposing belligerent. The matter is now chiefly of historical interest. *See also* blockade.

contribution principle. The principle applied in *international organizations that influence in decision-making and the allocation of posts in their *secretariats should reflect the size of members' budgetary contributions. *See also* geographical post; weighted voting.

contributor state. A state which contributes personnel to a *peace-keeping operation.

convention. A synonym for *treaty, used most often for multilateral treaties of general interest.

Convention
   on Consular Relations (1963)
   on Diplomatic Relations (1961)
   on the Law of Treaties (1969)
   on the Prevention and Punishment of Crimes against Internationally Protected Persons, including Diplomatic Agents (1973)
   on Privileges and Immunities of Specialized Agencies (1947)
   on the Privileges and Immunities of the United Nations (1946)
   on the Representation of States in their Relations with International Organizations of a Universal Character (1975)
   on Special Missions (1969)
   on the Status of Refugees (1951): *see that part of the title of the Convention which refers to its subject matter.* NB: the dates are those of

*signature or of *adoption by the UN *General Assembly, not the dates of *entry into force.

copie d'usage. See working copy (of credentials).

copie figurée. See working copy (of credentials).

coranto. See gazettes.

COREPER. The *COmité des REprésentants PERmanents* of the *European Union i.e. the Brussels-based ambassadors of the member states. The Committee of Permanent Representatives has two divisions: COREPER I, which deals with domestic affairs and is composed of the Deputy Permanent Representatives; and COREPER II, which handles external affairs and is made up of the Permanent Representatives themselves. The Permanent Representatives are almost always senior diplomats, though their own staffs are increasingly composed of officials from domestic – as opposed to foreign – ministries. COREPER, which among other things prepares meetings of the *Council of Ministers, is one of the most influential institutions within the EU framework.

COREUR. The system whereby telegrams and other forms of communication are regularly circulated around the foreign ministries of the member states of the *European Union. Supervised by their *political

directors, this is an important element in the Union's *Common Foreign and Security Policy.

corps diplomatiques. See diplomatic corps.

correspondence. (1) Letters. (2) The exchange of letters. (3) In the phrase to 'maintain a good correspondence' which was current until the end of the eighteenth century, a synonym for *diplomatic relations (sense 2).

correspondent. Another term for a member of a *warden network.

Council of Europe. Founded in 1949 as an association of European democracies, its membership expanded after the end of the *Cold War and presently stands at 44. It has a *Parliamentary Assembly made up of parliamentarians elected or appointed by their national parliaments, and a Committee of [Foreign]Ministers. The Assembly does not have legislative powers, but may make recommendations to the Committee of Ministers. The Committee can take decisions concerning the internal work of the Council, and make recommendations to the member states on matters that come under their authority. Among the main areas of Council activity are *human rights, social questions, culture, education, the environment, and legal cooperation, and it has successfully sponsored more than 150 *treaties in these and other fields. Under the European Convention on Human Rights (1950) an impressive amount of work has been done to safeguard fundamental rights and freedoms. Its headquarters and Secretariat are in Strasbourg, France.

Council of Ministers (European). The chief decision-making body of the *European Union where the *national interests of member states are represented, though it works to guidelines agreed by the *European Council. Its presidency changes every six months, though continuity was assisted until recently by the *troika arrangement. It meets in subject-based councils of which the most important is that composed of the foreign ministers of the member states, which normally meets monthly. (Officially referred to as the 'General Affairs Council', this is more generally known as the 'Foreign Affairs Council'.) Though in theory decisions may be taken by a simple majority vote, they are taken formally either by *unanimity or *qualified majority voting, and in reality most of them are taken by the *consensus method. Since the entry into force of the Treaty of *Maastricht, the Council of Ministers has been officially styled the 'Council of the European Union'. *See also* codecision procedure; high representative (example 1); Luxembourg compromise.

Council of the European Union. *See* Council of Ministers (European).

Council on Foreign Relations. The major American think tank on foreign policy which developed from the group of scholars summoned to advise President Woodrow *Wilson at the end of the First World War. It was formally established in 1921 and obtains its funds from corporations, foundations, and individual endowments. It publishes the journal *Foreign Affairs*.

counsellor. In *diplomatic ranks, that which lies beneath *minister (sense 2) (or, where it is used, beneath minister-counsellor) and above *first secretary. The spelling is 'counselor' in the US Foreign Service.

counter-espionage. The attempt to discover and neutralize specific foreign *espionage (*humint) attacks, typically by visual surveillance and *sigint interception of communications between *agents (sense 5) and their controllers.

counter-intelligence. (1) The attempt to destroy or weaken the effectiveness of foreign *espionage at its source, especially by penetration of its services. This is the older meaning of the term and the one still favoured by *humint professionals. (2) All methods, whether active or passive, designed to protect a state's secrets from any form of *intelligence gathering by foreign agencies.

countermeasure. A *reprisal which does not involve the use of armed force.

country team. The key committee in an American embassy. It is composed of the heads of any executive branch agencies operating in the country and is chaired by the ambassador. Designed to help US ambassadors reassert their authority following the colonization of their embassies during the *Cold War by a plethora of different Washington-based agencies, the twin principles of the country team idea are consensus and coordination. The term first came into use in 1951 following a report by General Lucius D. Clay. Nevertheless, the country team is only a 'management tool' and American ambassadors have never been required to employ it. The well known economist, J. K. Galbraith, who was sent by President Kennedy to be his ambassador to India in 1961, regarded it as indispensable only when he did not want to do anything.

courier. *See* diplomatic courier

Court of St James's. The manner in which the United Kingdom of Great Britain and Northern Ireland is referred to in the *letters of credence supplied to heads of *diplomatic missions being posted from or to that state: e.g. they are 'accredited to the Court of St James's'. This is because St James's Palace in Westminster remains the senior royal residence,

even though the sovereign has actually lived at Buckingham Palace since 1837. St James's Palace was built by Henry VIII in the 1530s and became the seat of the royal court in 1702 after fire destroyed the Palace of Whitehall. It is now the central London residence of the Prince of Wales and provides offices for, among others, the *Marshal of the Diplomatic Corps.

courtesy call. A visit made as a matter of courtesy by a newly arrived *head of mission to the *foreign minister of the *receiving state and, very possibly, to the head of government (where he or she is not also head of state). Such calls may also be made to other important personages in the capital city (e.g. the mayor), and sometimes in *federal states to such personages in the provincial capitals. Courtesy calls are also customarily made on other heads of mission. In capitals with a very large *diplomatic corps it may as a practical matter not be possible to visit all of them, though the expectation that all should receive a call remains high and those overlooked may well harbour an enduring resentment against the new head of mission.

court mourning. (1) The official period of mourning that follows the death of a monarch or other senior member of a royal family. (2) The dress code to be followed, among others by diplomats, during this period.

courtoisie. The correct subscription to a formal letter sent by a diplomat – e.g. 'I have the honour to be, Sir, Your obedient servant'. *See also appel*.

Covenant of the League of Nations. The 1919 instrument (which was part of the Versailles Peace Treaty) which provided for the establishment of the *League and set out what, in effect, was its constitution. *See also* Briand–Kellogg Pact.

covert action. Secret or at any rate deniable *intervention in the domestic politics or civil wars of other states, usually to defend a friendly government or overthrow a hostile one. An American term for what used to be known as 'political warfare', typically it involves supplying money or weapons to favoured groups, and is usually but not necessarily a task given to *intelligence agencies.

credence. *See* letters of credence.

credentials. A document which authenticates a person's status and competence. *See also* letter of introduction; letters of commission; letters of credence; permanent mission; presentation of credentials; working copy.

crisis. An international conflict which is so acute that it is believed by most governments concerned to carry a serious risk of *war. It will probably have a variety of sources but nevertheless be publicly focused on a specific issue, as in the *Cuban Missile Crisis. *See also* crisis management.

crisis management. The conduct of a *crisis by diplomacy, normally to dampen it down. The term was popularized by US Defense Secretary Robert McNamara, formerly a businessman, following the *Cuban Missile Crisis of 1962.

crossed bag. *See* diplomatic bag.

Crowe Report (1999). *See* Inman standards.

Crown dependency. The status enjoyed by the Channel Islands and the Isle of Man. As such, they are directly under the authority of the British monarch, and hence not within the jurisdiction of the British parliament. Britain, however, is responsible for their *international relations (sense 1) and defence. *See also* bailiwick.

cryptanalysis. *Cipher- and *code-breaking, or the craft of rendering into plain language an encrypted message. *See also* sigint.

cryptography. Secret writing, encrypting or writing in *cipher or *code, together with the protection of these systems.

cryptology. *Cryptanalysis plus *cryptography.

Cuban Missile Crisis. The *crisis that arose in October 1962 following the United States' demand that the Soviet Union remove the nuclear-headed missiles which it was in the process of installing in Cuba, a spot which Washington looked upon as well inside its 'backyard'. The crisis was the most serious which occurred during the *Cold War, East and West finding themselves *eyeball-to-eyeball. It only began to subside when Soviet vessels heading for the island finally turned back in the face of the cordon that the US Navy had thrown around it.

cultural diplomacy. The promotion abroad of a state's cultural achievements, in the case of France and Britain, among others, notably their languages. Cultural *attachés are posted to embassies; and dedicated organizations closely associated with the *diplomatic service, like the *British Council, are sometimes employed. Such organizations have their own offices and libraries in major foreign cities. Defined broadly to include the advertisement of achievements in science and technology as well as in the arts, humanities and social sciences, cultural diplomacy attaches special importance to promoting links between parallel institutions at home and abroad, for example between domestic and foreign universities.

cuneiform diplomacy. The diplomatic system in use between the kingdoms of the Near East from about 2500 to 500 BC, so called because it was based on the exchange of messages written, on tablets, in cuneiform characters. The system employed a common language, and had its own law, custom, and protocol. In its essentials, modern diplomacy can be seen as expressing the same needs and practices as the ancient cuneiform system. *See also* Amarna letters.

customary international law. General practices (also known as international customary law or general international customary law) which have grown up among states *and* which have become accepted as law – and hence as *binding on all states. Thus, mere usage is insufficient to translate a custom into law; the belief must also have developed that that usage has legal status. This last aspect of the matter is often referred to as *opinio iuris sive necessitatis* (or, for short, *opinio iuris*). Custom is one of the two main sources of *international law (the other being *treaties), and in historical and jurisprudential terms it is the more fundamental of the two. In quantitative terms, however, treaties have in recent times come to overshadow custom as a source of international law. *See also* special customary international law.

customs union. An association of states created for the purpose of promoting free trade among themselves behind a wall to the outside world represented by a common external tariff. *See also* Common Market; European Union; free trade area.

cut-price diplomacy. A term sometimes used to refer to *multiple accreditation (sense 1) and the maintenance of contact at the UN rather than through the establishment of a *resident mission.

D

damage. An injury suffered from an illegal act.

damages. The pecuniary sum payable by one state to another to compensate the latter following its successful *claim that a wrongful act has been done to it by the former. The award of damages is not necessarily linked with a pecuniary loss on the part of the wronged state. It should be noted that damages are not a form of punishment, *international law being, overwhelmingly, in the nature of civil law rather than *international criminal law. Consequently, damages are awarded as compensation for a wrong, not as punishment for a crime.

deadlock. *See* impasse.

dean. The representative of the *diplomatic corps on ceremonial occasions and its channel of communication on matters of common interest (especially *diplomatic privileges and immunities) with the government of the *receiving state.

The dean, or *doyen(ne)*, is generally the longest-serving member of the highest class of *diplomat accredited to the country in question. Exceptions to this rule are to be found in states where *precedence is by tradition granted to the papal *nuncio, and in certain other cases and circumstances. One such situation may occur when the most senior diplomat is head of a *non-resident mission – it being desirable, although not necessary, that the dean be resident in the capital in question.

In the late 1940s and early 1950s, when the status of *high commissioners in relation to the diplomatic corps was indeterminate, there was some uncertainty as to whether such a diplomat was eligible to be dean. Difficulties sometimes also arise when the dean represents a state or government that is not recognized by some of the other states that have *diplomatic missions accredited to the receiving state. (Notably, this problem arose in respect of the representatives of

China.) In this case, although a state may debar its ambassador from having any dealings whatsoever with the person who is dean, the usual solution is for the heads of these missions to deal with the individual concerned when he or she is acting in this capacity but to ignore all the individual's ambassadorial activity. However, acceptance of the office of dean implies a willingness to have dealings with *all* heads of mission accredited to the capital concerned. There is also a dean of the *consular corps.

See also vice-dean.

debellatio. Putting a forceful end to a *sovereign state by the *annexation of its territory. Such *aggression is no longer lawful.

décanat. The office of the *dean of the *diplomatic corps.

declaration. (1) A document which is not meant to have the *binding character of a *treaty but to have considerable political significance, e.g. the 1948 *Universal Declaration of Human Rights. Declarations of this kind, in addition to more general *communiqués, are now commonly issued on specific subjects following *summit meetings. (2) A now uncommon synonym for treaty, e.g. the Paris Declaration of 1856. (3) A formal statement by the *representative of a state which is meant to bind the state or is deemed so to have done. (4) A statement clarifying the position of a state regarding, for example, the interpretation of a particular provision of a just-agreed *treaty. Such a statement does not purport to exclude or modify the legal import of the provision in question.

declaration of war. *See* war.

Declaration on the Granting of Independence to Colonial Countries and Peoples. A *declaration (sense 1) of the UN *General Assembly made in December 1960 (resolution 1514 [XV]). It states that *colonialism is a denial of fundamental *human rights, and that inadequacy of political, economic, social, or educational preparedness for *independence (sense 1) is not a justification for delaying it. No state voted against the resolution, and only nine abstained. The Declaration is regarded as a landmark in the UN's campaign against colonialism. *See also* Committee of 24.

decorations. Any kind of personal adornment, for example a medal or chain. They may be presented by a foreign government to a diplomat. Unlike a 'present' or 'gift', it is valuable only for the honour that it signifies, usually membership of some prestigious order. Decorations, like presents, have long been employed by governments in an attempt to influence diplomats accredited to them. It is for this reason that many diplomatic services now prohibit acceptance of both decorations and presents, or permit their acceptance only under very restricted conditions or where refusal would cause serious offence and damage relations.

deductive method. (1) The process of *a priori* reasoning whereby, for example, principles of what is asserted to be *international law are deduced from certain broader principles. It is also called naturalism (with reference to the idea of natural law). (2) The approach to negotiation which, in contrast to *step-by-step diplomacy, favours seeking immediate agreement on general principles. If and when this is achieved, in the so-called *formula stage, the details are, loosely speaking, deduced from them.

de facto **recognition.** A form of *recognition of a government or of *recognition of a state which is provisional, either because of uncertainty regarding the immediate future of the recognized entity or because of political reluctance on the part of the recognizing state to accord the entity an unqualified status. If, later, unqualified status is granted, it will usually be referred to as **de jure* recognition. *See also* Estrada Doctrine.

defector. A prominent person, or one previously employed in a sensitive official position, who succeeds in fleeing, for whatever reason, to a state whose relationship with the country of origin is hostile or adversarial. Others who seek sanctuary in foreign states are simply known as refugees or asylum-seekers.

defence adviser. *See* service attaché.

defence attaché. (1) The senior service attaché at a *diplomatic mission. (2) Another term for a *service, or armed forces attaché.

defence diplomacy. The use of military personnel, including *service attachés, in support of conflict prevention and resolution. Among a great variety of activities, it includes providing assistance in the development of democratically accountable armed forces. This bland umbrella term appears to have been introduced by the British government's Strategic Defence Review, 1998, and is now officially employed by a few other states as well. It is not to be confused with *coercive diplomacy.

defence intelligence. (1) Information on the military power of foreign states and the international arms trade. (2) The agencies involved in the collection of this kind of information. *See also* Defense Intelligence Agency.

defence section. *See* defence staff.

defence staff. The body of *service attachés at a major embassy. The US Foreign Service describes it as the 'defense attaché's office', the British Diplomatic Service as the 'defence section'.

Defense Intelligence Agency (DIA). The all-service *intelligence organization which was superimposed on the three existing intelligence agencies of the United States' armed services in 1961.

definitive signature. *See* ratification; signature.

de jure **recognition.** *Recognition of a government or *recognition of a state which is unqualified. It is often so termed after a period during which the recognized entity has been accorded *de facto* recognition by the recognizing state. *See also* Estrada Doctrine.

delegate. An accredited member of a state's *delegation to an international *conference or other form of gathering. Support staff, such as translators and secretaries, are not delegates.

delegate-general. The head of a *general delegation.

delegation. A party sent to represent a state or some other body at an international *conference or other form of gathering. Such a group may be very large, especially if the conference is important and has a wide *agenda, and if the sending state is rich. Within the *UN system, however, rules of procedure limit the size of delegations, though the attitude to their advisers is usually more liberal. The most senior diplomat or politician is nor-mally styled 'head', or 'leader', of the delegation, and if it has been sent to negotiate a *treaty this person must be a *plenipotentiary.

delimitation. The drawing of a boundary on a map. The term is also often used to encompass *demarcation.

demarcation. The marking of a boundary on the ground.

démarche. A formal message, written or oral, to a *receiving state generally involving a protest, complaint or *ultimatum, delivered by one or more diplomats (sense 1).

démenti. A denial.

demilitarize. To agree that there shall be no military presence or function in a specified area (except, possibly, a *peacekeeping group); or, in the case of an area within one state's jurisdiction or control, to prohibit such activity. The area in question may then be referred to as a demilitarized zone (DMZ). If it is adjoined by two or more states it may be known as a *buffer zone.

demilitarized zone (DMZ). *See* demilitarize.

denunciation. *See* abrogation.

department. In the British *Foreign and Commonwealth Office, the administrative unit intermediate between a *desk and a *command.

The department is the basic organizational component of the ministry.

Department of State. *See* State Department.

dependent state. This phrase may be used synonymously with *protected state. But in contemporary usage it is more likely to have a political than a legal connotation, meaning a *state which is habitually subservient to another in respect of an important area or areas of policy. *See also* Brezhnev Doctrine; puppet state; satellite state; sphere of influence; vassal state.

dependent territory. A politically-correct term for such *colonies as remain, which has recently been replaced by one of even greater rectitude: 'overseas territory'. *See also* bailiwick.

deposit. *See* depositary.

depositary. A state or an international organization designated by a *treaty to receive and disseminate any formal written communications relating to it (such as *ratifications, *reservations, and *declarations (sense 4)), and to perform such other administrative functions as are specified by the treaty. A depositary is more likely to be appointed in respect of a multilateral than a bilateral treaty.

deputy chief of mission. The officer who is second in command in an American *diplomatic mission and responsible for its day-to-day running. Occupying a position closely analogous to the *deputy head of mission in a British mission, the DCM is *chargé d'affaires *ad interim* in the *ambassador's absence.

deputy head of mission. The term for the number two in almost all of Britain's embassies, who is now responsible for the managerial and coordinating work across all sections of the embassy formerly carried out by the *head of chancery. In British *high commissions the equivalent term is *deputy high commissioner, though the number two here as well as in embassies is referred to as the 'DHM'.

deputy high commission. The name which used sometimes to be given to the *office of a deputy high commissioner. It appears to have gone out of fashion.

deputy high commissioner. (1) The title sometimes given to the number two in a *high commission. In British high commissions, this title is used in even the smallest posts; but in the case of the high commissions of at least two other *Commonwealth states – Canada and South Africa – it is used only where the diplomat concerned is relatively senior. It is possible, although unusual, for more than one member of the staff of a high commission to be given this title. (2) The head of the *office of a deputy high commissioner.

deputy under-secretary of state. The second-most-senior official (as distinct from ministerial) position in Britain's *Foreign and Commonwealth Office, coming below the *permanent under-secretary of state and above the *assistant under-secretaries of state (now known as *directors).

desk. A small, if not the smallest, section of a ministry of *foreign affairs. *See also* desk officer.

desk officer. A traditional *State Department term for the person in the Department charged with oversight of relations with a particular foreign country. *See also* desk.

despatch. (1) In traditional British diplomatic usage, a formal and therefore stylized letter from a *head of mission abroad to the *Foreign Secretary, and vice versa; and also from one head of mission to another. (The *Oxford English Dictionary* prefers 'dispatch', as does the US Foreign Service.) Among the words of advice given on the writing of despatches in the earlier editions of *Satow's Guide* are these: 'Never place an adjective before a noun, if it can be spared; it only weakens the effect of a plain statement. Above all, do not attempt to be witty.' Today, however, despatches are not quite as formal as

they used to be. *See also* telegram, unofficial letter. (2) To send, as in to 'despatch a special envoy'.

détente. An easing of strained *diplomatic relations (sense 2). According to the *Oxford English Dictionary*, first used in this sense shortly before the First World War; it is also contained in the short glossary appended to the first edition of Harold Nicolson's *Diplomacy*, published in 1939. The term achieved great currency when it was employed to describe the relaxation of *Cold War tensions between the Soviet Union and the United States in the early 1970s.

developed vetting. *See* positive vetting.

difficult post allowance (DPA). *See* hardship post.

Dikko, Umaru. A member of an earlier Nigerian government who, in 1984, was kidnapped in London on Nigeria's authority. He was drugged and placed in a crate, which was intercepted as it was being loaded on to a Nigerian Airways plane. On the ground that it did not satisfy the criteria for a *diplomatic bag, British officials opened the crate, thus securing Dikko's release.

diplomacy. (1) The conduct of relations between *sovereign states through the medium of officials based at home or abroad, the latter being either members of their state's *diplomatic service or *temporary diplomats. Thus diplomacy includes the stationing of representatives at *international organizations. But the backbone of diplomacy has, for five centuries, been the despatch of *diplomatic missions to foreign states, and it is still very much the norm. As states are notional persons, they cannot communicate in the manner of individuals, but must do so through representative human persons. In principle, this can be done by such individuals speaking to each other at a distance through electronic devices. But there are large practical objections to the use of these as the sole or even the prime method of interstate communication. Diplomacy is therefore the principal means by which states communicate with each other, enabling them to have regular and complex relations. It is the communications system of the *international society. The label 'diplomacy' was first given to this system by Edmund Burke in 1796. *See also* channels of communication. (2) The use of tact in dealing with people. Diplomacy in this sense is a skill which is hugely important in the conduct of diplomacy. But there is a large distinction between an apt way of executing a task and its underlying function. (3) Any attempt to promote international *negotiations (particularly in circumstances of acute crisis), whether concerning inter- or intra-state conflicts; hence

*'track two diplomacy'. (4) Foreign policy. The use of the word 'diplomacy' as a synonym for foreign policy, which is especially common in the United States, can obscure the important distinction between policy and the (non-violent) means by which it is executed.

diplomat. (1) A person professionally engaged in the craft of *diplomacy (sense 1) as a member of a *diplomatic service, whether any aptitude for the craft is displayed or not. A diplomat may therefore be either a *diplomatic agent or an *official at a *foreign ministry. This is a worn-down version of the older word *diplomatist, which Britain's Diplomatic Service finally abandoned when it realized that the Americans had done so. (2) The term is also used in general speech of a person who is demonstrably possessed of those abilities traditionally associated with diplomacy, such as tact and moderation.

diplomatic agent. The head of a *diplomatic mission or a member of its staff having *diplomatic status.

diplomatic archives. (1) The records (in the pre-computer age, 'papers') of a *diplomatic mission, whatever form they may take and including any containers or other devices employed for their storage. The somewhat odd phrase 'archives and documents' was used in the Vienna Convention on *Diplomatic Relations to cover *draft* papers as well, these being regarded as not technically 'archives'. Diplomatic archives, and for that matter consular archives, are inviolable at any time and wherever they may be. *See also* chancelier; registry. (2) The official papers of a ministry of foreign affairs, the earlier ones of which might have been deposited in a national archive and be available for public inspection.

diplomatic asylum. The granting of refuge in diplomatic (and by extension in consular) premises to fugitives from the authority of the *receiving state when they are deemed by the *sending state to have given political rather than criminal offence. But whether a sending state is entitled to grant such asylum is controversial, not least because receiving states jib at allowing sending states to suggest that an alleged criminal is in fact a victim of political persecution. Hence no general agreement has been reached on the subject. However, it is always open to a limited number of states to agree among themselves on a right of diplomatic asylum, or to develop *customary law to that effect as among themselves, very possibly on a regional basis. It is frequently said that such regional rules exist in Latin America. Notwithstanding the lack of general agreement, diplomatic asylum is very occasionally given. It may be suggested that states are uneasy about agreeing to such a right (because of its recipro-

cal implications), but do not wish to impede their freedom to grant diplomatic asylum in exceptional circumstances. It should be noted that the issue of diplomatic asylum refers to a right which may be enjoyed by states; there is no question of a fugitive having the right to demand asylum. *See also* special international customary law.

diplomatic bag. A package which, to permit and protect *free communication between a state and its diplomats, may not be opened or detained en route, whether it contains classified material or not. (A diplomatic bag containing classified material and thus requiring special protection is known as a 'crossed bag' because its label is marked with a large black 'X'.) It is meant only for official diplomatic correspondence and articles intended exclusively for the use of a diplomatic or permanent mission. It must be clearly indicated as such, and secured with a *seal bearing the official stamp of the *sending state or mission. It may be in the charge of a *diplomatic courier or *diplomatic agent, but may also be sent by other means, such as by the hand of an aircraft's captain ('care-of-pilot'). It has no agreed maximum size or weight, so a diplomatic 'bag' may, and often does, consist of a crate or container. Because of the suspected (and sometimes documented) abuse of this facility to carry currency, drugs, weapons and even bombs, some states have asserted the right to place limits on the size of the bag, X-ray it, or return it to the sender. However, the protests of other states and the principle of *reciprocity go far to guarantee the inviolability and sure transmission of diplomatic bags.

In an effort to clarify disputed aspects of the relevant law, and to encourage a more uniform observance of it, the UN General Assembly, some 25 years ago, asked the *International Law Commission to examine the issue. In 1989 it produced a final text on the status of the diplomatic courier and the diplomatic bag not accompanied by diplomatic courier, and recommended that the Assembly convene a conference to study the matter. However, informal consultations revealed wide divergences of view (not least between Britain and the United States) on some of the draft articles, particularly the one relating to the inviolability of the diplomatic bag. In consequence, progress towards a treaty on the issue remains held up. But at the level of practice the situation is in almost all respects managed satisfactorily. *See also* casual courier; Dikko, Umaru; Queen's Messenger.

diplomatic classes. The classes into which *heads of mission are divided according to the Vienna Convention on *Diplomatic Relations (1961). The first class consists of *ambassadors or *nuncios, and other heads of mission of equivalent rank (notably *high commis-sioners); the second of envoys, *ministers (sense 1) and *internun-cios; and the third of *chargés d'affaires. The class to which a head of mission is assigned must be agreed by the *sending and *receiving states. Heads of mission in the first two classes are accredited to heads of state, while those in the third are accredited only to ministers of foreign affairs. The class of *minister resident, which had been added at the Congress of Aix-la-Chapelle in 1818 as the third out of four classes, was dropped in 1961. Today, heads of mission of the second rank are also a rarity. *See also* precedence; Regulation of Vienna (1815).

diplomatic communication. *See* channels of communication.

diplomatic corps. (1) The body of *diplomats of all states, including *attachés, who are resident at one *post. The term is a corruption of the French phrase *corps diplomatique*, which translates correctly as 'diplomatic body'. The designation 'body' is appropriate since, however insubstantial this may now be, the diplomats posted in the same capital still have a corporate existence founded on a common interest in defending their *privileges and immunities. The diplomatic corps is led by the *dean, has its own meetings, and is seen *en masse* at ceremonial occasions. (2) The *diplomatic service of a state. Use of the term 'diplomatic corps' as a synonym for diplomatic service has long been very common, not least among diplomats. However, it blurs an important distinction and is explicitly rejected by the most authoritative manuals.

diplomatic courier. A person employed, either on a regular or ad hoc basis, for the expressly limited purpose of carrying a *diplomatic bag. Hence a diplomatic courier is today not a *diplomatic agent such as a *special envoy, though in the ancient world the roles were usually fused in one individual. A diplomatic courier also carries identifying documents, usually a courier's passport (though in earlier times discreet badges were also found useful). This is important because a diplomatic courier is entitled to personal inviolability and immunity from arrest and detention; but he or she is not entitled to the more extensive privileges of a diplomatic agent. The immunities of an ad hoc courier cease when the diplomatic bag has been delivered to the consignee. Whether regular or ad hoc, the diplomatic courier must also carry a document indicating which bags are 'diplomatic' and which are not, since personal luggage may be searched at any frontier. This document, known as a 'way bill' or *lettre de part*, must also list every diplomatic bag. Though the work of the diplomatic courier is not, as a result of the revolution in transport and *telecommunications, by any means as important or as dangerous as in former times, it is still valued for

especially sensitive documents and other items – and couriers still occasionally disappear. A dedicated courier service was not permanently established by the United States until shortly before the Second World War. *See also* casual courier; express; freedom of communication; herald; Queen's Messenger; *staffeto*.

diplomatic designations. *See* diplomatic rank.

diplomatic flag. The flag used by a state on its *diplomatic premises and as the *personal standard flown on the means of transport used by its *heads of mission. It need not be identical with the national flag. Britain's diplomatic flag is the United Kingdom flag with the Royal Arms in the centre surrounded by a green garland. British *high commissioners, however, fly the United Kingdom flag. A *permanent mission is allowed the same flag-flying privileges as a diplomatic mission; and *special missions are generally treated in much the same way.

diplomatic functions. Far and away the most important function of the head and staff of a *diplomatic mission is to act as a permanent *channel of communication between the *sending state and the *receiving state, as it is only through such official human agencies that notional entities such as *states can speak to each other.

Sometimes such communication will take the very specific form of *negotiation; but usually it will be a matter of conveying and receiving statements of opinion and formal messages. Any such function is often referred to as that of *representation.

Additionally, a diplomatic mission has the task of reporting to its state on conditions and developments in the receiving state (though, in theory, information may only be obtained by 'lawful means'); and promoting and protecting the interests of the sending state and its nationals in the receiving state.

The Vienna Convention on *Diplomatic Relations states that one function of a diplomatic mission is to promote 'friendly relations' between the sending and the receiving state. At one level this is so, in the sense that a sending state always hopes that its representations will be accepted and appreciated. But the statement obscures the fact that in political terms a diplomatic mission is above all else in the business of advancing and defending its state's interests – which may sometimes necessitate an unfriendly or even a hostile stance towards the receiving state. In sum, this aspect of the Vienna Convention is more an expression of political correctitude than of reality.

See also espionage; permanent mission; special mission.

diplomatic history. Generally used to connote the history of relations between states, i.e. that in which diplomats are the executants. A diplomatic historian is therefore one who focuses on this subject. See also history of diplomacy.

diplomatic identity card. Many states issue accredited diplomats with such a card, in part with a view to minimizing difficulties between diplomats and law enforcement officers. See also silver car pass.

diplomatic illness. An illness feigned by a diplomat to avoid an official engagement that is likely to prove politically embarrassing.

diplomatic immunities. See diplomatic privileges and immunities.

diplomatic inviolability. See diplomatic privileges and immunities.

diplomatic language. (1) Special language employed in an effort to minimize the provocation likely to be caused by delivery of a sharp or unavoidably threatening message. It is typically mild, euphemistic, and circumlocutory. (2) The technical words and phrases of the craft of *diplomacy (sense 1). (3) The language most commonly employed for general communication in a *diplomatic system. For example, in the Ancient Near East this was Akkadian; in the European system it was first Latin and then French; and in today's world system it is English.

diplomatic law. The rules of *international law governing the conduct of *diplomacy (sense 1). Many of the rules regarding *diplomatic agents and *missions are embodied in the Vienna Convention on *Diplomatic Relations, 1961. *See also* Bynkershoek; Gentili; Grotius; Hotman; *Oppenheim's International Law*; *Satow's Guide to Diplomatic Practice*; Wicquefort.

diplomatic licence plates. The distinctive licence or number plates which are often attached to the official vehicles of *diplomatic missions and personal vehicles of *diplomatic staff. The plates on *consular vehicles are usually different, and in some countries different again for those belonging to *administrative and technical staff. Distinctive licence plates permit easy identification of a vehicle whose occupants probably enjoy *immunity from local process. However, since they also make it more likely that their vehicles will attract the attention of terrorists, the use of such plates has been discontinued in some states.

diplomatic list. The list maintained and (usually) published periodically by a *receiving state which gives the names of those who, being members of *resident or *non-resident diplomatic missions, enjoy *diplomatic status within that state. The names are grouped by mission, missions being listed on an alphabetical basis.

The order in which names are listed within each mission's list is indicative of the order of *precedence, within that mission, of its named *diplomatic agents. That order is entirely a matter for the *sending state, as is the designation of the agents. (The receiving state, however, determines the general format of the overall list.) When, as is often the case, the agents at a particular mission are members not just of the sending state's *foreign ministry but also of various other government departments, determining the mission's order of precedence can be a matter of controversy, between both the individuals and the departments concerned.

Should internal dissension within a state result in more than one diplomatic mission being sent to a second state, each claiming to represent the first state, the receiving state must decide which it regards as legitimate. Its decision will be reflected in its diplomatic list. If, however, it wishes to avoid or delay coming out in favour of one rather than the other but does not wish to acknowledge that fact, it may decline to publish a new diplomatic list until the matter has been resolved. This unusual state of affairs occurred in the Soviet Union in the early 1970s, when two embassies from Cambodia appeared in Moscow. However, it appears that the secretive Soviets had for some time not published a diplomatic list. The inconvenience to diplomats which this entailed was, from January 1965 at least into the early 1970s, made good by the inclusion of an unofficial list in a directory called *Information Moscow* which was regularly compiled for members of the foreign community by the British wife of a Soviet journalist.

An international organization to which *permanent missions have been sent by member states may publish its own list of the members of such missions. However, although those individuals will be in receipt of certain privileges and immunities they are not, formally speaking, regarded as enjoying 'diplomatic' status (although, at the level of practice, this is unlikely to be evident). Thus the organization's list may not use that term. The UN, for example, calls its list, 'Permanent Missions to the United Nations'. *See also* Sheriffs' List.

diplomatic mission. The diplomatic entity which permanently represents a *sending state in a *receiving state. However, some or all of a mission's members may be resident outside the receiving state. It is normal for missions to be established in the city from which the state is governed, and some receiving states insist on it. Thus the Netherlands requires that diplomatic missions be in The Hague, which is the seat of government, rather than in Amsterdam, the capital. Of the members of a diplomatic mission, only the *diplomatic staff enjoy *diplomatic status. Unless specific agreement has been reached to the contrary, the receiving state may require that the size of a mission be kept within limits which it deems reasonable and normal. This is particularly likely to happen where a mission is believed to have been involved in *espionage or *terrorism. Of course, such a requirement is likely to lead to reciprocal action by the sending state.

*Permanent missions to an *international organization and *special missions are also diplomatic missions, in the sense that they are engaged on diplomatic tasks and are largely staffed by *diplomats. But official *diplomatic language (sense 2) tends not to refer to them as diplomatic missions. There is reason for that, as the legal regimes which apply to them differ from that which applies to missions accredited to foreign states, and their roles are also somewhat different. Accordingly, in this *Dictionary*, the term diplomatic mission is applied only to a mission accredited to a foreign state. Permanent and special missions are referred to as such. *See also* chancery; resident mission; non-resident mission; multiple accreditation.

diplomatic overkill. Diplomatic representations which are so powerful that although they may achieve their immediate goal, they may in a longer term be counterproductive. The term has been used of President Johnson's letter of 5 June 1964 to

Prime Minister Ismet Inonu of Turkey, demanding that Turkey call off her plan to invade Cyprus. George Ball, Under-Secretary at the *State Department, called it 'the most brutal diplomatic note I have ever seen'.

diplomatic passport. A travel document issued by a state to the members of its *diplomatic service and their families, and also to government *ministers (sense 3) and their families and, where relevant, to royal personages. In some states *diplomats may be allowed to keep their diplomatic passports after their retirement; and favoured political figures may also be granted a 'diplomatic passport'. The holder of such a document may, as a matter of practice rather than of right, expect speedy and simplified treatment by customs and police officials at state borders. However, such a passport does not entitle the holder to *diplomatic privileges and immunities, as the former president of Chile, General Pinochet, discovered following his arrest in London in October 1998. Britain did not issue the members of its diplomatic service with diplomatic passports until 1995. *See also laisser passer.*

diplomatic premises. The buildings or parts of buildings used as a *diplomatic mission, including the *residence of the *head of mission. Such premises are inviolable, and may not therefore be entered by the *receiving state except with the consent of the head of mission. The receiving state also has an obligation to protect diplomatic premises. For its part, the *sending state is obliged not to use the premises in a manner which is incompatible with the functions of a diplomatic mission. Whether premises used for such purposes as an information centre, a tourist office, or an embassy school may be classified as 'diplomatic' is a matter to be agreed between the sending and the receiving state. In 1985 Britain decided that that she would no longer allow tourist offices and places used for educational activity to be classified as diplomatic premises. *See also* exterritoriality; Hotman.

diplomatic privileges and immunities. The special legal position accorded to *diplomatic agents by *receiving states is generally referred to by this phrase, with the words in the order given. The details are spelt out in the Vienna Convention on *Diplomatic Relations, but almost invariably require legislation by a receiving state for them to be operative domestically. The justification for treating *diplomats in this special way is that such measures are necessary for *diplomatic functions to be executed effectively. This is not always understood by a state's public opinion, which can lead to adverse comment on the matter. But the very potent consideration, which ensures that it is exceptionally rare for states not to endorse and honour this aspect of *diplomatic law, is the principle of *reciprocity. That is, if state A's diplomats are treated in a less-than-proper manner by state B, it is highly likely that state B's diplomats in state A will suffer the same fate. So important is the role played by diplomats, and so keen the wish of *sending states to guarantee their personal safety, that it is extremely unusual for a state not to take great care to guard against that eventuality.

The special legal position has three aspects. First, there are certain inviolabilities enjoyed by a *diplomatic mission and its *diplomatic staff. These apply to official premises and private residences, the mission's archives and documentation, and its correspondence, none of which may be entered or tampered with by the receiving state. The persons of diplomatic agents and of their *family members residing with them are also inviolable, in the sense that they may not be arrested or detained. Secondly, such individuals enjoy immunity from the criminal jurisdiction of the receiving state and, in most respects, from its civil and administrative jurisdiction. Thirdly, they enjoy certain privileges, such as exemption from dues, taxes, and many customs duties, from the liability to undertake public service, and (generally) from having to submit their baggage to inspection at frontier controls.

This special legal position applies only to diplomats who enjoy *diplomatic status within the receiving state, or who are in transit through third states on their way to or from such a posting. Thus they do not apply to diplomats who just happen to be in a foreign state.

It should be noted that diplomats' jurisdictional immunities do not place them outside the receiving state's legal system, but only beyond the normal consequences of alleged breaches of the law. Thus if a diplomat claims immunity in respect of an allegedly criminal act, it is well understood that he or she may be declared *persona non grata by the receiving state. Furthermore, if a diplomat appears to be in breach of an obligation which exists under the civil, and not the criminal, law, but claims diplomatic immunity, the receiving state may press the sending state to ensure that the obligation is fulfilled. In any particular case, either criminal or civil, a sending state may *waive a diplomatic agent's immunity.

One immunity that often gives rise to heated complaints by members of the public is that which allows diplomats to go unpunished for breaches of car-parking regulations. So much was this so in Britain that, in the mid-1980s, she made it known that she was going to keep a record of such matters and, ultimately, would ask for the removal of persistent offenders. This produced a dramatic reduction in such offences.

See also consular privileges and immunities; diplomatic bag; diplomatic law; diplomatic premises; first-arrival privileges.

diplomatic protection. (1) The measures taken by a *diplomatic agent to assist his or her state's subjects against the acts of or events in a foreign state – protection *by* diplomats. *See also* letter of protection. (2) Special police or army provision for the security of diplomatic agents and *diplomatic premises – protection *of* diplomats. In the United States this is one of the duties of the Secret Service Uniformed Division, while Britain has a specially-trained body of police, known as the Diplomatic Protection Group, for this task.

diplomatic quarter. The area within certain *capital cities where foreign states are required, encouraged, or simply choose to maintain their *diplomatic missions. For example, from the end of the sixteenth century until the 1920s the foreign embassies in Istanbul were concentrated in Pera on the heights above Galata on the northern side of the Golden Horn. In the early modern period certain of these quarters – notably in Rome and Madrid – claimed *franchise du quartier*, that is that the inviolability of the missions within them extended to the quarter as a whole. Though this extravagant assertion of *exterritoriality had been effectively extinguished in Europe by the end of the seventeenth century, it reappeared in somewhat different guise in the Far East in the nineteenth. The most remarkable case was provided by the legation quarter in Peking. This survived a prolonged siege during the Boxer uprising in 1900, and under Article VII of the Final Protocol imposed by the allied powers on China shortly afterwards was granted 'exclusive control' of its own affairs, including its own defence. Annex 14 contained a map showing the precise boundaries of this second 'forbidden city', which for once signified that exterritoriality meant what it said. The 1924 edition of the Tienstin Press *Guide to Peking and its Environs* states in matter-of-fact tones that 'In its present aspect Legation Quarter has the appearance of a small fortress of rectangular shape'. Control of the legation quarter was handed back to China in 1945.

diplomatic rank. (1) One customarily used within a *diplomatic or *permanent mission to indicate the holder's hierarchical place. In order of seniority such ranks are: *ambassador, *minister (sense 2), *minister-counsellor (used only by some states), *counsellor, *first secretary, *second secretary, and *third secretary; the rank of *attaché may be used at various levels of seniority. It should be noted that different ranks, based on a domestic grading system, are likely to be given to members of a *diplomatic service when they serve at home in their foreign ministry. Moreover, there is not necessarily a complete equivalence between the two ranking systems. Thus the head of a small *embassy may well hold a domestic rank less senior than that held by the head of a large one. It must also be noted that sometimes, for locally compelling reasons, a diplomatic agent may be given a rank which is senior to that which he or she would normally enjoy. This is known as 'local rank'. Ranks should not be confused with positions, e.g. head of *chancery or *deputy chief of mission. (2) Historically, a synonym for diplomatic *precedence, as in the statement that 'heads of mission take rank according to the date of the official notification of their arrival'. (3) Sometimes the term 'diplomatic rank' has also been used as a synonym for *diplomatic status.

diplomatic relations. (1) The situation enjoyed by two *states that can communicate with each other unhampered by any formal obstacles. This is the prerequisite for normal *diplomacy (sense 1), and states finding themselves in this situation are said to *have* or be *in* diplomatic relations with each other. Thus each may address the other, express views to the other, and reach agreements with the other, such business usually being done through *diplomatic agents. Moreover, those agents may interact freely with each other. In the absence of diplomatic relations none of these activities is likely to

be straightforward, and may even be impossible: when two states are not in diplomatic relations either is fully entitled to refuse any contact with the other. Thus, being in diplomatic relations is the usual (and easy) means of maintaining permanent contact between two states. Contrary to a popular view, diplomatic relations does not necessarily entail the despatch by either state of a *resident mission or even a *non-resident mission to the other. Such a development often follows the establishment of diplomatic relations, but there is no necessity for it to do so. Another misunderstanding is represented in the exchange of resident missions sometimes being spoken of as creating 'full' diplomatic relations. In fact, there are no degrees of diplomatic relations; any pair of states is either in this condition or not.

Diplomatic relations are established by agreement. That agreement is often explicit, but it may also be implicit. A precondition for it is the *recognition of each state by the other. Especially in the case of a new state, recognition and the establishment of diplomatic relations may take place simultaneously. More generally, it is now unusual for two states that recognize each other not to be in diplomatic relations.

As to the 'level' of diplomatic relations, this term is often employed when two states agree to exchange *diplomatic missions, the rank of the *heads of mission being said to be the level at which diplomatic relations exist. Thus two states may announce that they have established relations at ambassadorial level. Strictly speaking, however, the idea of levels is better applied to *diplomatic representation than to diplomatic relations, as its use in the latter context mistakenly suggests that diplomatic relations is a variable rather than an absolute concept.

Whereas the establishment of diplomatic relations is a bilateral affair, their downgrading or breach occurs through a decision to that effect by just one party to the relationship. 'Downgrading' is a non-technical term which refers to the temporary withdrawal of the *head of mission or (although now it rarely happens) to the replacement of a head of mission by one of lesser *diplomatic rank (sense 1). Such developments, however, are distinct from the breach of diplomatic relations. This is a formal, unilateral decision which has the *consequence* that neither state can maintain a diplomatic mission in or accredited to the other. By contrast, the mere withdrawal of a diplomatic mission, either temporarily or permanently, is *not* tantamount to a breach of diplomatic relations. It used to be the case that an outbreak of *war also involved the breaking of diplomatic relations. But this is no longer seen as an automatic accompaniment of *armed conflict (sense 1).

If two states have broken diplomatic relations it does not necessar-ily mean that they do not communicate with each other, despite the fact that that would seem to be the logical consequence of a breach. A form of relations may be continued through *protecting powers, the establishment of *interests sections in the missions of third states, occasional messages being passed via third parties, or through *signalling. Ad hoc meetings may also be arranged, or encounters may take place in third states or at *international organizations, the extent and openness of such contacts being dependent on the political relationship of the two states, and perhaps also on the personal relationship of the diplomats concerned. But in all these circumstances the diplomatic process is likely to be much more complex and tortuous, and perhaps less efficient, than it is when states are in diplomatic relations.

The re-establishment of diplomatic relations requires a new agreement – any proposal for which must, by custom, come from the state which instigated the breach.

(2) The condition of the political relationship between two states, as in the observation: 'there was a sharp deterioration in their diplomatic relations'.

Diplomatic Relations, Vienna Convention on. The outcome of a conference held in Vienna in 1961 at which 81 states were represented. Its object was to *codify and clarify the existing *customary international law regarding *diplomatic agents and *diplomatic missions exchanged between states, particularly their *privileges and immunities. The Convention *entered into force in 1964; virtually every sovereign state has become a party to it; and it is also generally regarded as expressive of customary international law on its subject matter.

It must be noted, however, that the Convention's formal acceptance by a state does not necessarily mean, and in practice very rarely means, that its provisions automatically take effect within that state's municipal law. For a municipal legal system to give effect to the exceptional expectations of diplomats arising from the privileges and immunities which the Convention says they should have, domestic legislation is almost invariably required. Only after such legislation has embodied these rules in a state's municipal law will its courts take formal notice of the rules. *See also* international law and municipal law.

Contrary to the implication of the title which was given the Convention, it has virtually nothing to say on *diplomatic relations (sense 1). For full text, see pp. 283ff.

diplomatic representation. The representation of one state in another by a *diplomatic mission. Contrary to what is sometimes thought, the establishment of *diplomatic relations (sense 1) between two states does not require this kind of representation, even by a *non-resident, let alone a *resident mission. (In other words, there is no *right of legation, representation in each direction being the product of agreement.) One state may also enjoy diplomatic representation in another without the second state being obliged to seek any representation in the first – what is sometimes called unilateral diplomacy. This situation is usually a product of a marked sense of material or moral superiority (or both) on the part of the *receiving state. Probably its most famous instance was the system conducted by the Ottoman Empire, which was admitting permanent foreign embassies within months of the fall of Constantinople in 1453 but did not condescend to send them abroad itself until 1793.

As there is there no requirement that representation should be reciprocal, so also there is none that it should be symmetrical. Thus, one state may be represented in another by a mission whose head is of the first *diplomatic class – that is, an *embassy (sense 1) headed by an *ambassador (sense 1) – while the second state may be represented in the first by a mission whose head is in the second diplomatic class – that is, a *legation, headed by a *minister (sense 1). However, asymmetrical representation was never customary. Furthermore, in the third quarter of the twentieth century representation by missions whose heads were in the second or third diplomatic class went speedily out of fashion, so that since then virtually all representation has taken place at ambassadorial level. It also seems that non-reciprocal representation has become a somewhat unusual situation, and that some states might see it as justifiable only in the presence of special circumstances. And certainly, unless there are strong and acceptable reasons for it, the refusal of a request for diplomatic representation might be seen as not in political keeping with the condition of being in diplomatic relations. The outcome of these developments is that, in striking contrast to the position a century ago, non-resident representation is by no means uncommon, and resident embassies vary hugely in size and importance.

diplomatic representative. Any properly accredited *diplomat, including a *delegate to an international *conference. See also diplomatic representation; representative; representative character.

diplomatics. The metatheory of diplomacy, that is, the theory in the light of which *diplomacy (sense 1) proceeds. It therefore includes such basic postulates as, for example, that states are (deemed to be) persons, that they are bound by international law, and that diplomats speak for their states.

diplomatic sanctions. See sanctions.

diplomatic service. The bureaucracy of the professional *diplomats of the state, usually embracing per-sonnel in the ministry of *foreign affairs as well as those employed at foreign postings. In the United States it is styled the *'Foreign Service', and its members as 'Foreign Service Officers' or 'FSOs'. It is now normal for strict nationality criteria to be employed in recruitment to the diplomatic service, though there was a time when practice was quite different. See also Diplomatic Service, British; Venetian diplomacy.

Diplomatic Service, British. (1) The body which now embraces those officials of the *Foreign and Commonwealth Office in London who have a liability to be posted overseas, as well as its staff in all British diplomatic and consular missions abroad, in both *Commonwealth and non-Commonwealth states. It was created at the beginning of 1965 by the merger of the former *Foreign Service with the Commonwealth and Trade Commissioner Services. (2) Until 1943, a term reserved exclusively for the diplomatic staff of Britain's *diplomatic missions abroad. The staffs of the Foreign Office and the Diplomatic Service were amalgamated after the First World War but the separate identities of the two bodies were retained until the Second World War. See also Foreign Office List.

diplomatic service list. The list of the members of a state's *diplomatic service. The British *Diplomatic*

Service List (successor to the *Foreign Office List*) is an annual publication detailing the staff of her *diplomatic and *permanent missions and of her *consular posts, and of the departments of the *Foreign and Commonwealth Office. A diplomatic service list should not be confused with a *diplomatic list, though they are sometimes printed in the same booklet.

diplomatic staff. The staff of a *diplomatic, *permanent or *special mission who enjoy *diplomatic status, as opposed to *administrative and technical staff and *service staff.

diplomatic status. The status held by a member of the staff of a *diplomatic mission who is classed as a *diplomatic agent. Those enjoying it, also called the *diplomatic staff, are thereby entitled to *diplomatic privileges and immunities, and are included in the *receiving state's *diplomatic list. It is for the *sending state to propose that an individual be so classified, and for the receiving state to agree. No problem arises with regard to members of the sending state's *diplomatic service; difficulties can, however, occur regarding members of other government departments who temporarily serve abroad. Usually there is pressure from such departments for their members to be given diplomatic status, especially as they are often quite senior. But the sending state's foreign ministry may be uneasy about that if such individuals are not obviously serving in a representational capacity; and those of its government departments charged with the administration of the law and the raising of revenue may also be unhappy at the thought of the reciprocal requests which may follow from the receiving state. For its part, the receiving state may raise at least an eyebrow at proposed expansions of the *diplomatic corps in its *capital which bear a doubtfully diplomatic character.

As between states, such issues generally seem to be settled without much difficulty, albeit at the cost of the inclusion in diplomatic lists of some unusual-sounding 'diplomatic' titles – as indicated in the entry dealing with attachés. Latterly, too, the matter appears to be handled with increasing liberality (provided that the individuals concerned can reasonably be said to be performing duties of a diplomatic nature). There are two associated reasons for this. One is the ever-potent principle of *reciprocity, which ensures equality of treatment as between any pair of states. The other is the worry that developed during the second half of the twentieth century about the safety, in many capitals, of the members of diplomatic missions. Inasmuch as the granting of diplomatic status provides such individuals with some additional safeguards, states became rather more willing to be generous in this respect. It is unlikely that that development will now be reversed.

In the normal way, a receiving state is unlikely to agree to grant diplomatic status to an *agent of a foreign state who is posted at a city within the receiving state which is not its capital. (*Consular officers, of course, enjoy *consular status, and are therefore not covered by this statement.) One exception to this approach, however, occurs with regard to the staff of the office of a *deputy high commissioner (sense 2). Diplomatic agents making up a *special mission or a *permanent mission to an international organization also enjoy a privileged status, but strictly it should not be called 'diplomatic' and its detailed nature is likely to differ from that accorded to the diplomatic staff of resident and non-resident missions.

diplomatic system. (1) The communications network linking *sovereign states which is expressive of the conduct of *diplomacy (sense 1). (2) The style of diplomacy (sense 1) in a given period. *See also* cuneiform diplomacy; history of diplomacy; states-system.

diplomatic theory. General inquiry into diplomacy (sense 1) which blends conceptual, ethical, legal, and historical analysis.

diplomatic titles. *See* diplomatic rank.

diplomatic uniform. Special formal dress, mostly of vaguely military appearance, often including a dress sword, designed for *diplomats (sense 1) to wear on certain ceremonial occasions in some states, mainly those where they are accredited to a royal court. Today it is rarely worn in *republics or in states which have become independent since the Second World War, or by the diplomats of such states regardless of where they are serving. However, in early 2002 it was reported that Russia was preparing to dress its diplomats in 'tsarist splendour'.

diplomat-in-residence. A *State Department title for senior *Foreign Service Officers assigned for one or two years to colleges and universities within the United States. DIRs do some teaching but their main purpose is to encourage and facilitate the recruitment of outstanding candidates to the Foreign Service. In the academic year 2002–2003 there were 14 of them.

diplomatist. A member of the diplomatic profession. This was the term preferred to 'diplomat' by the British Diplomatic Service at least until the 1960s, and is by no means entirely extinct. It is still often employed, for example, by *The Times* of London, the *New Cambridge Modern History* and the *Oxford Dictionary of National Biography, in association with the British Academy*. The term has the merit of underlining the important distinction between professionals and others engaged in *diplomacy (sense 1) – *ad hoc and *temporary diplomats. Nevertheless, the weight of usage is overwhelmingly in favour of 'diplomat' rather than 'diplomatist', and as a result this is the practice followed in this *Dictionary*.

direct dial diplomacy. Communications with some overseas body conducted by a ministry, for example defence or transport, which bypasses the ministry of *foreign affairs of the state from which the communications originate. Direct dial diplomacy is especially prevalent between member states of the *European Union. It is the great growth in this form of *channel of inter-state communication that has often led foreign ministries to assert the importance of their coordinating function.

director. A senior officer in Britain's *Foreign and Commonwealth Office who is responsible for the formulation of policy and deployment of resources within a particular area of *command. Formerly known as assistant under-secretaries of state, directors come immediately below deputy under-secretaries.

directorate-general. Another term for 'department', as in the *European Commission.

director-general. *See* secretary-general

Director of Central Intelligence. The DCI is both the Director of the *CIA and intelligence adviser to the President.

dispatch. *See* despatch.

dissenting opinion. The individual opinion of a member of the *International Court of Justice who disagrees with the operative part of a *judgment or *advisory opinion of the Court. *See also* separate opinion.

Ditchley. An eighteenth century country house (the full name of which is Ditchley Park) near Oxford, UK, at which the Ditchley Foundation holds small high-level conferences on matters of international concern. Typically, those invited are a mix of *ministers (sense 3), *officials, *diplomats (sense 1), and academics drawn largely but by no means exclusively from Britain and the United States.

domestic jurisdiction. This term refers to those matters arising within a *state on which it has no international legal obligations, and over which the state is therefore entitled to exercise an exclusive jurisdiction. By the same token, foreign states should not try to influence the handling of such matters. Of course, much controversy may arise over whether any particular issue in fact falls within a state's domestic jurisdiction. *See also* human rights; intervention.

domestic law. *See* municipal law.

dominions. The former British self-governing territories which emerged (gradually and often hesitantly) on to the international scene as *sovereign states in the 1920s and 1930s: Australia, Canada, Ireland, Newfoundland, New Zealand, and South Africa. Latterly during this period Ireland contested its dominion status. India, although a member of the *League of Nations, was not a dominion until its independence in 1947 and so did not participate in these constitutional developments. Newfoundland was not a member of the League, and lost its dominion status in 1934 as a result of financial difficulties (being in a kind of constitutional limbo until it joined Canada in 1949). By the end of the Second World War the connotation of *dominus*, or overlordship, was clearly out of date in regard to the dominions; and quite apart from its linguistic aspect, the use of the term was often an irritant in the states which were so described (New Zealand excepted). Thus in 1949 they and Britain agreed that the term 'dominion' would no longer receive official sanction or usage. Moreover, India's imminent assumption of republican status made the continued use of the term particularly inappropriate.

Dominions Office. The British department of state which from 1925 until 1947 was responsible for the conduct of her relations with the *dominions.

donner la main. To give a visitor the seat of honour, i.e. that which lies on the host's right hand. *See also* seating arrangements.

double majority voting. A voting system in which a decision requires both a majority of the total number of participants and a majority of some other kind. It is designed to ensure that decisions are achieved in a manner consistent with important political principles, or simply to carry the support of those without whose blessing (and money) effective implementation would be unlikely. The nature and size of the second majority will be determined by the goal that it is intended to achieve.

double veto. *See* Security Council.

downgrading of diplomatic relations. *See* diplomatic relations (sense 1).

doyen(ne). *See* dean.

doyenne. Either a female *dean of the *diplomatic corps, or the wife of a *doyen*.

dragoman. A person employed by the diplomatic missions and consulates in the Ottoman Empire as an interpreter, information gatherer and – above all – intermediary with the various central departments (the *Porte) and provincial agencies of the sultan's government. Often spelled 'druggerman' in the earlier years after these missions began to appear in the sixteenth century, the word is a corruption of the Ottoman *tercüman*, meaning translator or interpreter. Since so few ambassadors or their secretaries spoke Ottoman Turkish and so few of the sultan's officials initially spoke Italian (the Venetian-driven language of commerce in the Levant) or even French, the embassies found their dragomans, who were generally Italian, Greek or Armenian 'Levantines', indispensable. However, the temptations to sell information to the highest bidder and their vulnerability to pressure from the Porte (until the nineteenth century they were nearly all subjects or, rather, slaves of the sultan) were so great that they were generally regarded as untrustworthy and insufficiently forceful in presenting an ambassador's view. Various attempts were made to replace the native dragomans with young men sent out from home to learn the language, among them the *jeunes de langues* launched into the East by Louis XIV in 1669 and the handful of *oriental secretaries and attachés whom Britain began to despatch in the second decade of the nineteenth century. However, few of these experiments were very successful, and the embassies usually had as many native dragomans as they could afford. They were typically styled 'First (or Chief) Dragoman', 'Second Dragoman', and so on. However, the great growth in the facility of Turkish officials with the French language in the course of the nineteenth century and the introduction in Britain's case of the *Levant Consular Service in 1877 (the first members of which, though

British, were called 'student dragomans') were among the factors which spelled the end of the native dragomans. The title lapsed altogether after the Lausanne Treaty of 1923 finally ended *capitulations in the metropolitan remains of the Ottoman Empire (i.e. Turkey), in the administration and defence of which the dragomans had been so closely associated. *See also drogmanat*; oriental secretary.

drogmanat. More elegant than the English 'dragomanate' (a syllable too far), the *dragomans' section of an embassy in Istanbul, prior to the ending of the dragoman system after the First World War.

droit de chapelle. The right of a *diplomatic mission to maintain a chapel and conduct religious services on its premises. Developed as an essential protection for diplomats against the background of the religious intolerance of the sixteenth century, this right is now an aspect of the general inviolability of *diplomatic premises. *See also* diplomatic privileges and immunities.

drum. A medieval/early modern term for a small party sent with a drummer to speak to the opposing forces on or near the field of battle.

dual accreditation. *See* multiple accreditation.

Dumbarton Oaks. A mansion in Washington, DC, at which, during the latter part of 1944, the *major powers of the day laid the foundations for the *United Nations. This series of meetings was known as the Dumbarton Oaks Conference.

durbar. In British colonial practice, a *levee at the court of a native ruler or at the residence of certain governors.

duty officer. The officer or officers left in a *mission (sense 1) or ministry of *foreign affairs, or available on call, outside of normal office hours, i.e. during the night or over weekends and holiday periods. Duty officers have the important and ticklish task of deciding whether or not to postpone consideration of an incoming message of importance or immediately alert (sometimes meaning wake from sleep) a more senior officer or minister (sense 3). At US missions all officers, irrespective of their specialities, are required to take it in turns to serve in this role, usually for one week at a time. The duty officers in the British *Foreign & Commonwealth Office are known as the resident clerks.

E

Eastern bloc. The term which, during the *Cold War, was often used in the *West to refer to the Soviet Union and its East European *satellites. Also called the Soviet bloc. The term was frowned on by purists as implying greater homogeneity in domestic policies than was the case.

Echelon. The codename for the arrangement for pooling *sigint between the *intelligence agencies of the United States, Britain, Australia, Canada, and New Zealand. It has been in existence since 1948. *See also* CAZAB.

Economic and Social Council (ECOSOC). Designated by the UN *Charter as one of the UN's principal organs, ECOSOC is in effect subordinate to the UN *General Assembly, to which it makes recommendations on matters within its remit. Originally made up of 18 UN members, elected by the Assembly, it now consists of three times that number. Each member serves for a three-year term, and is eligible for immediate re-election. The Council acts on the basis of majority voting, each member having one vote. It generally meets once a year, alternately in New York and Geneva, and sits for five weeks. It has an extensive subordinate machinery of functional and regional commissions, standing and expert committees, and is responsible for certain UN bodies such as the Children's Fund (UNICEF), the *United Nations High Commissioner for Refugees, the World Food Programme, and the International Research and Training Institute for the Advancement of Women. *See also* consultative status.

economic attaché. *See* attaché.

Economic Community of West African States (ECOWAS). An association of most but not all of the states of West Africa. It has sixteen members: Benin, Burkina Faso, Cape Verde, Côte d'Ivoire, Gambia, Ghana, Guinea, Guinea-Bissau, Liberia, Mali,

Mauritania, Niger, Nigeria, Senegal, Sierra Leone, and Togo. It was founded in 1975, chiefly to promote economic cooperation and development, and holds yearly *summit meetings which rotate between the capitals of its members. Its *secretariat (headed by an executive secretary) is in Nigeria. In 1993 the founding treaty was revised to allow ECOWAS to engage in efforts to prevent and control regional conflict (in which, so far, it has not been very successful). Other far-reaching activity has also been provided for, but has not yet materialized.

economic diplomacy. (1) Diplomacy concerned with economic policy questions, including the work of delegations to conferences sponsored by bodies such as the *World Trade Organization. While distinct from the *commercial diplomacy of diplomatic missions, it also includes that part of their work concerned with monitoring and reporting on economic policies and developments in the receiving state and advising on how best to influence them. (2) Diplomacy which employs economic resources, either as rewards or sanctions, in pursuit of a particular *foreign policy objective. This is sometimes known as 'economic statecraft'.

economic officer. A US Foreign Service term for the head of the *economic section of a US diplomatic mission. Economic officers have broad responsibilities at posts that are too small to justify the appointment of a *commercial officer as well.

economic sanctions. See sanctions.

economic section. (1) A US Foreign Service term for the section of a US diplomatic mission dealing with trade, export promotion, finance, environmental matters (together with science and technology), investment, agriculture, energy, civil aviation, telecommunications, and international organizations. (2) A British Diplomatic Service term for the section in larger missions dealing with *economic diplomacy. See also commercial section.

economic statecraft. See economic diplomacy.

election assistance. The provision of technical or material support for the conducting of an election. Among other things, it may include legal guidance, voter and civic education, and the training of local observers. See also election monitoring; observer mission.

election monitoring. The independent and professional appraisal of an election process, with the related aims of deterring fraud and reinforcing the legitimacy of the result. See also election assistance; observer mission.

electronic voting. The use of an electronic device to record a vote, now often used in large meetings at *international organizations and *conferences. *See also* roll-call voting.

eleventh hour. A term sometimes used in *negotiations to indicate the approach of a *deadline. *See also* stopping the clock.

embargo. (1) A decision to block the sailing of vessels from a port, which was a traditional form of international *reprisal short of *war. (2) A prohibition on the release of something, for example arms shipments or the text of a speech prior to its delivery. (3) In the phrase 'trade embargo', a ban on all trade – imports as well as exports.

embassy. (1) The building occupied by the offices of a *diplomatic mission headed by an *ambassador, which is the modern meaning. (2) Among other earlier meanings, the envoy and the members of his *family (sense 2). (3) A synonym for a *diplomatic mission, especially one headed by an *ambassador (sense 1). *See also* chancery; legation; rapid reaction embassy; virtual embassy.

embassy of obedience. A lavish and ostentatious *special mission sent to Rome by a secular prince, including the emperor of the Holy Roman Empire, on the occasion of the election of a new pope. *Legationes obedientiae*, which had become customary by at least the eleventh century, were not only gestures of homage and religious affiliation but also marks of some degree of political subservience to the pope. They reached the high-point of their importance probably at the end of the fifteenth century and had all but died out by the end of the eighteenth. The enthusiasm of the Habsburgs for these missions diminished as the power of their house increased.

Embassy Row. The stretch of Massachusetts Avenue in Washington, DC, that extends out from Dupont Circle towards the National Cathedral. Along this are located many of the *embassies (sense 1) of states with *resident diplomatic missions to the United States.

emblem. *See* flag.

emergency room. The room (sometimes rooms) in a diplomatic mission located in a chronically unstable or hostile state, which is dedicated to coping with an emergency. In this event, its chief task is to provide reassurance and assistance to the *expatriate community and is manned 24 hours a day. Ideally, an emergency room should have, among other things, a bank of direct telephone lines ('hot lines'), television and internet connections. *See also* compound; Inman standards; warden network.

éminence grise. The power behind the throne. The archetypal grey eminence was Father Joseph, the Capuchin monk who provided spiritual reassurance as well as expert diplomatic assistance to Cardinal *Richelieu, the early seventeenth-century French statesman, who was eight years his junior.

eminent persons group. An unofficial or quasi-official advisory group consisting of influential figures from varied backgrounds. Such a group may be employed to advise a state or *international organization on a particular problem and disband when its task is completed. Employed in this sense, the term gained currency following the appointment of the *Commonwealth Group of Eminent Persons on Southern Africa, which reported in June 1986. Eminent persons groups may also be employed on a more enduring basis to advise on the conduct of a particular bilateral relationship, in which case a co-chair is provided by each side. India's oldest group of this kind is the India–Japan Study Group, created in the early 1960s. *See also* joint commission.

en clair. In plain language, that is, not in *code or *cypher. Though usually just the normal way of sending non-sensitive messages, communications are sometimes sent uncyphered in the expectation that they will be intercepted. For example, during tense Anglo-Ottoman negotiations over the disputed Aden frontier in 1902, the British ambassador in Istanbul asked that an order should be sent *en clair* to HMS *Harrier*, instructing the warship to remain at Hodeidah for the present. This was clearly envisaged as an unprovocative means of threatening the sultan with force.

endgame. The final or climactic phase of a *negotiation. An American term loosely adapted from chess, the metaphor is not a bad one since a chess game which is not concluded by a checkmate in the 'middle game' will extend into a contest where both players have few pieces left. In this 'endgame' there are certain resemblances to the final stage of a negotiation: each side has few options left, and the result may well be a draw.

en poste. The situation of a *head of mission who, whether formally or informally, has presented his or her *letters of credence to the receiving state and so can proceed with official duties. *See also* post; working copy.

entente. In contrast to an *alliance, a relationship between states in which military commitments are implicit rather than explicit. These may derive either from a formal agreement for consultation in the event of a crisis, or from some kind of practical military collaboration, for example in arms sales, military assistance agreements, military research and development, manoeuvres or arrangements for the use of bases. Ententes, in other words, suggest strongly that the parties are sympathetic to each other to the point that they will stand shoulder to shoulder in war but contain no international legal obligations. The modern concept derives from the Anglo-French *entente cordiale* of 1904. The relationship between the United States and Israel resembles a classic entente, as does NATO's *Partnership for Peace. *See also* Cambon, Paul.

entry into force. A term used in a *treaty stating the circumstances in which and the time at which the treaty will become operative.

In the case of a bilateral treaty which requires *ratification, the date in question will necessarily be linked with the treaty's ratification by both parties: it might be three calendar months after the exchange of instruments of ratification. In the case of a multilateral treaty requiring ratification, it might be a certain time after ratification by a stated number or a majority of the signatories, and that group may have to include certain specified signatories. In the case of a general multilateral treaty which is likely to receive many *signatures, it might be 30 days after the deposit of the fiftieth instrument of ratification or *accession. Some multilateral instruments, however, provide for entry into force as regards any particular state as and when that state accedes to the instrument. The General Convention on the *Privileges and Immunities of the United Nations is such an instrument.

When a multilateral treaty enters into force, it does so only between those states that have ratified it. However, a growing number of treaties permit any of the signatories to give provisional effect to the treaty's obligations prior to that state's ratification of the treaty, whether or not the treaty has entered into force. This can result in a treaty being brought provisionally into force – and some treaties even offer mechanisms for bringing them into force provisionally if there is an undue delay in obtaining the number of ratifications necessary to bring them formally into force.

envoy. A synonym for *diplomat (sense 1). *See also* envoy extraordinary and minister plenipotentiary.

envoy extraordinary and minister plenipotentiary. The full title of the *head of mission to a foreign state where that head, as among heads of mission, falls into the second *class. The head is, however, called *minister (sense 1); and his mission is called a *legation. While accredited to the head of state, a minister is not invested with 'the *representative character'. This rank had been noted by *Vattel and was subsequently codified in the *Regulation of Vienna (1815). However, this class of head of mission is now a historical curiosity, no state wishing to place its head of mission in anything other than the first class. *See also* envoy; foreign minister (sense 2).

equality of states. The principle that all *sovereign states, by virtue of the fact that they all enjoy *sovereignty (sense 1), are equal in status (notwithstanding the wide disparities of power and influence which exist between them). The principle often finds expression in diplomacy, for example in the rules regarding interstate *precedence. *See also* great power; major power; middle power; micro-state; superpower.

espionage. Obtaining *foreign intelligence by the employment of spies or *secret agents, as opposed to obtaining it by the 'technical means' which have become so important since the Second World War. Diplomats themselves have always been associated with this kind of work, either because they spied themselves, hired others to do it for them, or gave shelter in *diplomatic premises – under innocent-sounding titles – to spies in the secret service of their own state. (The last is the most common today.) Indeed, the acquisition of local information, by both legal and illegal means, was in general the most important of all of the functions of the first *resident missions, which is why they were regarded with great suspicion and why *diplomatic privileges and immunities developed only slowly. When the diplomat was described as an 'honourable spy', however, as was

common by the seventeenth century, reference was being made only to his role in the acquisition of information by lawful means. *See also* diplomatic functions; humint; intelligence; Kautilya.

estafette. See staffeto.

Estrada Doctrine. The doctrine that the *recognition of governments is superfluous and, indeed, is insulting in circumstances where it involves passing judgment on the legitimacy of a government which has come to power by unconstitutional means. Announced in 1930 by Don Genaro Estrada, the Foreign Minister of Mexico, this doctrine has grown in popularity over recent years. However, its adoption does not relieve states of the political necessity of deciding whether they are willing to enter into or continue *diplomatic relations (sense 1) with a new regime; nor of the need to decide, where two rival regimes appear, whether it should have dealings with both, one rather than the other, or neither. *See also de facto* recognition.

European Commission. The college of commissioners of the *European Union (who have risen in number with each enlargement), plus the civil servants who work for them. Each commissioner is responsible for one or more of the departments (known as directorates-general) into which the Commission is divided. Though unelected, a new college of commissioners now has to secure the approval of the *European Parliament. Guardian of the notion of a broader European interest, among its important tasks are ensuring that the Union's treaties are observed, initiating legislation, and executing decisions of the *Council of Ministers. The Commission is required to work under 'the political guidance of its President', and all major decisions are taken by *consensus. Its headquarters is located in the Berlaymont building in Brussels. *See also* comitology; representation.

European Community. The name officially given to the European Economic Community (previously and popularly *Common Market) in the *Maastricht Treaty. Technically it remains a separate entity from the *European Union (sense 2).

European Council. The serial *summit meeting (usually held three times a year) of the *European Union. Though its roots go back to European summits at the beginning of the 1960s, the Council began to meet informally in its current format in 1975 and it was regularized by the *Single European Act in 1986. The president of the *European Commission also attends, as do foreign ministers and – when appropriate – economic and finance ministers. The chief functions of the Council are to provide general political guidelines for the Union and resolve deadlocks which have developed at lower levels, especially in the *Council of Ministers. Decisions, which only occasionally are arrived at by voting, are presented as 'conclusions of the Presidency' and, where detailed agreements on points of substance are concerned, declarations.

European Economic Community. *See* European Community.

European Parliament. The directly elected assembly of the *European Union. It has 626 members, known as 'Members of the European Parliament' or MEPs. The meetings of the Parliament are held in Strasbourg but (most inconveniently) those of its standing committees take place in Brussels. Originally a very weak institution and largely consultative, the powers of the European Parliament have grown steadily and are now extensive. Apart from general supervision of the other institutions (including the power to dismiss the *European Commission), it has important budgetary and legislative powers. For these reasons and because it is directly elected, it is not a typical international *parliamentary assembly.

European Political Cooperation. *See* Common Foreign and Security Policy.

European Union (EU). (1) The goal of supporters of European 'integration': a European state. (2) Since the entry into force of the Treaty of *Maastricht in November 1993, the institutions involved in discharging the responsibilities of the *Council of Ministers for foreign and security policy (CFSP) and judicial and police affairs. On this technical definition of 'European Union' the term excludes the *European Community. (3) Popularly, the 'European Union' *plus* the 'European Community'.

ex aequo et bono. On the basis of justice and equity, as distinct from law. Thus, if an international tribunal is asked to adopt this principle it is then entitled (but not obliged) to disregard existing law in making its award.

excellency. A style used in addressing or referring to an *ambassador or *high commissioner (though today 'ambassador/high commissioner', sometimes prefixed by an indication of gender, is more common). When used referentially, it is prefixed by 'his' or 'her'. Originally intended only for the ambassadors of crowned heads of state, in the nineteenth century its use as regards ambassadors became general. In the twentieth century *ministers (sense 1) began to press for the style to be used with regard to them. It is for a receiving state to determine official usage within its jurisdiction, and practice varied. It was accorded to ministers in Latin American states (where the style 'excellency' was already distributed

with a generous hand), and in Britain and some *Commonwealth states, but South Africa resisted this instance of title creep (worrying, among other things, about the impact it might have on its domestic order of *precedence). In the United States ministers were called 'the honourable', not 'excellency'. High commissioners were accorded the style 'excellency' only after 1948, when it was decided that henceforth they would rank alongside ambassadors. With the general upgrading of *legations to *embassies at the middle of the century, the pressure for ministers to enjoy stylistic equality with ambassadors died a natural death. As already implied, high-ranking persons outside the world of *diplomacy (sense 1), such as *heads of state and government or government ministers, are also often accorded the style 'excellency'.

exchange of views. As opposed to a *negotiation, a diplomatic exchange limited to clarifying the attitudes of the parties towards a particular subject or range of subjects. In French, a *tour d'horizon*.

exclusion zone. An area declared by a party to a dispute to be one which its adversary's armed forces enter at their peril. Such declarations may well have little legal weight; but if (as is likely) the excluded party is the weaker of the two, they may have considerable effect. Such declarations were made in the Falklands War (1982), and in the 1990s in respect of parts of Iraq.

exclusive economic zone (EEZ). An area beyond but adjacent to a state's *territorial sea, not extending beyond 200 nautical miles from the baselines from which its territorial sea is measured. (A nautical mile is 1.1515 miles, or 1.852 kilometres.) The coastal state does not have the kind of general jurisdiction – i.e. *sovereignty (sense 2) – over the EEZ which it has over its territory; but it does have *sovereign rights over all the zone's economic resources: those in the waters above the sea-bed, on the sea-bed, and in its subsoil.

executive agreement. The term used by the United States for an international *agreement which, because of its technical nature, lesser importance, and perhaps also because of a domestic political difficulty, is to *enter into force upon or soon after *signature – that is, without *ratification. It is designated as an executive agreement rather than as a *treaty because the United States' constitution gives the Senate a key role in the ratification process – requiring that 'treaties' must be made with the Senate's 'advice and consent'. However, an agreement may be insufficiently significant to take up the Senate's time. And sometimes there is an additional reason for the use of a term other than treaty.

The separation of the executive and the legislature in the United States may result in the president being unable to ensure that the Senate will consent to an agreement which the executive is anxious to make, or to consent quickly to one which the executive deems to be urgent. If, therefore, the political content of such an agreement is not unduly high, it may be designated as an executive agreement rather than as a treaty. In *international law, however, any such agreement enjoys the same status as any other formal undertaking made on behalf of the United States, as the actual term which is used to designate an international agreement is irrelevant. Thus an executive agreement is *binding on the United States in the same way as a 'treaty' which has been approved by the Senate.

Nowadays it is not uncommon for states to make formal agreements which do not require ratification for them to become binding on the signatories. The content of such agreements may well be technical issues which do not need domestic legislation for their implementation. Legal *instruments of this kind, like all legally binding agreements, may or may not be designated as 'treaties'.

exequatur. The document supplied by the *receiving state to the head of a *consular post authorizing the officer to exercise consular functions within the post's district.

exhaustion of local remedies. The principle that someone who has suffered a loss or an injury for which a foreign state is allegedly responsible must generally seek redress through the courts of the state concerned before the aggrieved individual's state is entitled to take the matter up directly with the foreign state.

expatriate community. Citizens of one state who are temporarily or permanently resident in another, though they are not always as organized as the term implies. The welfare of such communities is a particular concern of *diplomatic missions and consular posts, especially during crises and emergencies. *See also* emergency room; national day; warden network.

express. A *messenger riding on horseback who carried mails at the fastest speed possible. In England at the end of the seventeenth century the 'ordinary' post travelled at an average speed of about four miles an hour, while an express messenger would travel at between five and seven miles an hour depending on his burden and the quality of the fresh horses available at the staging posts on his route. (An express would sometimes consist of one rider carrying the message for the whole journey, sometimes of relays of riders; in either event, he would often be accompanied by a guide and, if necessary, by one or more armed guards.) Nevertheless, the chief advantage of an express lay in its ability – for a price – to depart as soon as letters were ready for despatch. For urgent messages this was essential since ordinary international posts were regulated by schedules with days or even weeks intervening between departures. The slowly increasing frequency of the ordinary posts together with dramatic technical developments (better roads and mail coaches, railways, steamships and finally the *telegraph) made expresses outmoded by the first half of the nineteenth century. Until then, however, they were of the greatest value to the diplomatic services of Europe when it was, for example, necessary to issue fresh *instructions to envoys and for the latter to return urgent *despatches. *Machiavelli had much admired their employment by the Duke Valentino at the beginning of the sixteenth century. Nevertheless, their use was restricted not only because they were very expensive but also because, like *special envoys, they were inclined to attract attention and excite rumour. Some of the members of the British government's own express service, the *Queen's/King's Messengers, became quite well known and their arrivals were announced in the press. At the end of the nineteenth century there was even a cartoon of the senior messenger, Captain Conway F. C. Seymour, published by 'Spy' in the popular periodical *Vanity Fair*.

external affairs, ministry or department of. A less common name for a ministry of *foreign affairs. 'External' is preferred to 'foreign' by some states to avoid the implication that fellow members of some close and intimate association such as the *Commonwealth or EU are 'foreign'. Occasional attempts by British governments to restore to the *Foreign and Commonwealth Office its historic title of 'Foreign Office' have so far always run aground on, in part, the objection of Commonwealth states to the suggestion that they are 'foreign'.

exterritoriality. Sometimes spelled 'extraterritoriality', the fiction that in law the *diplomatic agent abroad remains at home, and certainly outside of the territory of the state to which he or she is accredited. The term itself probably originated with an observation of *Grotius in his *De Jure Belli ac Pacis* (1625). Now a quality most commonly associated with *diplomatic premises and still sometimes believed or at least pretended, not least by professional diplomats, to be an important explanation of *diplomatic privileges and immunities, exterritoriality is in fact no more than a very loose *description* of them. As *Vattel wrote in *Le Droit des Gens* in 1758, 'this is only a figurative way of expressing his [the ambassador's] independence of the jurisdiction of the country and his possession of all the rights necessary to the due success of the embassy'. Lawyers have attached little importance to exterritoriality since at least the nineteenth century and it is nowhere mentioned in the Vienna Convention on *Diplomatic Relations (1961). Nevertheless, it remains, as has been said, a 'striking image' and thus a useful political buttress to diplomatic immunity. *See also* functional approach.

extradition. The process whereby one state surrenders to another (on the latter's request) a person accused or convicted of a criminal offence against the law of the requesting state. Extradition usually takes place on the basis of a bilateral *treaty but may also proceed under multilateral conventions relating to serious crime.

extraordinaries. A term going back to the early modern period for what would now be called a diplomat's 'expenses'.

extraordinary. Originally an additional title given to an *ambassador on a *special mission, it became the custom also to attach it to the title of resident ambassadors and *envoys. Now it is part of the full title of most *heads of mission of the first and second *class. However, British *high commissioners do not have the word included in their title. Instead they are spoken of as an 'accredited Representative and Plenipotentiary'. (Not all *Commonwealth states distinguish in this way, or in others, between the titles of their ambassadors and high commissioners.)

extraterritoriality. A synonym for *exterritoriality.

eyeball-to-eyeball. Mutual *brinkmanship.

F

facilitator. A modern term for a *third party who provides *good offices (sense 1) in an attempt to facilitate or assist the settlement of an international or intrastate conflict.

fact finding. *See* inquiry.

factor. In early modern Europe: (1) a trader (*see also* factory); or (2) an agent acting on an employer's behalf.

factory. In early modern Europe, the body of *factors (sense 1) established at any one place, usually a port, a trading settlement. Hence for example 'the English factory at Smyrna'. The affairs of a factory were a major responsibility of the *consul of the state of which the factors were citizens.

fait accompli. A decision reached or action accomplished, usually in the context of anticipated opposition.

fall-back position. In *negotiations, the most a party is willing to concede, and the least it will accept in return, as the basis for concluding an agreement. For obvious reasons, formally drafted fall-back positions – unless drawn up for purposes of deception – are best kept secret. Those who are doubtful that secrecy can ever be maintained and believe that professional diplomats are in any case always too ready to *compromise, believe that fall-back positions should never be produced at all.

family of a diplomatic agent. (1) The spouse or partner of a *diplomat, together with their dependent children and any other relative (usually in the 'immediate' family) admitted to this category by negotiation with the *receiving state at the time of the relative's arrival. This definition of what used to be known as the 'domestic family' is based on current practice rather than the 1961 Vienna Convention on Diplomatic Relations, as it was not then possible to reach detailed agreement on what proved a controversial subject. But it was accepted that those recognized as members of the agent's family should enjoy the same privileges and immunities as the agent. (2) Until well into the nineteenth century, however, the head of mission's 'family' meant his entire embassy (sense 2), and thus included what was known as his 'official family', usually a *secretary of embassy/legation, *attachés, servants, and so on. *See also* administrative and technical staff; service staff.

farewell call. One made by a departing *head of mission on the *head of the state to which the diplomat concerned has been accredited, or to any other dignitary with whom he or she has had dealings. In most, but not all, countries *protocol does not require a call on the head of state, but some circumstances may result in one being made: close ties between the two states concerned, a personal relationship between the departing head of mission and the head of state, or just the expressed wish of the head of mission. In the last case, as well as when a farewell call is a protocol requirement, the diplomat may find that the diary of the head of state is somewhat congested. This is a real likelihood if he or she is also *head of government, and a delay possibly extending to months before a convenient time for a farewell call can be found may well be the result. Any such call is likely

to be less formal than the initial one employed by a head of mission to present *letters of credence to the head of state. Farewell calls on the *receiving state's foreign minister are more likely to be made than on the head of state. Also known as a farewell audience.

farewell despatch. *See* valedictory despatch.

Farnesina. The Italian Ministry of Foreign Affairs, so-called because it has occupied the *Palazzo della Farnesina* in Rome since 1959.

federal state. A *sovereign state the constitution of which assigns a significant measure of self-rule to the state's main constituent territorial parts. That measure may include the right to engage in limited international activity, so that the agents of the constituent parts may sometimes play a superficially diplomatic role, in connection with which they may be accorded certain privileges and immunities by the *receiving state. However, as the constituent units are not sovereign (sense 1) their international activity is not diplomacy (sense 1), and hence their agents are not classified as *diplomats and *diplomatic law does not apply to them. *See also* agent-general.

ferman. Sometimes *'firman'*, this was an official decree handed down by the Ottoman sultan – an imperial edict.

fetial priest. A member of the Roman college, the *fetiales*, which was responsible for the ceremonial associated with diplomatic moves of high significance, such as forming an *alliance, issuing an *ultimatum, surrendering a prisoner, or concluding a *peace. In his *De Legationibus Libri Tres* (1585), Alberico *Gentili, drawing chiefly on Livy, devotes two chapters in his first book to the fecial [*sic*] priests, noting, *inter alia*, that 'redress was sought through fecial priests on those occasions when other kinds of embassies had failed to get any satisfaction'. *See also* heralds.

final act. A summary of the proceedings of an international *conference, which typically lists any *agreements reached and resolutions adopted. A final act of this – the usual – sort is not itself a *treaty, but a treaty is very occasionally called a final act.

fin de non-recevoir. Rejection of an official representation (usually a complaint or a demand) without looking into its merits: an evasive reply or a brushing off.

first-arrival privileges. The exemption from customs duties and taxes which the *receiving state is obliged to grant in respect of such personal and household goods as are brought into the state by a *diplomatic agent accredited to that state and by members of his or her *family on the occasion of their first arrival.

first person note. *See* note (sense 2).

first poster. A diplomat preparing for, or already at, his or her first overseas posting.

first secretary. In *diplomatic ranks, that which lies beneath *counsellor and above *second secretary. *See also* secretary of embassy/legation.

flag. *See* diplomatic flag.

flag of convenience. The registration of a ship in a state with which it has no other connection, but whose shipping regulations or international legal obligations are significantly less onerous than those of other states, so making it advantageous for the ship owners to register their ship in that state. In other words, the flag the ship flies is no more than one of convenience.

The UN Convention on the Law of the Sea (1982) provides that there must be a genuine link between a ship and its flag state. But such a link is often less than clear.

flag of truce. One under which, during the course of hostilities, a messenger from one side approaches the other, the flag being designed to ensure the messenger's safe passage. *See also* herald.

flag state. The state whose flag is flown by a ship. A ship must register to sail under the flag of one state only, and then has the nationality of that state. *See also* flag of convenience.

flash telegram. A *telegram of the highest priority.

flat-pack embassy. *See* rapid reaction embassy.

flying a kite. In *negotiation, putting out a feeler or leaking a radical proposal with a view to examining the reaction of the other side. If this is not too hostile, the kite-flyer may well assume that its *interlocutor may be able to afford acceptance of something like this proposal (kite), and in this event the kite (proposal) is wound in, straightened out and presented across the table. The French equivalent is *envoyer un ballon d'essai*.

flying seal. *See* under flying seal.

Foggy Bottom. The flat ground by the Potomac River in Washington, DC, where the current *State Department building was erected after the Second World War and hence the name sometimes used by members of the US *Foreign Service for the Department itself.

force commander. *See* commander.

force majeure. An irresistible force. The defence of *force majeure* is sometimes used by states to justify a failure to execute an obligation or the commission of an apparently unlawful act.

foreign affairs community. The departments and executive agencies located in Washington which are involved in the formulation and execution of American foreign policy. The term eloquently signifies the diminished influence of the *State Department but finds official favour because it suggests a cooperative spirit which, in practice, is often lacking. In recent years this lack has often been particularly obvious in the relationship between the State Department and the *National Security Council.

Foreign Affairs Council. The term currently applied to the EU *Council of Ministers when a meeting under this head is composed of foreign ministers as opposed, say, to transport ministers.

foreign affairs, ministry of. The government department usually charged with taking the lead in the conduct of a state's foreign policy, and hence with its *diplomacy (sense 1); and ideally, too, with coordinating all of the state's international activity. It is now commonly referred to as the 'MFA'. *See also* channel of communication; direct dial diplomacy; external affairs, ministry or department of; Richelieu.

foreign aid. Economic resources (including interest-free/low-interest loans) transferred from one state to another, either at significantly less than market price, or without anticipation of payment, or as a gift. *International organizations may also extend such aid.

Foreign and Commonwealth Office (FCO). Britain's ministry of *foreign affairs. Its political head is called the Secretary of State for Foreign and Commonwealth Affairs; its head official, the Permanent Under-Secretary of State and Head of the *Diplomatic Service. The FCO's name derives from the merger in 1968 of two former departments, the *Foreign Office and the Commonwealth Office (which had earlier been the *Commonwealth Relations Office). However, the FCO is now routinely referred to in the media by the earlier and shorter name – 'Foreign Office'. *See also* Whitehall.

Foreign Buildings Operations (FBO), Office of. *See* Larkin, Frederick A.

foreign intelligence. (1) All information on foreign targets obtained by intelligence agencies, including *defence intelligence. (2) All information on foreign targets obtained by intelligence agencies excluding defence intelligence. (3) The intelligence agencies of foreign states. It will thus be clear that this is a highly treacherous term. Apart from the difference in the first two meanings, the phrase 'foreign intelligence agencies' can mean either (a) agencies specializing in gathering *intelligence on foreign targets, or (b) the

intelligence agencies of foreign powers.

foreign minister. (1) The governmental *minister (sense 3) in charge of a state's ministry of *foreign affairs, though actual titles vary from country to country. (2) Historically, any *diplomat or *public minister. Thus at the coronation of King George V and Queen Mary in June 1911 the programme and foreign guest list produced by the Foreign Office listed, for example, *ambassadors, *envoys extraordinary and ministers plenipotentiary under the heading 'Foreign Ministers at this Court in order of their precedence in each class'.

Foreign Office. The British department of state responsible from its establishment in 1782 until 1968 for the execution (except in relation to members of the *Commonwealth) of the country's foreign policy. Thereafter this responsibility across the whole foreign spectrum lay with the *Foreign and Commonwealth Office. Prior to 1919–20 the members of the Foreign Office served only in London, Britain's diplomatic posts abroad being staffed by members of the separate *Diplomatic Service. *See also* external affairs, ministry of.

Foreign Office certificate. The traditional British term for a communication from the Foreign Office (now the *Foreign and Commonwealth Office) to a court of law setting out the former's understanding as to some factual matter, such as whether a state has been *recognized by Britain, whether Britain is at *war with another state, and whether a person enjoys *diplomatic status. British courts accept such statements as conclusive. Also known as a secretary of state's certificate.

Foreign Office List. The short name by which Britain's Diplomatic Service List used to be known up to and including 1965, though the full title was more revealing: *The Foreign Office List and Diplomatic and Consular Year Book*. It was first published in 1852. *See also* diplomatic list; diplomatic service list.

foreign policy. (1) The political and security policies adopted by a state in relation to the outside world. (2) All of the policies (including economic policies) adopted by a state in relation to the outside world.

Foreign Secretary. A synonym, in Britain, for *foreign minister (sense 1). In some other states it is the title of the head official of the ministry of *foreign affairs.

foreign service. *See* diplomatic service; Diplomatic Service, British; Foreign Service, British; Foreign Service, US.

Foreign Service, British. The body created in 1943 by the amalgamation of the Foreign Office and Diplomatic Service, the Consular Service and the Commercial Diplomatic Service. It ceased to exist at the end of 1964, when it was itself amalgamated with other services to form part of the new British *Diplomatic Service.

Foreign Service Institute (FSI). Founded in 1946, the FSI is the primary training institute for the US *foreign affairs community.

foreign service list. *See* diplomatic service list.

foreign service national. A US Foreign Service term for a member of a *diplomatic mission's *locally engaged staff.

foreign service reserves. *See* attaché (sense 2).

Foreign Service, US. The diplomatic (including consular) service of the United States. As in the case of Britain, the United States originally had separate diplomatic and consular services but these were merged into a unified service – the US Foreign Service – when the Rogers Act became law on 24 May 1924. Under this Act, which was also of great significance for putting the service for the first time on a secure professional basis, permanent officers under the rank of minister were designated Foreign Service Officers (FSOs). A further amalgamation, analogous to that which had taken place in Britain after the First World War, occurred when, following the

Wriston Report of 1954, the Foreign Service absorbed the personnel of the hitherto separate *State Department. *See also* career ambassador; career minister; career officer; diplomat-in-residence; Foggy Bottom; Larkin; senior foreign service.

foreign trade service. The governmental agency which, quite separately from the *diplomatic and *consular services, often used to be charged with the promotion of a state's foreign trade. Nowadays, even if such a distinct agency is maintained domestically, its work abroad is likely to be closely integrated with that of the diplomatic service, and those of its members serving abroad are likely to enjoy *diplomatic or *consular status. *See also* Commercial Diplomatic Service.

formula. In *negotiations, the broad principles of a settlement, which ideally should be comprehensive, balanced, and flexible. 'Guidelines', 'framework for agreement', and 'set of ideas' are other terms for a formula. *See also* framework treaty.

forum. (1) Any international gathering. (2) An informal international gathering which has a fairly sharp focus for discussion and is often held at high level. For example, the Regional Forum of the *Association of South-East Asian Nations meets annually at foreign minister level to exchange views on regional security

and has resisted external pressure to develop organizational features and concerted policies. Membership of such a forum provides opportunities for influence and *intelligence-gathering while imposing few obligations on members and signalling little more than interest in its subject matter. As a result, the opportunity for participation is rarely missed. In many ways a forum is a *functionalist conception.

forum shopping. Raising the same issue in a variety of different multilateral bodies (typically UN agencies or *regional organizations) to see which of them is likely to serve best the interests of the state concerned.

Fourteen Points. *See* Wilson, Woodrow.

frais de représentation. The allowances of a *head of mission, including entertainment allowances.

framework for agreement. *See* formula.

framework treaty. A multilateral *treaty usually setting out obligations only in general terms, the assumption being that the parties will fill out the details either in subsequent treaties (usually called protocols), or national legislation. *See also* formula.

franchise de l'hotel. A *diplomatic mission's right to use its premises for their prescribed purpose. *See also* diplomatic privileges and immunities; diplomatic premises.

franchise du quartier. See diplomatic quarter.

francophonie. The collectivity of French-speaking states and communities. Support for the idea of *la francophonie* revived strongly at the beginning of the 1960s, and now finds expression in a variety of institutions, most visibly the annual Franco-African *summit. *See also* French Community.

free city. *See* internationalization.

freedom of communication. *Receiving states are obliged to permit and protect free communication by *diplomatic missions for all official purposes – although there is evidence that this obligation has sometimes been broken through the use of *listening devices. However, the permission of the receiving state is required for the installation and use of a 'wireless [i.e. radio] transmitter' – unless, as in the case of Britain, the receiving state's general policy is not to require such permission. *See also* bubble; diplomatic bag; diplomatic courier; Queen's Messenger.

freedom of movement. The entitlement of all members of a *diplomatic mission to move freely in the territory of the *receiving state. However, for reasons of national security that state is entitled to pro-

hibit or regulate entry into certain areas. Sometimes receiving states have interpreted this entitlement very broadly, but the principle of *reciprocity tends to place limits on such developments.

free port. An area of a state into which goods may be imported for processing or manufacture without payment of customs duty, provided that they are later directly exported from the free port.

free trade. Trade between states which is unhindered by such devices as tariffs and import quotas, and probably also by export subsidies. *See also* free trade area.

free trade area. An association of states created to promote *free trade among its members while, in contrast to a *customs union, leaving each of them at liberty to conduct different trade policies towards other states.

French Community. A device instituted by President de Gaulle in 1958 in the hope of staving off the full impact of the decolonization movement on France's overseas territories. However, within two years all the French colonies in sub-Saharan Africa had demanded and received sovereignty (sense 1), and the *Communauté Française* was adjusted to resemble the *Commonwealth. A number of the former French possessions in Africa have seceded from it, but most of them, whether Community members or not, continue to have close financial, economic, and technical ties with France, and sometimes military ones, too. *See also francophonie.*

French Political Academy. *See* Torcy.

French system of diplomacy. *See* old diplomacy.

friendly relations. States often speak of being in friendly relations and of having friends. By these terms they generally refer to contacts which are at the least marked by easy and unfettered diplomatic links and at the most by productive liaisons in a variety of spheres. Thus the terms tend to have the connotation of 'normal' relations. However, while the Vienna Convention on *Diplomatic Relations lists the promotion of 'friendly relations' as one of the functions of a diplomatic mission, it should be noted that relations between states are based on utility, not liking. International 'friendship' is therefore quite different from the phenomenon which, as among humans, is usually indicated by the use of that term. Accordingly, rather than 'friends' and 'friendly' such terms as 'associates' and 'associative' would be more appropriate at the international level. But there is little chance of them supplanting the current usage. *See also* diplomatic functions.

friends. (1) The term employed in the British *Diplomatic Service to refer to the *Secret Intelligence Service (SIS) in general and, in particular, to those on the staff of a British *diplomatic mission who, although purportedly professional diplomats, and also often acting as such in practice, are in fact members of SIS. (2) An informal grouping of states which bands together in support of another state or international organization, typically one engaged in a *mediation. Hence, in the UN context, the 'group of friends' or 'Friends of the Secretary-General' on such-and-such an issue. *See also* contact group.

FSB. The Russian Federal Security Service, the main successor body to the *KGB in counter-intelligence. *See also* SVR.

fudging. *See* constructive ambiguity.

full and frank discussion. A diplomatic exchange which fails to elicit agreement on anything at all, with the possible exception of the need to 'resume' the discussion at 'some future date'. This is a good example of the kind of standard *diplomatic language (sense 1) employed in press releases and *communiqués.

full diplomatic relations. *See* diplomatic relations (sense 1).

full powers. The capacity to sign a *treaty. Usually it consists of a specific written authorization granted by a state to one of its *diplomatic agents. Such full powers must be available for inspection by the other party or parties to the treaty, and may be exchanged for theirs. However, a *head of state, *head of government, and *foreign minister (sense 1) enjoy full powers by virtue of their offices. Someone with full powers is known as a plenipotentiary. The inclusion of that term in the full title of an *ambassador indicates that such an official does not need full powers to agree the text of a treaty between the *sending and the *receiving state. *See also* general full powers.

functional approach. (1) The view that *diplomatic privileges and immunities are accorded and justified because they permit the effective execution of *diplomatic functions. (2) An activity exemplifying the principle of *functionalism.

functional department. In a ministry of *foreign affairs, a department dealing with a general issue, such as the environment, arms control, or drugs, as distinct from a *geographical department.

functionalism. The belief that international conflict can be eliminated by the development of institutionalized international cooperation in the economic and social spheres. The idea is that such cooperation will 'spill over' into areas of greater 'political' significance, though there is not much evidence in its support. It is a theory which was advanced and strongly advocated by David Mitrany (1888–1975).

functions of diplomacy. *See* diplomatic functions.

funeral diplomacy. *See* working funeral.

G

Gaimushō. The Japanese Ministry of Foreign Affairs. The ministry was established in 1868, although it was not called the *Gaimushō* until 1885.

gazette. A printed news sheet produced by governments and sold to the public, the gazette first appeared in the early seventeenth century and was so called because in Venice it was sold for a *gazeta*, a coin of small value. Also sometimes referred to as a 'coranto' or 'couranto' (from the French *courante* – running), it contained government proclamations and the official version of domestic and foreign events. The foreign news was obtained largely from manuscript *newsletters and other gazettes, as well as from diplomatic and consular *despatches. Their content made them of interest to envoys themselves, though as obvious organs of *propaganda they were not generally held by them in high regard. Notable examples were the *Gazette de France* (the mouthpiece of Cardinal *Richelieu), the *Relations Véritables* of Brussels, the *Oprechte Haerlemse Dingsdaegse Courant* (known in England as the *Haarlem Gazette*), and – late on the scene – the *London Gazette*, which did not appear until the mid-1660s. As their monopolies of the news gradually weakened, especially in the nineteenth century, official gazettes changed their form, lost their political importance and became not much more than vehicles for governmental statements (including official appointments) and legal notices – very often, material which would be given publicity nowhere else, but for which some kind of formal announcement and record is highly desirable.

GCHQ. *See* Government Communications Headquarters; sigint.

general act. (1) A synonym for a *treaty, usually a multilateral one of widespread interest. (2) Detailed regulations deriving from general principles contained in a treaty.

General Assembly. The chief deliberative organ of the *United

Nations. It consists of all UN members, each of them having one vote. The Assembly's resolutions are passed by either a two-thirds or a simple majority of those present and voting. On external matters its resolutions are only recommendatory, but on matters internal to the UN – such as budgetary questions and the election of non-permanent members of the UN *Security Council – the Assembly's resolutions are *binding on the members and the organization.

The General Assembly meets each year in regular session between mid-September and late December; sometimes this session is continued in the next calendar year. Special sessions of the Assembly are convoked at the request of the Security Council or of a majority of UN members.

The fact that since about 1960 most of the world's states have been UN members, and hence represented in the Assembly, has resulted in a tendency to refer to some of its most popular themes as expressive of world public opinion. More cogently, what they represent is the numerical balance of the opinion of member states, which some observers have called diplomatic opinion. However, there can be little doubt that the work of the Assembly had a powerful influence on moulding some of the key ideas of the latter part of the twentieth century, such as the need to remedy economic inequality and, especially, the impropriety of *colonialism and racism.

See also Committee of 24; Declaration on the Granting of Independence to Colonial Countries and Peoples; multilateral diplomacy; open diplomacy; self-determination.

general delegation. A group of *non-diplomatic agents.

general full powers. *Full powers of a general kind which may be granted by a state to its *permanent representatives to those *international organizations (such as the *United Nations, the *European Union, and the *Council of Europe) whose work gives rise to a relatively large number of *treaties. Possession of such powers permits the *signature of these treaties without the specific documentary authorization which would otherwise be required.

general international customary law. *See* customary international law.

general principles of law. The Statute of the *International Court of Justice states that in settling disputes in accordance with *international law it shall apply not just *treaties and *customary international law but also the general principles of law recognized by civilized nations. It may be that this 1945 statement was the last official expression (in public) of the belief that some nations are less than civilized.

Geneva Conventions. *See* Red Cross Conventions.

genocide. A term invented in 1944 by a Polish Jewish lawyer, Raphael Lemkin, which the *Genocide Convention defined as 'acts committed with intent to destroy, in whole or in part, a national, ethnical, racial or religious group'.

Genocide Convention. Adopted by the UN *General Assembly in 1948, this establishes rules for the punishment of persons committing the *international crime of *genocide. The Convention entered into force in 1951.

Gentili, Alberico (1552–1608). An Italian lawyer of Protestant conviction who in 1580 sought refuge from the Inquisition in the England of Elizabeth I. He found employment at Oxford University and from 1587 until 1600 was Regius Professor of Civil Law. His chief interest for students of diplomacy is his remarkable work *De Legationibus Libri Tres*, which has been justly described by Peter Haggenmacher as 'undoubtedly the first successful attempt to encompass diplomatic law as a coherent whole'. Published in 1585, it was inspired by his involvement in the case of the Spanish ambassador, Don Bernadino de Mendoza, who had been accused in the previous year of complicity in the Throckmorton plot against the queen. Contrary to the view of Elizabeth's privy council, who wished to punish Don Bernadino, Gentili, together with *Hotman, held that the ambassador's status gave him immunity. This was

accepted and he was simply expelled from the country. Thereafter Gentili's work focused on the law of war. He is generally believed to have been a considerable influence on the thought of *Grotius.

geographical department. In a ministry of *foreign affairs, a department dealing with a particular state or region, as distinct from a *functional department. In some MFAs, for example that of India, such a department is known as a 'territorial division'.

geographical post. A post in the *secretariat of an *international organization which is allotted to a specific member state so that at least in non-specialist areas the organization's staff might provide evidence of 'equitable geographical distribution'. *See also* contribution principle.

giovanni di lingua. Student *dragomans attached to embassies and consulates in the Ottoman Empire.

GlavUpDK. The 'Main Administration for Service to the Diplomatic Corps under the Ministry of Foreign Affairs of the Russian Federation', i.e. a foreign ministry agency devoted to providing the members of the Moscow *diplomatic corps with day-to-day living, travel, and recreational requirements. It also publishes a monthly journal called *Diplomat*. Assisting with the provision of *service staff to embassies, at least during the *Cold War the

UpDK was in effect a branch of the *KGB, designed to assist its surveillance and control of foreign diplomatic activity.

global governance. A misleading term for the collective activities of *international organizations with a more or less universal membership. Such activities by no means equate to the usual meaning of the word governance.

globalization. The vague but omnipresent term for the changes – especially in the areas of finance, trade, investment and communications – which over recent decades have limited the effective economic freedom of *sovereign states. The extreme claim is that linked but nevertheless previously separate national economies have been replaced by a 'global economy' and that national cultures are being slowly replaced by a 'global culture'. In this process the activities of the *multinational corporation are given pride of place, and the collapse of Communism and the deregulatory policies of some of the leading free-market economies are held to have given it added impetus. Nevertheless, it is difficult to envisage globalization overcoming *nationalism (sense 1) as there is as yet little evidence that the latter is withering as quickly as the former is alleged to be growing.

globalism. The idea that worldwide problems should be approached on a world-wide basis. It is

thus little more than a semantically fashionable expression of the obvious.

Goethe-Institut. The *Goethe-Institut Inter Nationes e. V.*, founded in 1951, is the vehicle of German *cultural diplomacy.

Gondomar, Count Diego (1567–1626). The outstanding Spanish ambassador to the court of James I of England from 1613 until 1622, who became an intimate friend of the king. Though Gondomar's influence over him was exaggerated at the time and has been since, it remained considerable. His most spectacular success came in 1618, when he persuaded James to execute Sir Walter Raleigh for infringing the King of Spain's monopoly in America.

good offices. (1) Diplomatic intervention by a *neutral *third party (or 'facilitator') in an international or intrastate conflict which is usually limited to providing assistance in bringing the rival parties into direct negotiations but may extend to suggesting a *formula for a settlement. Good offices (*bons offices*) do not, however, extend to active participation in discussions once they are beyond the procedural stage; if this develops, as sometimes happens, the provision of good offices has changed into *mediation. In his *Guide to Diplomatic Practice*, where he devoted separate chapters to 'good offices' and 'mediation', *Satow was rightly impatient with those who could not grasp this distinction, and added the acute observation that, unlike mediation, good offices could be exerted at the request of only one party to a dispute, 'since the essential character of such a step is the presentation to the other party of reasons for a particular course of action which he is invited to take into consideration and adopt'. This is the earlier notion of good offices. *See also* venue. (2) A synonym for mediation. Support for this usage pre-dated Satow and is now, largely thanks to the UN, widespread. Gone is the separate chapter on good offices in the latest edition of *Satow's Guide* and the extremely active role of the UN *Secretary-General in the Cyprus conflict is officially described as his 'mission of good offices'.

goodwill visit. A visit by the representative of one state to another, which is formally limited, or at any rate primarily devoted, to improving the atmosphere in relations between them or to confirming an already *friendly relationship. Generally conducted at a senior level, it may also produce useful personal contacts. Goodwill visits are not formally concerned with *negotiations. In reality, they are sometimes used to mask sensitive negotiations or, when the term is used after the event, to conceal the fact that they have failed: 'it was only a goodwill visit'.

Government Communications Headquarters (GCHQ). The title of Britain's national *sigint collection agency. A largely civilian organization, it grew from the Government Code and Cypher School established after the First World War.

government-in-exile. A body which claims to be the legitimate government of a state, but which is unable to establish itself in the state in question. It may be *recognized as such by other states – at the cost, of course, of that decision being seen as a hostile act by the government actually in control of the state.

governor-general. The official who represents and acts on behalf and in the place of the *head of state in those (now relatively few) members of the *Commonwealth who accept the British monarch as their formal head. Originally, the governor-general was the representative, and always a national, of Britain in a British *dominion (and in some dependent territories – usually those with a *federal structure), and was the senior person in the self-governing territory's administrative structure. But as the Commonwealth underwent constitutional development, and the dominions became *sovereign states, the office of governor-general changed, so that in all essential respects its holder became, in relation to the Commonwealth member in question, the on-the-spot substitute for the member's head of state. Thus a governor-general was never a *diplomat; and in the twentieth century the holder of this office ceased to be the representative or agent of the British government. He or she is appointed by the monarch on the advice of the government of the state concerned. In the federal state of Australia the monarch is represented at the federal level by a governor-general, and in each of Australia's constituent States by a governor; and in each of the Provinces of the federal state of Canada by a lieutenant-governor, while also being represented at the federal level by a governor-general. *See also* high commissioner.

grand vizier. The head, under the sultan, of the former Ottoman government; in other words, his senior slave. *See also* Sublime Porte.

great power. Until the end of the Second World War, the term for a power of the first rank in terms of reputation for military strength. The great powers always dominated the peace conferences following major wars and assumed special rights and obligations in any formal machinery created to preserve international peace and security. *See also* major power; middle power; permanent members; Security Council; superpower.

Great Seal. *See* seal.

green line. A phrase sometimes used for a *ceasefire line, or a line of division within a state between hostile communities. It derives from a line drawn on a map in Cyprus in 1963 with a chinagraph pencil of this colour. However, its use is not confined to post-1963 lines.

Greenwich Mean Time (GMT). The local time at the 0 degree meridian passing through Greenwich, London. It is standard time throughout the United Kingdom, and the basis for establishing standard time in each of the 24 time zones into which the world is divided – although since 1986 the term has been replaced internationally by *UTC. In diplomatic (and military) communications which cross time zones, GMT is sometimes used to give the time of despatch rather than the local time. This is indicated by placing the letter Z after the time. Alternatively, the letter A signifies a local time of GMT + one hour; the letter B, GMT + two hours; and so on.

greeter. A colloquial term for the *protocol official who welcomes visiting dignitaries. *See also* Marshal of the Diplomatic Corps.

Grotius, Hugo (1583–1645). A Dutchman born Huig de Groot, Grotius was a great scholar and lawyer. However, he was also a politician and diplomat and between 1607 and 1618 served in both of these capacities under the patronage of Oldenbarnevelt, the powerful Advocate of Holland. When Oldenbarnevelt fell in 1618 Grotius fell with him and was condemned to life imprisonment. Nevertheless, he escaped in 1621 and fled into exile in France, where he was given a pension and encouraged to make his home. In 1634, following negotiations with the Swedish Chancellor, Axel Oxenstierna, he agreed to become Sweden's ambassador in Paris. This position – 'the top post in the Swedish diplomatic service' – was occupied by Grotius until 1644, the year before his death.

Grotius was a prolific writer, but among his works pride of place is generally given to his magisterial *De Jure Belli ac Pacis Libri Tres* (*Three Books On the Law of War and Peace*). This first appeared in 1625 and was the fruit of his first years of exile in France. It was subsequently republished many times. Though students of jurisprudence argue over the scope and general significance of *De Jure Belli ac Pacis*, there is now wide agreement that it was of great importance in the general development of *international law, the theory of the just war, and the notion of an *international society. Though *diplomatic law itself is not much more than a long footnote in *De Jure Belli ac Pacis* (Chapter 18 of Book 2, which Grotius entitled 'The Right of Legation'), it has been well said that in this account 'the outlines of the modern law are for the first time clearly discernible'. *See also* Hotman.

Group of Eight (G8). The G8 countries are a self-styled informal club of 'leading industrialized democracies' which meets annually at the *summit and in a separate cycle of meetings during the year at finance minister level. (The pre-meeting *caucuses before the gatherings of the International Monetary Fund and the World Bank each September are particularly important.) It sprang from an Economic Summit convened by President Valéry Giscard d'Estaing of France at Rambouillet in November 1975 and until recently was an essentially Western grouping which consisted of Britain, Canada, France, Germany, Italy, Japan and the United States (plus the president of the *European Commission); it was known accordingly as the G7. However, the end of the *Cold War was followed by the gradual integration of Russia into the group and the meeting held in Britain at Birmingham in May 1998 was the first 'G8 Summit'. Originally focused only on economic questions, the G8 agenda broadened in the 1980s to include political issues, and an agreed *communiqué, drafted beforehand by the *sherpas, also became a feature of the annual summits.

group of friends. *See* friends.

Group of Seven (G7). *See* Group of Eight (G8).

Group of 77. A UN grouping (now many more than 77, but the original number is still used) of the less developed countries of the *Third World. *See also* parliamentary diplomacy.

guarantee. This does not have a technical meaning in international law and diplomacy. But it generally indicates a legal undertaking by a relatively strong state or states to protect – by force unless otherwise specified – the independence and territorial integrity of another and usually weaker state, or some other important aspect of its condition.

By a 1960 Treaty of Guarantee between Cyprus, Britain, Greece, and Turkey, the last three guaranteed the independence, territorial integrity, and security of the first, and the same three states also guaranteed Cyprus's renunciation of union with Greece (*enosis*) and of partition (*taksim*) between Turkey and Greece. The guarantee also covered the basic articles of the Cypriot constitution, which attempted to balance the interests of the Greek Cypriot majority and the Turkish Cypriot minority. Given the keen interest of Greece and Turkey in the internal affairs of Cyprus, they were highly unsuitable as guarantors; and Britain was unlikely to take armed action against either of them. Indeed, there was no obligation on the guarantors to take armed action under the guarantee, only a right to do so, either jointly or severally. As a guarantee, therefore, the arrangement was extremely dubious; and in practice it has proved little better

than worthless. Generally in *international relations (sense 2), guarantees are more an indication of a contemporary political disposition than a reliable indication of future behaviour. *See also* neutralization.

guardship. *See stationnaire.*

Guicciardini, Francesco (1483–1540). A Florentine patrician, Guicciardini trained and then practised successfully as a lawyer, though he subsequently acquired much experience of the world of diplomacy. He was ambassador in Spain from 1512 until 1514 and, in his later capacity as a papal lord-lieutenant, he received envoys and despatched his own, including his friend *Machiavelli. Guicciardini is remembered today chiefly for his great works of history, especially his *History of Italy*, in which he displayed a taste for methods well ahead of his time. Nevertheless, he also committed to paper some interesting general reflections on diplomacy. A few of these are to be found in his sympathetic but cautionary observations on Machiavelli's *Discourses*. Most however are located in a volume entitled the *Ricordi*, which consists of a list of more or less elaborated maxims and observations on a miscellaneous range of topics which he began to write during his sojourn in Spain and periodically revised until 1530, when the final version, known as 'Series C', was produced. This contains 221 *ricordi* in all, about 50 of which are of relevance to the student of diplomacy. The *Ricordi* are important because they reveal the thinking about certain key elements of diplomacy of one of the greatest minds of the Italian Renaissance at precisely the time that *diplomacy (sense 1) was being established. They are also a valuable antidote to the elegant caricature of the 'Italian method' of negotiation offered by Harold *Nicolson.

guidance telegram. A *telegram issued by a foreign ministry to many or all of its diplomatic missions giving guidance on the state's policy towards a major issue of the day and the reasoning behind that policy.

Gulf War. (1) Although it was not commonly so called at the time, the war between Iran and Iraq which lasted from 1980 until 1988 is now often referred to as the First Gulf War. (2) The Second Gulf War (or simply the Gulf War, as many still call it) was the 1991 expulsion of Iraq from Kuwait by a UN-authorized group, led by the United States. It was arguably a rare case of authentic *collective security.

gunboat diplomacy. The use of naval power in support of diplomacy (sense 1). A form of what would now be called *coercive diplomacy, this became common in the second half of the nineteenth century, not least along the China coast. Though by no means the only kind of vessel employed even at that time for this purpose, gunboats were ideally suited to it. They were small and lightly armed but had a shallow draught and great manoeuvrability deriving from their steam and screw-driven propulsion. These design features made it possible for them to enter rivers, estuaries and shallow coastal waters either to 'show the flag' or go into action. *See also* bomber diplomacy; *stationnaire*.

gun salute. The aspect of national ceremonial which involves the firing of guns in honour of distinguished visitors or to mark important occasions. Such a salute may be given on the occasion of an official visit by a *diplomatic agent to a warship from home when it is berthed in a port of the state to which he or she is accredited.

H

Hague Conferences. Held at the instigation of the Tsar of Russia in 1899 and 1907 to try to reach agreements on disarmament, the mitigation of the horrors of war, and the *pacific settlement of disputes. No progress was made on the first of these aims; on the second, a number of *conventions were agreed; and in pursuit of the third, the *Permanent Court of Arbitration was established.

handed his/her passports. A phrase sometimes used to refer to the fact that a *head of mission has been requested by the *receiving state to leave the country immediately. It has long been anachronistic, dating from the time when governments issued passports to permit foreigners to both enter and leave their territories. To be 'handed a passport' was in effect to be handed an exit *visa. *See also* ask for passports.

hardship post. A diplomatic posting which either for its unhealthy climate, lack of amenities, inaccessibility or – especially today – physical danger, is deemed to be exceptionally 'difficult'. For working at such posts diplomats are sometimes given compensations of different kinds, including special financial allowances varying according to the difficulty of the post. Until a few years ago the provision of extra pensionable periods was the normal form of compensation employed in the British Diplomatic Service. It was then replaced by a 'Difficult Post Allowance (DPA)'. In the US Foreign Service the comparable allowances are called 'post differentials'. Tours of duty in hardship posts may also be much shorter than usual. *See also* bid list.

Harris, Sir James (1746–1820). Sir James Harris was one of the most notable British diplomats of the late eighteenth century. St Petersburg, where he resided from 1777 until 1783, is the posting for which he is chiefly remembered. This is because the handsome ambassador made such an impression on Catherine the Great that the setting of his diplomacy moved to her 'boudoir' – the *representational function taken to its logical conclusion. Harris had a general reputation for exceptional audacity in obtaining information and was one of the first Englishmen to be regarded as a professional specialist in diplomacy. In 1800 he was created Earl of Malmesbury. *See also* boudoir diplomacy.

H.E. Short for 'His Excellency', the way in which the members of a British diplomatic mission commonly used to refer to their ambassador. Since the late 1970s (and the *diktat* of the then Foreign and Commonwealth Secretary, Dr David Owen) it has gone out of use, 'HMA' (Her Majesty's Ambassador) generally being substituted for it. As British *high commissioners have never been formally described as 'Her Majesty's', the abbreviation HMHC has never been used. *See also* excellency.

head of chancery. A recently abolished post in the British *Diplomatic Service, the head of *chancery was not only head of the political section of a British mission but *ex officio* general manager of the whole mission. He or she was responsible for coordinating all the work of all of the sections, identifying and eliminating policy deviations by individuals or sections, ensuring that all sections had the necessary resources to do their jobs,

promoting cooperation between sections, and other such matters. The general managerial role is now the responsibility of the *deputy head of mission. The head of chancery was normally a *counsellor in a large or medium-sized embassy and a *first or *second secretary in a smaller one. The negotiating team employed on an important and protracted negotiation was also managed by a head of chancery.

head of department. In many ministries of *foreign affairs, the middle-ranking official who is in charge of a particular geographical or functional area.

head of government. A title used to describe the head of the executive branch of the central government of a *state where this position is separate, as in the United Kingdom, from that of a largely ceremonial *head of state. In Britain the prime minister is the head of government (by virtue of commanding the support of a majority of members of the House of Commons), while the monarch is the head of state. In certain countries, for example the United States, the head of government is also the head of state, i.e. the president. It should however be noted that where, as also in the United States, there is a genuine separation of powers, this person can have no position in and is subject to significant constraints by the legislative and judicial branches. Heads of government now play an important part in *summitry, as do heads of state who are also heads of government. Persons who are merely ceremonial heads of state do not, though their symbolic potency is of value on other diplomatic occasions. The phrase 'heads of state and government' to describe those who take the lead at multilateral summits neatly covers these possibilities.

head of mission. The person charged by the *sending state with the duty of acting in that capacity in a *resident or *non-resident mission. (In British parlance, the head of a *consulate or other subordinate post is described as a 'head of post'.) Heads of mission fall into one or other of three diplomatic *classes, and within each class take *precedence in the chronological order in which they took up their functions. Other than in respect of precedence and etiquette, there is no difference between heads of mission by reason of their class – yet classes two and three have been virtually abandoned. *See also* ambassador (sense 1); chargé d'affaires *en titre*; envoy extraordinary and minister plenipotentiary; high commissioner; minister resident; nuncio.

head of post. *See* head of mission.

head of state. The person who, on the basis of a *state's constitution or of other effective internal proce-

dures, is designated as its head. This individual may possess supreme executive power, as in the case of the President of the United States, or retain largely ceremonial functions, as in the case of the Queen of the United Kingdom of Great Britain and Northern Ireland. *See also* governor-general; head of government; summitry.

headquarters agreement. One regulating the relationship between an *international organization and its *host state (sense 2). One example is the Agreement between the UN and the USA regarding the *Headquarters of the United Nations.

Headquarters of the United Nations, Agreement between the United Nations and the United States of America regarding the Status of the United Nations in New York, Convention on (1947). This agreement (also known as the Headquarters Agreement, the Host-Country Agreement, and the Host-State Agreement) deals with the position of the UN's headquarters in New York. A headquarters district was defined, placed under the control and authority of the UN, and declared to be inviolable. The UN was given the power to make such regulations for the district as the UN's functions required, any US laws and regulations which were inconsistent with them were declared to be inapplicable within the district, but otherwise US law was to apply. Provision was made for the UN to establish communication facilities, and the representatives of its members and its officials were to enjoy freedom of transit through the United States to and from the headquarters. The members of *permanent missions to the UN were to have the privileges and immunities in the United States which that state accorded to accredited diplomats. In sum, the UN headquarters was to be treated in much the same manner as an embassy.

heads of agreement. A form of *interim agreement, but one which is not necessarily *binding.

Helsinki Conference. *See* Organization for Security and Cooperation in Europe.

Henderson, Loy Wesley (1892–1986). A diplomat who achieved such stature in the American profession that he came to be known as 'Mr Foreign Service'. Henderson was a founder member of the *State Department's influential 'Soviet Service', serving in Riga and Moscow as well as in Washington. However, he was profoundly out of sympathy with Roosevelt's wartime policy of friendship towards Stalin and in July 1943 threw up his expertise in Soviet questions to become head of mission in Iraq. This led to a concentration on the Middle East which culminated in his appointment as ambassador to

Iran in 1951, though – following a disagreement with the Truman administration over policy towards Israel – he had been diverted to India for the three years preceding this.

By 1955 a grandee of the profession, in that year Henderson was appointed deputy under-secretary of state for administration. This gave him responsibility for two issues which were of cardinal importance to the morale and efficiency of American diplomacy: the merger of the *Foreign Service with the personnel of the State Department which had been recommended in the Wriston Report of the previous year; and the Department's foreign building programme, which had been launched so successfully by *Larkin after the war but was now facing mounting congressional resistance. In 1956 Henderson was given the coveted rank of *career ambassador; he retired in 1961.

herald. In the ancient world, a member of a profession responsible, among other things, for declaring *war, seeking permission for the removal of the dead from a battlefield, and securing agreement to the safe passage of envoys. Regarded in ancient Greece as the offspring of Hermes, the messenger of the gods, and bearing a staff as the symbol of their office, heralds were believed to enjoy divine protection at a time when ordinary envoys could not regard this as axiomatic and had to rely more on codes of hospitality. It was this special immunity which made it possible for heralds to take on the most dangerous of all diplomatic tasks. Heralds were last seen in medieval Europe, where they acted under and on behalf of the code of chivalry of the feudal nobility. However, these heralds lacked the status of those of the ancient world and possessed no more immunity than *nuncii and *plenipotentiaries, the two principal kinds of envoy of this period. *See also* diplomatic courier; diplomatic privileges and immunities; fetial priests.

hidden agenda. *See* agenda.

high commissioner. The title given to the *head of mission of the first class sent by one member of the *Commonwealth to another. Apart from terminology, and some small additional privileges and ceremonial differentiation in London, a high commissioner is in exactly the same position and has exactly the same role as an *ambassador (sense 1). However, the *credentials carried by high commissioners are not the more usual letters of credence. Where both the *sending and *receiving states are of the *Queen's Realms – that is, where both of them have the same *head of state – the high commissioner carries a letter of introduction from the sending state's head of government (the prime minister) to the receiving state's head of government (the prime minister). This is because it is

not deemed possible for a head of state to accredit a representative to herself or himself, nor for the Queen to accredit someone to her *governor-general or for a governor-general to accredit someone to his or her Queen. It may be supposed that a similar procedure would have taken place in the case of (now extinct) *personal unions. Unlike ambassadors (who are *of* the sending state *to* the receiving state), such high commissioners may be described as high commissioner *for* (the sending state) *in* (the receiving state). Where either the sending state or the receiving state is not of the Queen's Realms – that is, it is a *republic or a *monarchy with a head of state other than the British Queen – the high commissioner carries a letter of commission from the sending state's head of state to the head of state of the receiving state. In another terminological twist, such high commissioners are often described as high commissioner *for* (the sending state) *to* (the receiving state).

All British high commissioners (whether in the Queen's Realms or otherwise) are called just that – never Her Majesty's high commissioner. The reason for this is that British high commissioners do not hold commissions or warrants of appointment from the Queen, which alone would entitle them to be described as 'Her Majesty's'. It is thought that this usage stems from the origins of the office, when all high commissioners, whether representing the *dominions in London or vice versa, were subjects of the Crown. Hence they were not representatives of one *sovereign state to another, and thus did not require to be commissioned to represent their sovereign at a foreign court. Additionally, all British high commissioners fly the United Kingdom flag, never the British *diplomatic flag.

Given that the point is very frequently misunderstood, it perhaps bears emphasizing that as between two states of the Queen's Realms their high commissioners represent *not* their (common) head of state but their heads of government. Thus, when the Queen visits one of her other Realms, she is neither accommodated nor escorted by the British high commissioner, but by her *governor-general.

The title of high commissioner derives from the late nineteenth century, when the oldest British dominion (Canada) first sought representation in London. As the territory was not a *sovereign state it could not appoint a *diplomatic representative, and hence a different terminology was adopted – which was later used for the representatives of other dominions. When, later still (in the 1920s) Britain began to appoint political representatives to the dominions, the same title was used. Soon afterwards, the dominions slowly became accepted as sovereign states, and in some dominion quarters there was unease at the continued use of the colonial-sounding title of high commissioner, and at the fact that such representatives were not members of the *diplomatic corps or entitled to the usual *diplomatic privileges and immunities. Suggestions emerged that the title be replaced by that of ambassador. However, some of these (by now Commonwealth) states were unenthusiastic about a change, and the impetus behind it was largely removed, in the late 1940s, by high commissioners being integrated into the diplomatic corps of the relevant states and made heads of mission of the first class. Since then there has been no serious opposition to the title; and now its distinctive character is often viewed very positively. *See also* presentation of credentials.

It is perhaps worth adding that although it is only in intra-Commonwealth relations that the title of 'high commissioner' is a genuinely diplomatic one, historically it has also served as a convenient title to give to senior officials with at least quasi-diplomatic responsibilities, not least when working in unusual circumstances. These include (i) some governors of dependent territories not formally part of an empire, as in the former British 'high commission territories' in southern Africa, and certain League of Nations *mandates; (ii) representatives of victorious states sent to a defeated territory to conduct relations with its authorities and oversee its civil administration, as for example in Turkey after the First

World War and Germany after the Second; (iii) representatives to unrecognized governments which nevertheless the sending state wished to support, as for example with the short-lived anti-Bolshevik government of Admiral Kolchak in Siberia during the Russian civil war; and (iv) some international civil servants with overall responsibility for certain humanitarian matters, such as the *United Nations High Commissioner for Human Rights and *United Nations High Commissioner for Refugees.

High Commissioner on National Minorities. *See* minorities treaties.

high contracting parties. The way in which *heads of state are referred to in a *treaty which is expressed as being an agreement between them, other than when they are referred to by name.

high representative. A title that began to become popular at the end of the twentieth century, though it was given to individuals with markedly different tasks, for example: (1) The senior assistant on *Common Foreign and Security Policy to the member state currently holding the presidency of the *European Union. Created by the Treaty of Amsterdam (1997), the position of 'High Representative for CFSP' is held by the head of the General Secretariat of the *Council of Ministers – its secretary-general. The High Representative also helps in formulating, preparing, and implementing policy decisions, and engages in diplomacy with third parties. Responsibility for running the General Secretariat now rests with the secretary-general's deputy. *See also* policy planning department. (2) The virtually *proconsular High Representative for Bosnia, whose task is nation-building. This position was created by the Dayton Peace Accords (1995).

high seas. Traditionally, that part of the sea which lies beyond states' *territorial sea; but now only that part of the sea which lies beyond the *exclusive economic zones (EEZs) of coastal states.

history of diplomacy. The historical study of the methods of diplomacy (sense 1), or the study of diplomatic methods in different periods and in different civilizations in the same period. Thus quite distinct in focus from *diplomatic history, the history of diplomacy embraces the study of *diplomatic systems. These include those in the ancient world (notably Greece, the Near East and Asia), medieval Europe, renaissance Italy (the birth of the resident embassy), Europe together with the Ottoman Empire (during which long period according to Harold *Nicolson the Italian method was greatly improved, chiefly by the French), and in the world as a whole following the First World War (when *open diplomacy made its first major appearance). *See* *also* Amarna letters; Byzantine diplomacy; Kautilya; Ottoman diplomacy; Venetian diplomacy.

Holy See. (1) A synonym for the Vatican City State which is commonly found in *diplomatic lists. (2) The government of the Roman Catholic Church, based in the *Vatican City State. (The City State itself is administered by a separate body appointed by the pope.) The highest of the Holy See's Sacred Congregations is the Secretariat of State and within this it is the Second Section which deals with Vatican relations with foreign states.

Homans's theorem. This, according to the sociologist George Homans, asserts that in a negotiation 'The more the items at stake can be divided into goods valued more by one party than they cost to the other and goods valued more by the other party than they cost to the first, the greater the chances of successful outcomes'. In other words it is not likely to be difficult for a negotiation to be successfully concluded between a meat-loving weight-watcher embarrassed by a gift of chocolates and a sweet-toothed vegetarian with a joint of beef won in a raffle. *See also* linkage.

honorary attaché. *See* attaché.

honorary consul. (1) A generic term which refers to any rank of *honorary consular officer. (2) The rank of honorary consular officer intermediate between honorary consul-general and honorary vice-consul.

honorary consular officer. An officer performing *consular functions in an honorary capacity. Such an officer is normally a citizen of or permanently resident in the *receiving state, and is not a member of the *sending state's *diplomatic service. However, some substantial connection with that state is usual. An honorary consular officer may, and generally does, head a *consular post, and that post may be at any consular level. Thus these officers are encountered as honorary consuls-general, honorary consuls, honorary vice-consuls, or as honorary consular agents, but most commonly as one of the middle two of these four ranks.

Where a state has an honorary consular officer in a capital city in which it has no other residential representation (because no diplomatic mission has been accredited to the state in question or because all the members of its mission are *non-resident), the receiving state may, as a convenience, include any such officers in an annex to its *diplomatic list. This is Britain's practice. It reflects the fact that consular facilities in capital cities now appear almost invariably to be provided through the *consular sections of embassies rather than through separate consulates. Accordingly, consular lists in respect of capital cities – in which such honorary consular officers would normally be included – seem to be a rarity, or even extinct. In the case of those few *Commonwealth states which do not exchange 'consuls', an honorary officer performing consular functions is usually called an *honorary representative (sense 2). A state may decline to receive honorary consular officers. In the past, honorary consular officers have sometimes been known as 'trading consuls'. *See also* consular privileges and immunities; *proxenos*.

honorary consular representative. A title occasionally given to those who serve as *honorary consular officers.

honorary representative. (1) A position analogous to that of *honorary consular officer sometimes established by a state in one where it is not *recognized. (2) A term used by those *Commonwealth states which do not exchange 'consuls' for an honorary officer who performs consular functions. *See also* non-diplomatic relations; representative office.

honour. A term which states have often associated with *vital interests – 'honour and vital interests' – to indicate that they regarded the matter in question as having the gravest importance.

honourable spy, diplomat as. *See* espionage.

hostage. (1) In some ancient diplomatic systems, a valuable person (for example, the heir to a throne) temporarily surrendered, to guarantee, or at least make it more likely, that a treaty would be honoured. This was an important institution in relations between different courts, and *Kautilya wrote a whole chapter on the subject in the *Arthashastra*. In the Ottoman Empire, ambassadors permanently resident in Istanbul were themselves regarded as hostages for the good behaviour of their princes until at least the end of the eighteenth century. In the event of hostilities breaking out between the Turks and the sending state, the ambassador concerned was removed to the prison of the Seven Towers. (2) More recently, in the context of diplomacy, the term has come to signify a person seized by a *terrorist group in an attempt to get something to trade in exchange for the gratification of its political demands. Diplomats are often involved in the consequent negotiations, and sometimes they have been victims of hostage taking.

host-country agreement. *See* headquarters agreement.

host state. (1) A synonym for *receiving state. (2) More appropriately, a state which has agreed to an *international organization having offices on its territory, or to a *peacekeeping body or an *observer mission operating there, or to an *ad hoc conference being held there. In the last event, it is customary for its foreign minister or principal delegate to be the president of the conference. With responsibilities which include the chairing of *plenary sessions and perhaps the drafting of any final report, this gives the host state a position of some influence.

host-state agreement. *See* headquarters agreement.

hôtel de l'ambassadeur. A term which, for much of the modern period, was used to refer both to the *residence of an *ambassador and the *chancery of his *embassy (sense 2).

hot line. (1) The popular term for the emergency communications link between the White House and the *Kremlin during the *Cold War. This was first proposed by the *State Department's Gerard C. Smith in 1960 and installed under a memorandum of understanding of 20 June 1963 following the alarm caused by the *Cuban Missile Crisis of the previous October. Known formally as the 'Direct Communications Link', this was a precautionary measure which was designed to help cope with the consequences of accidental or unauthorized use of nuclear weapons. It consisted of a wire-telegraph circuit which was routed Washington–London–Copenhagen –Stockholm–Helsinki–Moscow, and a back-up radio-telegraph circuit routed Washington–Tangier–Moscow. At each end were teleprinter terminals through which encoded messages in the sender's language were received. It had apparently proved its worth during at least one crisis but had weaknesses, one of which became apparent when the landline link in Finland was put out of action by a farmer's plough. As a result the hot line was upgraded with satellite circuits under an *executive agreement (negotiated during the SALT I talks) which came into force upon signature on 30 September 1971. It soon proved useful again, especially during the Arab–Israeli war in October 1973. Interestingly enough, however, the hot line continued to have no 'voice capability' on the grounds that oral exchanges, with their requirement for simultaneous translation, would have been less accurate than the written message. Harold *Nicolson, who maintained that diplomacy was essentially a written art, would have approved of this. The hot line was further reinforced in the late 1980s by the creation of 'risk reduction centres', which directly linked the American and Soviet defence establishments. (2) Over recent years this term has also come to be employed figuratively to signify any close relationship, especially between *heads of state or government, which is supported by rapid direct communication links capable, in an emergency or when extreme confidentiality is required, of bypassing advisers and officials. When recorded, these communications links are sometimes known as 'black box hot lines'. This is because they can be examined for an explanation, as with the black box flight recorder on an aircraft, in the event that the relationship 'crashes'. (3) Telephones manned 24 hours a day in the *emergency room of a diplomatic mission during an emergency.

Hotman, Jean (1552–1636). A French diplomat and devout Calvinist, Jean was the eldest son of the famous Huguenot revolutionary and scholar, François Hotman. An anglophile, his father sent him to study law at Oxford. This led directly to a distinguished five-year career as secretary to the Earl of Leicester in the first half of the 1580s. Learned and influential, and with a familiarity with embassy life acquired a few years earlier when he was a tutor in the household of the English ambassador in Paris, Hotman (like *Gentili) had been consulted in the Mendoza case in 1584. By students of diplomacy he is now remembered chiefly as the author of *L'Ambassadeur*, published in 1603 and expanded and corrected in the following year under the title *De la charge et dignité de l'ambassadeur*. This work was important for being the first to argue that the inviolability of *diplomatic premises, as opposed to the person of the envoy, was a central compo-

nent of *diplomatic law. Though other jurists were soon to accept this view, it was still unacknowledged by *Grotius two decades later.

hot pursuit. This phrase refers to the right of a coastal state to pursue and arrest a foreign ship which is believed to have violated the laws and regulations of that state. The pursued ship must have received an order to stop when it was within the area covered by the coastal state's laws and regulations; the pursuit must be uninterrupted; and it must cease once the pursued ship enters the *territorial sea of its *flag state or of a third state. Pursuit may take place by air.

humanitarian intervention. *See* intervention.

human rights. The modern term for what political theorists used to called 'natural rights', that is, rights alleged to belong 'naturally' to all human beings irrespective of what positive law has to say on the matter. On this view, human rights should be replicated in legal rights, though often they are not. Nevertheless, stimulated by the reaction to the Holocaust during the Second World War, *international law has come to embody a substantial body of human rights *treaty law (plus machinery for implementation) via both the *United Nations system and regional bodies such as the *European Union, the *Organization of American States and the Organization of African Unity (now replaced by the *African Union). It is also held by international human rights lawyers that in addition to treaty instruments such as the European Convention for the Protection of Human Rights and Fundamental Freedoms (1950), the Covenants on Civil and Political Rights and on Economic, Social and Cultural Rights (both adopted by the UN General Assembly in 1966, and both *entering into force ten years later), certain human rights are now enshrined in *customary international law in consequence of state practice. Notable among these are the prohibitions on *genocide, slavery and torture and the principle of non-discrimination. Long a controversial question within Western political theory and jurisprudence, human rights is now a controversial question in interstate relations. It presents a particularly testing problem for diplomats from states concerned about human rights who are resident in those which are not,

or which are concerned but subscribe either to a different list of human rights or to the sophistry that 'collective human rights' (as determined by the government) take precedence over 'individual human rights'. *See also* domestic jurisdiction; inter vention; United Nations High Commissioner for Human Rights.

humint. This inelegant abbreviation stands for 'human intelligence' and is originally a *CIA term, now in common use, meaning the collection of *intelligence *directly* from human beings, as opposed, say, to radio signals. Such persons may include refugees, prisoners of war or – best of all – *agents in place. Not surprisingly, intelligence agencies which use this kind of source tend to rely heavily on human beings (agents) to make contact with them and this is a second connotation of the term. The CIA's Directorate of Operations is the principal American humint organization. *See also* KGB; Secret Intelligence Service.

I

idealism. Used in the study of *international relations (sense 3) to refer to views or policies which are deemed to reflect ideals rather than practicality. It is a charge which has often been leveled against scholars and politicians of the 1918 to 1939 period. *See also* realism (sense 1).

identic notes. *Notes addressed separately to a government by the *diplomatic agents of two or more states which contain essentially the same message though they may be expressed somewhat differently. They are presented as nearly as possible simultaneously. Designed like the *collective note to give maximum impact to a joint representation, the strategy of the *notes identiques* is to achieve this with less risk of an appearance of ganging up.

imagery. *Intelligence obtained from photographic and other images, including radar echoes. In peacetime at least, satellites are now the main source of intelligence from imagery.

immunity. *See* consular privileges and immunities; diplomatic privileges and immunities; permanent mission.

impasse. A point in a negotiation, or on one item on the agenda of a negotiation, when the parties acknowledge that they cannot agree. This need not lead to a breakdown and abandonment of the talks but only to their suspension. If the item concerned is not vital, it may merely lead them to move on to another subject.

imperialism. (1) A synonym for *colonialism. (2) Aggressive behaviour, especially that which is intended to establish long-term dominance.

incident. An event which causes a sharp deterioration in diplomatic relations (sense 2) and may or may not lead to a *crisis. The 'Yangtze Incident', when the British vessel HMS *Amethyst* was fired on by Communist batteries as it was attempting to reach the British Embassy at Nanking in 1949, is a case of an incident which did not lead to a crisis.

independence. (1) Used in a legal sense to refer to a *state's lack of constitutional subordination to another state, i.e. to its *sovereignty (sense 1). In this sense, independence has an absolute character. (2) Used in a political sense to refer to a state's degree of effective freedom in its dealings with other states. In this sense, independence has a relative character – but measuring the extent of a state's independence is enormously difficult.

independent state. A synonym for *sovereign state. States commonly refer to themselves and other states as 'sovereign and independent'.

inductive method. (1) The establishment of general rules on the basis of particular instances. It is also called positivism. Many lawyers see *international law as established by this method, although some are uneasy about its wholesale and uncritical use. Contrast, *deductive method. (2) In negotiations, a synonym for *step-by-step diplomacy.

informal consultations. In the UN context: (1) Private meetings of the *Security Council not governed (as are those concerned for example with the appointment of a *Secretary-General) by the Charter or the Council's provisional *rules of procedure. This class of private meetings is usually referred to as 'informal consultations of the whole' or 'informals', and they take place in the Consultation Room, which is adjacent to the Council Chamber where the public meetings of the Security Council are held. Built in 1978, the Consultation Room is now the scene of most of the serious work done by this key organ of the United Nations. No official records are kept of informal consultations. (2) *Any* informal meeting in connection with the work of the Security Council, including those of *caucus groups, groups of *friends, *contact groups, and *Arria formula meetings.

initialling. Usually this represents an interim authentication by the state concerned of the draft text of a *treaty, the formal or 'full' *signature to follow later. However, initialling may, in special circumstances, amount to signature. Even when it does not, it may well give sufficient confidence in the treaty to the parties concerned for them to take limited steps in fulfilment of its provisions. For example, the initialling of the Hong Kong Airport Agreement by Britain and the People's Republic of China on 30 June 1991 led to the immediate commencement of work on two urgent contracts. *See also* plenipotentiary.

Inman standards. The security-driven design and building standards for new US diplomatic and consular properties introduced in the late 1980s. This development came in the train of a steady escalation in violent ground assaults after the mid-1960s, which culminated in the suicide bomb attack on the American embassy *compound in Beirut on 18 April 1983. (A van containing over 400lb of explosives was driven into the side of the embassy, killing approximately 60 people and injuring 120, and completely destroying the central consular section of the building. The 17 US nationals killed included marine guards, senior embassy staff, and CIA employees; in the last category was Robert Ames, director of the CIA's office of analysis for the Near East and South Asia.) The new standards were named after Admiral Bobby R. Inman, former head of the *National Security Agency and Chairman of the Advisory Panel on Overseas Security which reported in June 1985 (though the detailed work was done in a separate study by the National Research Council).

Inman standards called for missions to be located at remote sites (optimally 15 acres in size), a setback of 100 feet from any surrounding streets, blast-proof construction, an absence of hand-holds of any kind within 15 feet of the ground, windows limited to 15 per cent of the total wall area, safe havens for all embassy personnel including foreign nationals, perimeter walls, electronic vehicle arrest barriers, electronic locks, cameras, and monitors. All of this was far removed from the look of American embassies of the late 1940s and 1950s, buildings which typically featured glass walls, visual openness, and easy access, and were the fruit of a programme directed by Fritz *Larkin. Nevertheless, with the Beirut attack still a vivid memory, congressional appropriations of $948 million were made available to build new embassies to these standards and 61 new projects were under way by 1986. Most of these were completed by the early 1990s, but it had become apparent that the financial burden of continuing to impose Inman architecture was becoming insupportable and that a heavy diplomatic price would also be paid if all of America's 'downtown' embassies in cities such as Rome and Paris were replaced by inaccessible suburban fortresses. However, the *State Department's subsequent attempt to compromise between the needs of security and diplomacy was called into question following the bombings of the American embassies in Nairobi and Dar es Salaam in 1998. Two Accountability Review Boards directed by Admiral William J. Crowe reviewed these major incidents (the first of which saw great loss of life) and presented recommendations in January 1999. Since that time, the State Department has been reassessing how to upgrade security at its projects worldwide. *See also* emergency room; warden network.

innocent passage. This refers to the ancient right of the ships of all states to traverse *territorial sea provided that their passage is reasonably continuous and expeditious and is not prejudicial to the peace, good order, and security of the coastal state. Ships so engaged must also observe any relevant laws and regulations of the coastal state. Submarines on innocent passage must proceed on the surface and show the flag of their *flag state. The right of innocent passage is the only general limitation on the *sovereignty (sense 2) of the coastal state over its territorial sea. Foreign aircraft are not entitled to innocent passage through the air space of territorial sea. The term innocent passage has also been used to refer to the passing through third states of *diplomatic agents on their way to and from a *post. Nowadays this is known – somewhat misleadingly – as the *right of transit.

inquiry. A method of promoting *pacific settlement by appointing a commission to inquire into the facts of a dispute and report on them (but not to make recommendations for its solution). The commission may be appointed by the parties or, with their agreement, by an *international organization. It is then for the parties to decide what effect, if any, is to be given to the report, or for the appointing organization to decide on what recommendations should be made to the parties. Such a commission may also be described

as one of fact-finding or of investigation. *See also* conciliation; good offices; mediation.

instant. Of this month, as in 'Thank you for your *despatch of the 19th instant.' Often abbreviated to 'inst.' Now only historical.

instructions. (1) Any orders issued, at whatever level and in whatever form, by a diplomat's head office at home. It is common for a diplomat in talking to an *interlocutor of the *receiving state to stress that he or she is acting or speaking either 'on instructions' or 'personally', i.e. not 'on instructions'. In the last event, the diplomat may have to return later and say either that what he or she did or said had been confirmed from home or else that a different view had been taken and that he or she can now act or speak 'on instructions'. (2) A stylized letter to one of his diplomats from a *head of state (or secretary with responsibility for foreign affairs), the core component of which was a list of the aims to be pursued at his post. Sometimes described as containing 'general instructions', this was handed to him, along with his *letters of credence, prior to his departure. Essentially a feature of the pre-telegraphic era, instructions in this form, even when very detailed, invariably permitted the diplomat a fair degree of discretion in pursuing the directives which they contained since 'fresh instructions' could take weeks and, at distant posts, even months to obtain. A British diplomat's instructions also reminded him to maintain good relations with the other members of the *diplomatic corps, maintain a correspondence with British diplomats at other posts, and send regular reports home. On the assumption that it might be expedient on occasion to reveal his instructions at the court to which he was accredited, a diplomat was sometimes issued with a second, secret set of instructions designed for his more precise guidance. Instructions were generally more detailed when the diplomat being despatched was charged with an important negotiation at his post, which is why they continued to be given to *delegates to *congresses and *conferences for long after they had generally become obsolete, at least in their traditional form, for *resident ambassadors. It is still certainly not unknown for ambassadors and high commissioners to be given written guidance before departing on a mission, though this may now be styled a 'directive' or 'letter of appointment'. *See also* sponsion.

instrument. A formal legal document, such as a *treaty.

insurgency. A status sometimes accorded by *third parties under the traditional law of *war to an insurgent group which, while not in a sufficiently strong position to justify recognition of its *belligerency, is nonetheless in effective occupation of and constitutes the de facto authority in a large part of the territory of the *state in question. For a recognizing third party, the grant of insurgency may be a prerequisite for the protection of its interests in the territory which the insurgents control, as it is a means of establishing formal communication with them. In the second half of the twentieth century the recognition of insurgency went out of fashion, reflecting the lessened formality of the times and their greater hostility to anything which might undermine the territorial integrity of existing states.

intelligence. (1) Information, whether foreign or defence, political or economic, secret or openly available. (2) The government organization or organizations ('intelligence agencies' or 'secret intelligence agencies') which collect, analyse and disseminate this information, which is chiefly about actually or potentially hostile foreign countries. What gives the final assessments of these agencies special authority and their activities a special flavour is that (a) they seek the most sensitive and highly classified information and (b) they seek it by means which are themselves either secret or, as with orbiting satellites, employed without the consent of their targets. This meaning began to emerge in the late nineteenth century. *See also* agent in place; CIA; Echelon;

foreign intelligence; intelligence community; intelligencer; KGB; Secret Intelligence Service.

intelligence assessment. *See* all-source analysis.

intelligence community. The entire range of *intelligence agencies responsible to one government. In Britain and the United States, where the term gained currency during the *Cold War, it also implies the existence of high-level mechanisms for the coordination of the work of these agencies and *all-source assessment. The American intelligence community is composed of over twenty organizations, with the Office of the Director of Central Intelligence at the top, immediately below the *National Security Council. *See also* CIA; Echelon; Joint Intelligence Committee.

intelligencer. A term employed in the early modern period for any supplier of *intelligence to a diplomatic mission or directly to a government. An intelligencer was typically one of its own *consuls, or an official attached to a foreign court who was paid a retainer by an envoy. *See also* Wicquefort.

interests section. A small group of *diplomats of one state working under the flag of a second on the territory of a third, the interests section is an elaboration of the much older diplomatic institution of the *protecting power. There were harbingers of this development in Istanbul at least as early as the beginning of the nineteenth century. When an embassy in the city was forced to close, sometimes one of its *dragomans would be transferred to the embassy or consulate-general of the protecting power, where he would continue his previous work. However, the first proper interests sections were not established until May 1965 (in Cairo and Bonn), following the decision of Egypt to break *diplomatic relations (sense 1) with West Germany in retaliation for the decision of the latter to open them with Israel. Designed to maintain communication in the absence of diplomatic relations, the interests section permits the *sending state to retain its own diplomats in the *receiving state by the ruse of attaching them *in law*, together with their mission premises, to the embassy of a protecting power. (Previously, the protecting power's own embassy staff had to do the work of protection.) The idea quickly caught on, and interests sections have since been widely used as half-way houses to the restoration of diplomatic relations as well as to cope with their recent breach. Thus South Africa and the Soviet Union, which had severed diplomatic relations in 1955, each opened an interests section in the other's capital (under the protection of Austria) in February 1991. In the receiving state's *diplomatic list, an interests section appears as part of the diplomatic mission of the protecting power.

Though some American interests sections are very large, it is a mistake to regard them as embassies in all but name. Interests sections are usually very small (two or three diplomats); it appears necessary for all of their members to receive *agrément*; and *service attachés are barred.

intergovernmental conference (IGC). In the *European Union, a major negotiation between the member states with a view to amending its institutional and legal structure.

intergovernmental organization. Another, but less common, way of referring to an *international organization. It has the (limited) virtue of being in semantic harmony with the term *non-governmental organization.

interim agreement. The modern term for what used to be called a *modus vivendi*, this is a temporary or provisional *agreement which is designed ostensibly to be replaced later on by one which is possibly more detailed, probably more comprehensive, and certainly more permanent. Interim agreements tend to be popular because they can be presented both as the only way to advance to a final settlement and the only way to forestall one. *See*

also framework treaty; heads of agreement; step-by-step diplomacy.

interlocutor. A party to a dialogue.

intermediary. *See* mediation.

international. That which pertains to the sphere of interstate activity rather than to the domestic sphere.

international actor. The ambit of this term is dependent on the content given to the word 'international'. If, as in the field within which *diplomacy (sense 1) occurs, it is defined with reference to the interaction of *sovereign states, international actors are primarily the states themselves, and secondarily the *international organizations which they have established. Intermittent actorhood is also exhibited by *non-governmental organizations and groups as and when they have dealings with states or an impact on their behaviour.

International Atomic Energy Agency (IAEA). Established in 1957 as an autonomous agency under the aegis of the UN (and hence not a *specialized agency – although very like one), the IAE's purpose is to accelerate and enlarge the peaceful uses of atomic energy, and to ensure that such assistance as it gives in this area is not used for military purposes. Towards this end it has an elaborate 'safeguards' system operating in conjunction with its extensive programme of technical assistance in the nuclear field.

international civil servant. A member of the *secretariat of an *international organization, who is thus obliged to be professionally loyal to the organization rather than serve the interests of a member state. The likelihood of this obligation being observed is thought to be enhanced if secretariat members are directly employed by the organization rather than temporarily seconded from national civil services. Such a practice was begun by the *League of Nations, being strongly advocated by its first *Secretary-General, Sir Eric Drummond, who persuaded the League's Council to endorse it. Since then this concept of a genuinely international civil service has been generally accepted by international organizations – but that is not to say that member states and secretariat members always live up to it. *See also* International Civil Service Commission.

International Civil Service Commission (ICSC). This body, established by the UN *General Assembly in 1974, regulates and coordinates the conditions of service of the UN *common system. The Commission is composed of 15 members appointed by the General Assembly in their personal capacity. *See also* international civil service.

International Committee of the Red Cross (ICRC). A *non-govern-mental organization established by Henry Dunant (1828–1910) in 1863. Its headquarters is in Geneva, Switzerland, but it has a permanent presence in over 50 countries. Its 'exclusively humanitarian mission is to protect the lives and dignity of victims of war and internal violence and to provide them with assistance'. The ICRC has no authority over the national Red Cross or Red Crescent societies but as the original such organization it is often seen as having a tutelary role in regard to them.

international community. The collectivity of *states. The term is often thought to suggest a greater degree of warmth and harmony than the alternative term, *international society, and for that reason is judged by many scholars to be less appropriate. However, it is much favoured by states' political leaders, and hence is frequently used by diplomats.

International Court of Justice (ICJ). Although formally an organ of the *United Nations, the ICJ is an independent judicial body. It sits (full-time) at The Hague (in the Netherlands) and is composed of 15 judges, no two of whom may be nationals of the same state. They are elected for nine-year terms by the UN *General Assembly and *Security Council, voting separately. The Court has jurisdiction to decide contentious cases and to give *advisory opinions. In respect of the former, only states may be parties before the Court, which has the duty of judging on the basis of *international law (unless the parties request a decision *ex aequo et bono*). Accordingly, the ICJ is in the nature of a civil, and not a criminal, court: it does not, on behalf of the whole *international society, punish wrongdoing, but resolves argument as to the rectitude of a *claim made by one state on another. A party which does not have a judge of its nationality on the ICJ is entitled to choose a person to sit in that capacity. The Court decides by majority vote, and its judgment is final. Judges may issue *separate or *dissenting opinions. Cases are referred to the ICJ on the basis of agreement between the parties. Thus no state is obliged to go to the Court against its will. But states may agree in advance to accept the *compulsory jurisdiction of the ICJ either by *treaty or by way of the *Optional Clause procedure. Although a decision of the Court only has *binding force as between the parties and in respect of that particular dispute, the judgments of the ICJ and its advisory opinions make an important contribution to the clarification and development of general international law. The ICJ is the only general organ of *judicial settlement available to the international society. It has one predecessor, the *Permanent Court of International Justice.

international crime. *See* international criminal law; International Criminal Court.

International Criminal Court. In 1998 an international conference in Rome adopted a statute for such a Court. The statute came into effect on 1 July 2002, 60 days after its 60th *ratification, and the Court was formally opened on 11 March 2003. Its seat is at The Hague. Britain, along with all other *European Union member states, has ratified the statute, and thus become a *party to it. As of May 2003, however, the United States, although a signatory to the statute, has not yet ratified it, and has shown a marked reluctance to do so. The same is true of Israel.

The Court has jurisdiction over individuals charged with the most serious crimes of international concern: *genocide, crimes against humanity, and *war crimes, and also the crime of *aggression once an acceptable definition for the Court's jurisdiction over it is adopted. The alleged crime, however, must have taken place on the territory of a party to the Court, and the relevant national legal system must have indicated an inability or unwillingness to prosecute the individual concerned. A prosecution may then be initiated by the UN *Security Council, by a state party to the Court, or by the Court's Prosecutor. The Court does not have retrospective jurisdiction. *See also* international criminal law.

international criminal law. That part of *international law which establishes crimes of international concern, for the breach of which individuals may be held directly responsible. Generally speaking, international law applies between *states. To that extent, only states can make *claims against each other; this is what is meant by references to a state as enjoying *international personality, and as a subject of international law. Correspondingly, individuals are objects of that law, and so cannot assert rights against a state at the international level, nor be sued or prosecuted by a state for the breach of an international obligation. However, some *war crimes are a well-recognized exception to this rule. And since the Second World War, crimes against humanity, *aggression, and *genocide have been added to the content of what has now become known as international criminal law. But the prosecution of individuals charged with the breach of this law has, for a variety of reasons, always presented difficulties, or laid itself open to the charge of 'victor's justice'. For this reason, the *Security Council established ad hoc International Criminal Tribunals for the Former Yugoslavia in 1993 and for Rwanda in 1994. And in 1998 an international conference voted for the establishment of a permanent *International Criminal Court.

international customary law. *See* customary international law.

international friendship. *See* friendly relations.

international humanitarian law. The term by which, during the last quarter of the twentieth century, the 'laws of war' became known. This law places limits on the force which may be used against combatants and civilians during *war or *armed conflict, and enunciates rules regarding the treatment of prisoners-of-war. Larger states generally provide their senior military staff with *military manuals which set out and interpret the chief aspects of international humanitarian law. Laws of war date from the Middle Ages. They used to have a *customary basis, but since the middle of the nineteenth century have increasingly been embodied in *treaties, latterly in what are known as the Geneva or *Red Cross Conventions. *See also* armed conflict; belligerency; blockade; contraband; genocide; human rights; insurgency; International Committee of the Red Cross; *ius ad bellum*; *ius in bello*; war.

international institution. (1) A synonym for *international organization. (2) A more or less standardized pattern of behaviour evolved to achieve certain generally accepted international goals. *Diplomacy (sense 1), *international law, and the *balance of power (sense 3) are good examples of international institutions in this sense.

internationalization. The idea that an area should not form part of a *sovereign state but be given an international status by, for example, being permanently placed under the aegis of an organ of the *United Nations. Such schemes have been proposed for the city and environs of Trieste and for Jerusalem (both in 1947). However, although to uninvolved outsiders it can seem a fair way of dealing with an area subject to hotly competing claims, it has much less appeal to the stronger claimant and its supporters, and to those in the minority in the relevant UN organ. Largely for these sorts of reason, neither of the above schemes bore fruit. A version of this idea operated during the interwar period in respect of the former German city of Danzig (now Gdansk), which was established as a Free City under the *guarantee of the *League of Nations. However, it was not a happy experience, and the city was reoccupied by Germany in 1939. During the interwar period the territory of the Saar was internationalized for 15 years (its governing commission being appointed by and responsible to the League of Nations). One other case of temporary internationalization concerned the Colombian district of Leticia, which was administered by the League for a year. The Serbian province of Kosovo is currently under a form of internationalization.

internationalism. The policy of maximizing cooperation with other states and support for the decisions of *international organizations. Internationalist claims are nowadays fashionable, but where the *national interest clearly points in the opposite direction internationalism will not prevail. However, certain *middle powers, such as Canada and the Scandinavian states, can reasonably assert that more than most their foreign policies have a distinctive internationalist tinge.

international law. The body of rules and principles of action which are *binding on *sovereign states in their relations with each other. The last half-century or so has also seen the extension of international law to include the rules relating to the activity of *international organizations and to individuals and *non-governmental organizations to the extent to which their activity comes within the ambit of international law (as, for example, in connection with *international criminal law). However, international law remains primarily an expression of the rights and duties of states *inter se*. And overwhelmingly it is in the nature of civil rather than criminal law. International law derives from two main sources: international custom (of the sort which creates *customary international law) and *treaties. Jurisprudentially, the former is the more fundamental; but quantitatively the latter is now dominant. As between its signatories (unless it is in breach of *ius cogens*), a treaty supersedes any relevant customary law. A third source of international law is *general principles of law. And it should be noted that the Statute of the *International Court of Justice makes reference to judicial precedents and the work of highly qualified writers as 'subsidiary means for the determination' of international law. Like all systems of law, the essential purpose of international law is to provide an accepted framework for behaviour, enabling states to know what they may do, what they must not do, and how they may lawfully seek to achieve certain goals. Provided, therefore (as is in fact the case), international law is generally observed, it supplies the element of predictability which is absolutely essential for the maintenance of *international order. Without it, relations between states would necessarily be minimal or chaotic. In this sense, international law is a crucial constituent of the *international society.

international law and municipal law. The fact that a *state is bound by a provision of *international law by no means necessarily results in that law thereby being valid within the state, and hence binding on domestic governmental organs and enforceable by the municipal courts. The relationship between the two legal systems is governed, municipally, by the state's constitution. Given the variety of the relevant constitutional provisions which exist, generalization about them is hazardous. Broadly speak-

ing, however, it may be said that *customary international law is valid within states, provided it does not conflict with municipal law; but that *treaties often require legislation for them to be brought into force within the state, and almost invariably so if their operation would modify existing law or affect the private rights of the state's citizens. Inasmuch, therefore, as *diplomatic law gives *diplomats special privileges, it is extremely rare for it to become operative municipally without enabling legislation. *See also* Act of Anne.

The problem of the relationship between the two systems of law can be particularly acute in *federal states, inasmuch as the state's treaty-making power is almost always the sole preserve of the central government, but the right to make any required enabling legislation may well lie with the territorial units composing the federation. Germany and the United States are just two such states which often encounter this difficulty. It may result either in the state declining to become a *party to a treaty, notwithstanding the wish of the federal government to do so; or in it becoming internationally bound (possibly through the development of customary international law or a *European Union directive) but unable fully to implement the obligation. It should be noted, however, that if a state's municipal law prevents it from executing an international obligation, that is no defence, internationally, to a *claim by the injured state or international organization – although in some quarters it may of course be seen as a mitigating factor.

International Law Commission. The UN organ charged with the task of promoting the *progressive development of *international law and its *codification. Established in 1947, it has twice been enlarged and now has 34 members; these sit in their individual capacity and not as representatives of their states. It meets each year for a session of 12 weeks, and works on the preparation of draft articles on topics of general international concern. These drafts are submitted to the *General Assembly, which may (among other courses) decide to convene an international conference to consider a draft with a view to the conclusion of a *treaty. The Vienna Conventions on *Diplomatic Relations and on *Consular Relations emerged in this way.

international legislation. A term sometimes used to refer to multilateral *treaties which have been widely accepted. However, inasmuch as the term legislation usually entails the enactment of generally-applicable law by majority vote, its use at the international level can be misleading, for a majority of states cannot impose an obligation on those states who do not consent to it.

international minimum standards. Legal standards below which a state is not entitled to treat citizens of other states, even if its own citizens are subject to such treatment. In principle, it is accepted that a state is entitled to seek redress if its citizens have been so treated, and if they have *exhausted local remedies in their effort to obtain local satisfaction. But in practice it is a difficult and sensitive area – as is indicated by the fact that the standards in question used to be spoken of as reflecting the 'standard of civilization'.

international order. (1) A non-technical term which refers to the absence of chaos in the relations of states. This state of affairs is obtained through there being agreement on the criterion for being an *international actor – which takes the form of *sovereignty (sense 1); a means for these notional entities to communicate with each other – which is supplied by *diplomacy (sense 1); and a normative framework for their relations – which is supplied by *international law. (2) Occasionally used as a synonym for *international society or *international system.

international organization. An association of *states deriving its organizational character from its permanence, its quasi-governmental organs, and (generally speaking) its employment of *international civil servants. Thus an international organization is likely to have an executive committee composed of a relatively small number of its member states, a general deliberative body in which all the members participate, and a *secretariat headed by a *secretary-general. It may be more-or-less universal in membership, have a *regional focus, or even be composed of just two or three states. No less various is the subject matter of an international organization: it can be wide-ranging or have a narrow specialist character, or anything in between. There are probably about three hundred such bodies, the *United Nations, the *European Union, the *Organization of American States, the *African Union, and *NATO being among the best known.

An international organization is established by *treaty, which defines and limits the organization's legal competence. This points to a fundamental difference between a state and an international organization: the latter possesses only such powers as are granted to it by its constituent document, and cannot legally act beyond those powers, whereas a *sovereign state possesses the totality of rights and duties recognized by *international law and, subject to the provisions of that law, can engage in almost any activity that it chooses.

International organizations reflect the need that has been felt for certain matters to be permanently handled on a *multilateral basis. Thus they began to be established in the latter part of the nineteenth century when it was realized that the efficient conduct of postal and telegraphic communication across the world required something more than a myriad of bilateral arrangements. In the twentieth century attempts were made to ensure the maintenance of world peace through general international organizations in the shape, first, of the *League of Nations and then of the UN.

In political terms, international organizations are in a weak position, in that they depend on their member states for finance and, in respect of any external activity that they conduct, for personnel. Thus any particular proposed activity is dependent on a sufficient number of member states thinking that it is in their individual *national interests. Nonetheless, in certain limited respects some organizations may be more than the sum of their members. For example, a resolution of the UN *General Assembly may be generally seen as representing something more than the views of the states who voted for it; or the UN Secretary-General may be seen not just as a paid official but also as the independent spokesman for the ideals which the UN espouses.

International organizations used often to be called international institutions but, except perhaps among lawyers, the term 'organization' is now widely preferred. It should be noted that scholars frequently use 'International Organization' to refer to the study of such bodies.

international person. (1) Used non-technically, a notional entity which is spoken of as acting internationally as if it were a person. In this sense, *states are notional persons. (2) An entity which enjoys *international personality.

international personality. The status held by an entity which possesses rights and duties under *international law. *Sovereign states are the principal holders of international personality. But *international organizations have also been granted international personality by their members; and to a limited extent individuals, too, have been accorded this status in connection with their responsibilities under *international criminal law.

international politics. A less-common way of referring to *international relations (all senses).

International Red Cross and Red Crescent Movement. The umbrella term for the *International Committee of the Red Cross, the International Federation of Red Cross and Red Crescent Societies, and the National Red Cross and Red Crescent Societies. A conference of these bodies, together with representatives of states party to the *Red Cross Conventions, normally meets every four years.

international regime. The rules and procedures relating to a specific international activity, geographical area, or economic resource.

international relations. (1) ·A *state's dealings and contacts with other states, and with *international organizations. (2) The general sphere of bilateral and multilateral interstate activity. (3) When the first letters are in capitals, the study of international relations (sense 2).

international society. A term used to refer to the collectivity of *sovereign states. Historically, it was often used in writing about *international relations (sense 2), and at this level finds much contemporary favour in Britain. 'International society' certainly has some advantages over the alternative terms, *international community, *international system, and *states-system. For example, it hints at the associative character of international relations, yet does not invest them with the intimacy implied by the word community. Then, too, the general idea of society focuses attention on the fact that it is individuals who take decisions on behalf of states, and do so on the basis of volition, whereas the idea of system carries more than a whiff of automaticity. And, unlike system, the term society directly suggests the ideas of admission and exclusivity, thus pointing to the fact that there is a very specific criterion – *sovereignty (sense 1) – which must be met before a territorial entity is eligible for participation in international relations. *See also* international institution (sense 2); international order; Westphalia, Congress of (1644–48).

international system. The network of relationships which exists at the *international level, including therefore the role in those relationships of *international organizations, *non-governmental organizations, and other *non-state actors. Inasmuch as sovereign states play the leading role in these relationships, the term international system is often used, particularly in American writing, to refer to the collectivity of *states. However, the content and reverberations of the term *international society better convey certain basic features of the collectivity of states than does the term international system.

International Telecommunication Union (ITU). The ITU was created in 1865 in response to the invention of the electric *telegraph and the need to facilitate the connection of the different national telegraphic systems subsequently established. It is now a UN *specialized agency with headquarters in Geneva, Switzerland. *See also* telecommunication.

internuncio. (1) A papal *head of mission of the second class, who thus has the same rank as an *envoy extraordinary and minister plenipotentiary. (2) Between the Middle Ages and the seventeenth century, however, the title was in more general use by temporal powers, the Austrians clinging to it for their *resident at Istanbul – the 'Imperial Internuncio' – until the middle of the nineteenth. The motive, it appears, was to avoid disputes over *precedence with the *Porte's long most favoured friend, the French ambassador. The Polish representative in Istanbul also bore the title 'internuncio'.

Inter-Parliamentary Union. *See* parliamentary diplomacy (sense 2).

interpretative declaration. *See* reservation.

interstate. A synonym for *international (but within *federal states it may also have a domestic connotation).

intervention. Sometimes described as 'interference', action directed at a state from outside with the immediate intention either of influencing some aspect of its domestic policy or of changing its regime. Another desired outcome – especially in the latter case – may be to modify its foreign policy as well. The author of the intervention may be another state, an *alliance, or an *international organization. The act of intervention and the means involved always attract contention, on both political and legal grounds. But for some years there has been increasing support for the view that intervention is permitted in certain circumstances, provided the UN *Security Council has authorized such action. (The recent view that this authorization is unnecessary appears to be very much a minority position.) The first case is that in which intervention is deemed to be the only means of ending massive and sustained abuse of *human rights. (The claim that intervention is justified to avert an *anticipated* humanitarian disaster is much more controversial.) The second case is that where intervention (usually to achieve regime-change) is deemed to be essential to *self-defence, that is, where it is believed to be necessary to pre-empt imminent and devastating *aggression. Both of these doctrines are, of course, open to gross abuse. There is also, thirdly, some support for the claim that intervention is justified where it is a *counter*-intervention in a civil war designed to restore the balance between the internal parties upset by an initial outside intervention. Intervention is distinguishable from *annexation. *See also* sovereignty; sphere of influence.

investigation. *See* inquiry.

introduction. *See* letter of introduction.

Iron Curtain. A term which was popularly used to describe the *Cold War division in Europe between the *West and the *Eastern bloc. It had been famously used by Winston Churchill, the once and future British prime minister, in a speech in the United States (at Fulton, Missouri) on 5 March 1946.

isolationism. The policy of non-participation in contentious international matters. It is particularly associated with the United States, which acted on its basis throughout the nineteenth century and for much of the first half of the twentieth. The policy contributed to that state's refusal ever to join the League of Nations, and was only abandoned after the United States was brought into the Second World War by Japan's attack on Pearl Harbor (Hawaii) in December 1941. *See also* neutrality; non-alignment; splendid isolation.

Itamaraty. The Brazilian Foreign Office, so called because its headquarters are located in the Itamaraty Palace in Brasilia. Until 1970 they were housed in the original Itamaraty Palace in Rio de Janeiro, which is still used for certain purposes (including archival storage) by the ministry.

ius ad bellum. The legal right to go to *war. During the twentieth century this traditional right was much circumscribed, especially after the signing of the UN Charter in 1945. Thus in general terms, offensive war is now permissible in law only in response to a breach of *ius cogens*, and many commentators would add that it is at least highly desirable that such a breach be certified as such by the *Security Council. Of course, a state attacked unlawfully retains the right to defend itself, and other states the right to assist it. *See also* aggression; collective security; peace enforcement; self-defence.

ius cogens. That part of *international law which is peremptory in character. Accordingly, it is not permissible for two or more states, as among themselves, to modify such law. The idea that some part of international law is of this nature was referred to with great frequency during the second half of the twentieth century, and can thus be said to have become orthodox. However, the identification of the relevant legal norms is a matter of some difficulty. It has been suggested that they include rules of a fundamental kind regarding the maintenance of *peace, humanitarian issues, the territorial integrity and political *independence of states, and the right of all states to enjoy certain common resources (such as those which lie on the bed of the high seas). It is unclear, however, what practical benefits follow from the designation of such widely accepted norms as ones of *ius cogens*; and some think that the concept might even be disadvantageous, in that it could facilitate the breach of onerous obligations, or be used to justify interference in matters of *domestic jurisdiction. But it remains that, formally speaking, the concept of *ius cogens* has entered the language of international law and diplomacy. Possibly it reflects the rhetorical popularity of the idea of an *international community despite, or even because of, the fact that to many observers *international relations (sense 2) fall some way short of that condition.

ius in bello. The laws which govern the conduct of *war and *armed conflict. *See also* international humanitarian law.

J

Japanese secretary. *See* oriental secretary.

joint commission. (1) A body consisting of representatives of two states designed to keep under review some issue that is a more or less permanent feature of their relationship. Often quite large in membership and provided with a co-chair by each side, the joint commission usually meets on a regular basis although the interval between meetings may be a year or even more. (2) A body established to oversee the implementation of an agreement, especially one produced by a diplomatic breakthrough on a narrow front between still-hostile parties. Joint commissions of this sort are composed preponderantly of specialist representatives of the parties concerned and may include a neutral element as well. If the disputed issue concerned armed personnel, the ameliorative body might be called a joint military commission or committee. Now an important, though surprisingly

unremarked, feature of diplomacy, such bodies (like *peacekeeping operations of a traditional kind) are evidence that the world has taken to heart the wisdom contained in the following *ricordo* of *Guicciardini: 'it is not enough to begin things, give them their direction, and get them moving; you must also follow them up and stay with them until the end.' The joint commission created under the Angola/Namibia accords of December 1988 played a critical role in keeping them on course after the renewal of fighting in northern Namibia early in the following year. *See also* eminent persons group; international organization.

Joint Intelligence Committee (JIC). This committee sits at the apex of the British *intelligence community. It serves as both its manager and the means by which *intelligence from all sources is pooled and weighed to provide the most objective and complete assessment of the most important targets.

In the last role it is assisted by the assessments staff of the Cabinet Office; it reports directly to the Cabinet Secretary. The core membership of the JIC consists of the heads of the intelligence agencies, together with senior officials from the *Foreign and Commonwealth Office, the Ministry of Defence and the Treasury. It is usually chaired by an FCO official.

judgment. The *binding decision (or 'award') of an *international judicial organization or of an arbitral tribunal on a dispute which has been submitted to it. *See also* advisory opinion.

judicial settlement. The settlement of a dispute by a permanent *international judicial body as distinct from resort to *arbitration. Except to the extent to which two or more states have agreed in advance that a specified class of disputes shall be subject to a particular court's *compulsory jurisdiction, this device for *pacific settlement can only be used when the parties agree to it. The agreement by which this is done is called a *compromis* or, alternatively, a special agreement. Judicial settlement is generally conducted on the basis of *international law. But if they wish, states resorting to it may provide that the tribunal proceed *ex aequo et bono. See also* International Court of Justice.

justiciable dispute. One which is considered by the parties to be capable of settlement by *adjudication – that is, by *arbitration or *judicial settlement. In principle, any dispute can be settled on this basis. But if the core of the dispute is not about the application or interpretation of existing *international law but reflects dissatisfaction with it, resort to adjudication will not provide a real settlement. Nor will it do so unless each of the parties is willing to apply an adverse *judgment. Justiciable disputes are sometimes known as legal disputes. *See also* non-justiciable dispute.

K

Kaunitz, Count Wenzel Anton von (1711–94). After a career as a highly successful Austrian diplomat, Kaunitz served as chancellor and foreign minister under three Habsburg rulers from 1753 until his retirement in 1792. He is regarded as one of the ablest statesmen of the eighteenth century. He was also responsible for modernizing the *Ballhausplatz and inspiring the foundation of the *Akademie der Orientalischen Sprachen* in 1753, from which developed Austria's training school for consuls and diplomats. *See also* Vienna, Diplomatic Academy of.

Kautilya. Also known as Chanakya and Vishnugupta, Kautilya is generally believed to have lived somewhere between approximately 300 BC and AD 300 and to have been the friend, adviser and first minister of Chandragupta Maurya, whom he helped install as King of Magadha in northern India. Kautilya is remembered today chiefly for his reputed authorship (there is controversy on this question) of a long Sanskrit text on the science of government which came to modern eyes only in 1904. Known as the *Arthashastra*, this is without doubt one of the earliest extant works of its kind and has long sections dealing with foreign policy and war. Kautilya's teaching on *statecraft assumes that kings will always want to expand their territory and should thus regard any with whom they share a common border as a 'natural enemy'. Since his interest is the small state (including the 'weak king'), he places great emphasis on the use of the *envoy, the duties of whom include 'sending information to his king, ensuring maintenance of the terms of a treaty, upholding his king's honour, acquiring allies, instigating dissension among the friends of the enemy, conveying secret agents and troops, suborning the kinsmen of the enemy to his own king's side, acquiring clandestinely gems and other valuable material for his own king, ascertaining secret information and showing valour in liberating hostages'. Envoys were also of great value in playing for time. Kautilya taught that an envoy should never be killed even if an outcast, though he condoned the imprisonment of one who had brought an unwelcome message. Though the list of duties prescribed for the envoy by Kautilya do not suggest that the average mission would be brief, it is also clear that he was not speaking of an envoy who was properly permanently resident at a foreign court. Any lengthy stay was because he had been refused permission to leave, in which case he should use every resource at his disposal to subvert the local king. Though Kautilya felt that the giving of *hostages was the least satisfactory way of guaranteeing a treaty, the fact that he devoted a whole chapter to the subject suggests, as has been pointed out, that this was a common practice in his time. (The first person to offer as a hostage is a treacherous minister, the last oneself; in between, daughters rather than sons, brave sons rather than wise ones, and so on.) As for the ethics of his statecraft, these are so repellent that it must be said that the common description of Kautilya as the 'Indian *Machiavelli' is a serious libel on the Florentine Secretary. The *Arthashastra* is a work of great pedantry and replete with banalities and circular statements. Though of little if any enduring theoretical significance, it is nevertheless of great historical interest. A modern translation with the text helpfully rearranged and interpreted was produced by the former Indian ambassador L. N. Rangarajan in 1992.

Kellogg Pact. *See* Briand–Kellogg Pact.

KGB. The former Soviet agency for the collection and analysis of both *security and *foreign intelligence; also responsible for *counter-espionage, *counter-intelligence and *covert action. The acronym is from the Russian: *Komitet Gosudarstvennoye Bezopasnosti* (Committee for State Security). Military intelligence was chiefly the responsibility of the *Glavnoye Razvedyvatelnoye Upravleniye* (GRU). The KGB's tasks are now executed by the *FSB and the *SVR. *See also* GlavUpDK.

King's Messenger. *See* Queen's Messenger; diplomatic courier.

Kissinger, Henry (1923–). Born of German-Jewish parents who fled to America in 1938, Henry (formerly 'Heinz') Kissinger was a professor of international relations at Harvard University until he was invited to be *National Security Advisor by Richard Nixon after his victory in the US presidential election in November 1968. In August 1973 he also became *secretary of state, a position he held until the Republicans surrendered the White House at the beginning of 1977.

A student and admirer of *Metternich, Kissinger brought to the formulation of US foreign policy a strong belief in the idea of the *balance of power (sense 3) at the point in America's fortunes when it seemed that she was becoming just another *major power. During his early years as National Security Advisor, Kissinger was also famous for activities, often highly secret, as a *special envoy, particularly in the negotiations which led to the ending of the *Vietnam War (for which, together with Le Duc Tho, he won the *Nobel Peace Prize in 1973) and the opening to the People's Republic of China. It was this side of his activities which led, as he became a major international celebrity, to the popularization of the term *linkage, and – at least in this extreme form – the invention of *shuttle diplomacy.

For students of Kissinger's views on diplomacy and his theory of international relations, probably the most important of his many writings are his doctoral thesis, subsequently published under the title *A World Restored: Metternich, Castlereagh and the Problems of Peace 1812–22* (1957); the first of his three volumes of memoirs, *The White House Years* (1979); and *Diplomacy* (1994) – in that order.

See also salami tactics; step-by-step diplomacy; triangular diplomacy.

kissing hands. The British ceremony at which the head of state appoints an *ambassador or *high commissioner (other than one to the *Queen's Realms). Nowadays, hands are no longer kissed – but the terminology is retained.

Korean War. The 1950–53 war in which the United States and a number of her allies fought, under the auspices of the *United Nations, to repel the invasion of the western-oriented South Korea by the Communist regime in North Korea.

kowtow. The manner in which a *tributary ruler physically abased himself before the Emperor of China. The kowtow involved three separate kneelings, each followed by three successive prostrations of the body in which the nose came into intimate contact with the ground: in all, three kneelings and nine prostrations. This was not popular with the European envoys who visited the court of the Celestial Empire. *See also* audience.

Kreisky, Bruno (1911–90). Austrian socialist politician, diplomat, and statesman. On returning to Austria from war exile in Sweden, Kreisky was sent back to serve at the Austrian *legation in Stockholm, where he remained from 1947 until 1950. In 1951 he joined the Foreign Affairs Department of the Chancellery in Vienna, and remained there until elected to the National Assembly at the beginning of 1956. In 1959 he became chair of the *Sozialdemokratische Partei Österreichs* (*SPÖ*). In the same year he was appointed foreign minister and secured the upgrading of the Foreign Affairs Department to a cabinet ministry in its own right. He remained foreign minister until 1966. In 1967 he was elected leader of the *SPÖ* and in 1970 chancellor of Austria. He held both positions until his retirement in 1983. Pursuing a policy of 'active *neutrality' abroad, Kreisky was a highly regarded *mediator and without doubt one of the most gifted statesmen of the second half of the twentieth century.

Kremlin. The ancient citadel in Moscow within which, among other buildings, the offices of the Russian government are located. It has thus become shorthand for the Russian, formerly Soviet, government.

L

laisser passer. (1) A letter of recommendation to the customs authorities asking that the luggage and effects of a *diplomat or *diplomatic courier be allowed to pass through without inspection; it is issued by the embassy of the country which it is proposed to enter. (2) A travel document issued by *international organizations to its officials, which some states treat as the equivalent of a passport. (3) In some states, a document issued to persons residing within its border who are not citizens. *See also* diplomatic passport.

Larkin, Frederick A. (1887–1975). Originally a construction industry engineer, from 1936 until his retirement in 1952 Larkin directed the purchase and sale of America's diplomatic real estate as head of what latterly came to be known as the US *State Department's Office of Foreign Buildings Operations (FBO). It was Larkin who first proposed and then vigorously supported the plan to finance America's post-war building of new diplomatic and

consular properties abroad from the vast reservoir of foreign credits accumulated by the United States during the Second World War. Following congressional approval in 1946, the result was an unprecedented surge in US diplomatic building and considerable architectural licence in its design. By the time he retired Larkin, who had travelled the world making deals, could boast that the Foreign Service had acquired 737 buildings abroad, purchased 92 additional sites, and had 36 new buildings already under construction. *See also* Inman standards.

Lateran Treaties. The three agreements which settled the disputes prompted by the absorption of the Papal States by the new state of Italy in the second half of the nineteenth century. They were signed in the palace of St John Lateran on 11 February 1929 by the Italian dictator, Benito Mussolini, and the Pope's secretary of state, Cardinal Gasparri. In addition to a *Concordat and a Financial Convention, a Political Treaty provided for the full and independent *sovereignty (sense 1) of the papacy within the territory it still retained: *Vatican City.

law-making treaty. One to which many states are parties, and so has become widely applicable. However, it is an unfortunate term in that it implies, incorrectly, that a bilateral treaty or one with few parties does not, for those parties, constitute law.

Law of Treaties, Vienna Convention on. This Convention, which was signed in May 1969, brought together and tidied up most of the rules of *customary international law regarding *treaties, and extended a good number of them. It was the product of much preparatory work by the *International Law Commission. It *entered into force in 1980, but has so far been *ratified or acceded to by slightly fewer than half the world's sovereign states. However, in large measure it is generally seen as expressive of customary law on the subject, and to that extent is *binding on all states.

laws of war. *See* international humanitarian law.

lead ministry. The ministry with formal responsibility for a negotiation. In a negotiation where one ministry is allowed to 'take the lead', others are naturally involved; formal responsibility does not, therefore, imply exclusive influence. It is usually the *line ministries (e.g. transport, agriculture) that are described as the lead ministries in their particular sectors within the EU, though obviously there is nothing to prevent a ministry of *foreign affairs from being the lead ministry in a particular negotiation.

league. (1) An old term for an *alliance, as in the anti-Venetian League of Cambrai which saw the forces of Pope Julius II, Louis of France, Ferdinand of Spain and the Emperor Maximilian rout the republic at Aguadello in 1509. (2) An old term for a *confederation, as in the cases of Switzerland and the Swabian League (created in 1488 and boasting regular meetings, tribunals and a common force of infantry and horse). This is the meaning employed by *Machiavelli in the section of his *Discourses* where he considers the various methods which a republic might employ in order to expand. (3) An *international organization, either universal in aspiration, as in the *League of Nations, or regional in scope, as in the *League of Arab States.

League of Arab States. Founded in 1945 by the seven then-sovereign Arab states, it now has 22 members, including the as yet non-sovereign Palestine. It seeks to promote closer ties between the members and to coordinate their cultural, economic, and security policies. Proposals towards this end are the responsibility of the League Council, on which each member is represented and holds one vote. The Council may meet in the capital of any member state. The League also has a number of specialized ministerial committees which may make suggestions to the Council. However, especially on issues with a higher profile, the League has rarely made much effective (as distinct from rhetorical) progress, due to the considerable animosity which often exists within the Arab world. The League's headquarters and hence its *secretariat are in Cairo, Egypt. During the 1980s, however, they were in Tunis, as Egypt was then suspended from the League on account of her having agreed a peace treaty with Israel.

League of Nations. Provided for by the peace treaty of 1919 – the Treaty of Versailles – which brought the Great War to an end, the League of Nations was the first general *international organization to be charged with the maintenance of *peace. In this area it represented the breakthrough into the *international society of the idea of *collective security, suggesting that state practice on the fundamental issues of peace and *war would in future proceed on a radically different basis from what had hitherto been orthodox. However, the League's *Covenant also reflected the *realism (sense 1) of its makers in that it did not try to embody a full-blown version of collective security. And the events leading to the Second World War showed that states did not feel able fully to honour even the Covenant's limited expression of the idea. Thus so far as its primary purpose is concerned, the League is often said to have failed. But it did not fail in this all the time, nor in respect of all its other purposes. And at the level of ideas the League undoubtedly reflected something in the nature of a revolution which, in the second half of the twentieth century, was to be confirmed and extended – notably by the *United Nations.

The League came into being in 1920 with 42 members. Subsequently, 20 other states were admitted; 17 departed (as was their right); and one (the Soviet Union) was deemed to have been expelled. All members were represented (with one vote each) in the League Assembly, which immediately insisted on meeting annually, and gave rise to what later became known as *multilateral (or parliamentary) diplomacy. The major victorious powers were permanent members of the League Council (except that the United States could not take its seat, as it failed to *ratify the Treaty of Versailles), and they were later added to; there were also some non-permanent (and, later, semi-permanent) Council members. The League was based in Geneva, Switzerland, where a truly international *secretariat was established for the first time. A splendid building was eventually constructed there as the League's headquarters and meeting place, which was ready for occupation in the late 1930s just when the League was fast going downhill. (It is now the UN's Geneva Office.) The League was formally wound up in 1946.

The League was responsible for the supervision of the *mandate system; was given certain protective tasks in respect of *minorities; acted as the governing authority of two territories which were subject to temporary *internationalization; engaged in much work of a 'technical' kind; sponsored a number of 'auxiliary' organizations (some of which were the forerunners of the UN's *specialized agencies); and had a close relationship with the *Permanent Court of International Justice. *See also* Briand–Kellogg Pact.

Least Developed Country (LDC). One of the 50 or so countries deemed by the UN Conference on Trade and Development to be among the 'least developed' countries in the world. Originally described as the Least [Developed] of the Less Developed Countries (LLDCs). Two-thirds of them are in Africa. *See also* Third World.

ledger ambassador. *See* lieger.

legal adviser. (1) The head of the office within a ministry of *foreign affairs responsible for advice on *international law. The equivalent officer within the UN is called the legal counsel. Since 1989 the legal advisers of many states have held informal meetings in the margins of meetings of the Sixth Committee (Legal) of the UN *General Assembly in New York. (2) Any member of a legal adviser's office.

legal dispute. *See* justiciable dispute.

legalization. Confirmation that a public official's signature, seal (sense 1), or stamp is genuine. A document emanating from within one state – a university degree certificate, for example, or a statement made before a legal official, or a birth certificate – may not be accepted in another state without an assurance by the first state of its authenticity. Such an assurance may be provided (for a fee) by the attachment of a legalization certificate (also called an apostille) to the document by the legalization office of a ministry of *foreign affairs.

legalization office. *See* legalization.

legate. (1) From the ancient world until the early modern period, any person sent by any other on diplomatic business. In his *De Legationibus Libri Tres* (1585), *Gentili tells us that 'In Roman law the technical term for ambassadors is *legati* from *legare* "to send with a commission"'. (2) A papal emissary. Entrenched in canon law, the term 'legate' was still being used by the *Holy See in the twentieth century, long after it had fallen into disuse elsewhere. A papal legate *a latere* (literally, 'from the side of the Pope') is usually a cardinal entrusted with a *special mission. The legate *missus* is now described as a *nuncio, while the legate *natus* has no diplomatic status. *See also* legation; right of legation.

legate *a latere*. *See* legate.

legation. A *resident or *non-resident *diplomatic mission headed by a *minister (sense 1) – that is, by a *head of mission of the second *diplomatic class. Ordinarily, the minister's full title is *envoy extraordinary and minister plenipotentiary. Legations used to be the usual type of diplomatic mission, *embassies being exchanged only between *major powers. However, since the Second World War they have gone dramatically out of fashion. The process seems to have begun during the war, when, with the agreement of the *receiving state, virtually all legations in Washington were raised to embassies in an effort by *sending states to emphasize the importance they attached to their relationship with the United States. Later, the speedy ending of colonialism greatly accelerated the process, as the ex-colonial territories which were now *sovereign states regarded it as damaging to their pride and dignity to be represented at anything short of the highest level. Thus whereas embassies were once notable for their pomp – in respect of both their premises and their display – it is now by no means uncommon for such missions to be exceedingly small and generally lacking in ostentation.

legation quarter. *See* diplomatic quarter.

Less Developed Country (LDC). *See* Least Developed Country.

Lesser Developed Country (LDC). A term now used in the United States for *Least Developed Country.

letter of introduction. (1) Where both the *sending and *receiving states are of the *Queen's Realms – that is, where The Queen who is ordinarily resident in Britain is the *head of state of both of them – it is not thought possible for a new *head of mission to carry a *letter of commission addressed by The Queen (as head of state of the sending state) to herself (as head of state of the receiving state). Instead, the head of mission is supplied with a letter of introduction written by the sending state's *head of government (the prime minister) to his or her counterpart in the receiving state. This letter is not deemed to be a formal document and therefore, in being described, is referred to with the first letters of the words 'letter' and 'introduction' in lower case (unlike the usual letters relating to accreditation, which attract capital letters). Such a head of mission, being from one *Commonwealth state to another, will be called a *high commissioner. This form of accreditation was adopted in the early 1950s, when the adoption of letters of commission for the exchange of heads of mission between certain Commonwealth states focused attention on the fact that as between other such states there was no standard form of accreditation for heads of mission. It emerged that some heads were supplied with a letter from their prime minister to the receiving state's prime minister; others with a letter from their *foreign minister to the receiving state's foreign minister; and yet others with no form of accreditation at all. The general adoption of a letter of introduction by the relevant states thus tidied up this aspect of diplomatic procedure. *See also* letters of recall. (2) The term used by Britain for the *credentials given to her *permanent representatives to *international organizations.

letter of protection. (1) A document testifying that the bearer enjoys the diplomatic and consular protection of the issuing authority, normally a foreign state. Letters of this kind have played a significant role in modern history and, not surprisingly, have proved controversial. The *berāt* of the Ottoman Empire, which was commonly sold to a subject of the sultan by an embassy in Istanbul, is a notable example. Originally deriving from the *exequaturs* issued by the Ottoman authorities through the embassies in the city and intended for the protection of consuls and *dragomans, these documents came to be the object of serious abuse in the eighteenth century. Among others who had not the remotest connection with diplomatic or consular work, non-Muslim merchants, such as Armenians and Greeks, were especially attracted by the *berāt* because it exempted them from Ottoman taxes, the discriminatory practices of the sultan's courts, and the non-Muslim dress code, which advertised their minority status in a crowd and thus sometimes put their safety at risk. For their part, the ambassadors saw the *berāts* as an important source of income, selling them for substantial sums and expecting presents from their *berātli* (holders of *berāts*) when newly arrived in the city. In the eighteenth century Istanbul and cities such as Aleppo were awash with holders of *berāts*, the market prices of which were an accurate barometer of the degree of respect in which the *Sublime Porte held the issuing embassy. At the beginning of the nineteenth century Russian *berāts* were the most expensive. The Ottoman government hated the system, as did some ambassadors, and it was finally abolished in the early nineteenth century. Another notable letter of protection was the *schutzbrief,* over 50,000 of which were famously issued to Jews by Carl Lutz, Swiss Consul in Budapest during the last years of the Second World War. They provided a guarantee that the bearer was under the protection of Switzerland until he or she was able to leave Hungary. Diplomats of many other nationalities resident in Nazi-occupied Europe also issued, without authority from home, thousands of *visas to Jews threatened with the death camps, at considerable risk to their careers and in some cases their lives. *See also* protecting power; safe-conduct. (2) A letter that confirmed that all of the lands and possessions of an envoy were under the special protection of his monarch while he was absent on diplomatic business. Issued to envoys prior to their departure, these were no doubt designed to reduce resistance to this kind of employment. Such letters were a particular feature of the medieval period.

letters of commission. Except where a *letter of introduction is appropriate, a new *head of mission sent by one *Commonwealth state to another carries letters of commission from the *sending state's *head of state to the *receiving state's head of state. The term came into use as from 1950 to accommodate the presence, for the first time, of a republic – India – as a member of the Commonwealth. The exact phraseology which was adopted (at India's suggestion) reflected the fact that the head of mission sent by one Commonwealth state to another was (and is) called a *high commissioner; and the thought that the more usual term for such documents, *letters of credence, was inappropriate for the special relationship which was then deemed to exist between Commonwealth members, even when one of those members had broken with tradition by becoming a republic. Now, republics are in a large majority in the Commonwealth; and it may be doubted whether the relationship between Commonwealth states is, in political terms, particularly special. Nonetheless, the terminology adopted in 1950 is maintained (although in informal contexts the document may be referred to as 'credentials'). The use of the plural, 'letters', in this context is in imitation of its general use in the term, 'letters of credence'. But sometimes the singular form, 'letter of commission', is encountered.

letters of credence. The *credentials with which a newly appointed *ambassador (as distinct from a *high commissioner) is furnished. They take the form of a letter (although the plural is generally used) in which (to use typical wording) the *sending state's *head of state asks his or her counterpart in the *receiving state to 'give entire credence to all that [the ambassador] shall have occasion to communicate to you in my name'. They are a specific (and often rather colourful) instance of the general rule that any *agent (senses 1 and 2) needs to carry documents of authentication. It should be noted, however, that in the case of the despatch of an ambassador by one of the *Queen's Realms, the letters may – if the sending state so wishes – be signed by its *governor-general in the name and on behalf of the head of state (the Queen). And in some other monarchical states the letters may be countersigned by the prime minister or foreign minister.

In the days when *ministers (sense 1) were appointed as *heads of mission, they too carried letters of credence of the type given to ambassadors, announcing the minister as the representative of the sending state's head of state. But a *chargé d'affaires *en titre* (another virtually extinct breed of head of mission) was accredited not to the head of state but to the receiving state's foreign minister. Accordingly, his credentials were furnished by the sending state's foreign minister for presentation to his counterpart in the receiving state.

Traditionally, a head of mission could not assume his full functions until he had presented his credentials. This could and still can sometimes result in a fairly lengthy period in limbo for the head of mission designate, while he awaited the convenience of the receiving state's head of state. Taking advantage of an ambiguity in the *Regulation of Vienna (1815), some states therefore adopted the practice of treating the head of mission as fully *en poste* as from the date on which (as was customary) he notified the receiving state's foreign ministry of his arrival and furnished the ministry with a *working copy of his letters of credence. This has now been accepted as legitimate, and appears to be quite widely followed. However, each receiving state must adopt a uniform practice in the matter.

It is not known whether the Democratic Republic of the Congo (the ex-Belgian Congo) had, by 1965, adopted the practice of allowing an ambassador to act as such before presenting his letters of credence. (Its attitude to such matters was said to have been 'flexible'.) But in that year the country's President asked the newly arrived Canadian Ambassador to visit him urgently in advance of the credentials ceremony. He had a small favour to ask: the transmission by diplomatic bag of $400 (US) to his son, who was studying in Ottawa and had run short of cash. The Ambassador readily agreed. A few hours later news arrived at the Embassy that a new, and earlier, date had been fixed for the presentation of the Ambassador's letters of credence.

See also letters of commission; letter of introduction; presentation of credentials; representative character.

letters of recall. The formal letter (although the plural is generally used) sent by the *sending state's *head of state to that of the *receiving state announcing that a *head of mission is being *recalled (sense 2). Usually that letter is presented to the head of state by the incoming head of mission, together with his or her *letters of credence. It should be noted, however, that the departure of a *high commissioner from one of the *Queen's Realms to another (who, on appointment, is furnished not with letters of credence but with a *letter of introduction) is not marked by the issue of the equivalent of letters of recall. *See also* recredential.

letter of request. *See* rogatory letter.

letter rogatory. *See* rogatory letter.

lettre de cabinet. Compared to the *lettre de chancellerie*, a relatively familiar and informal style of communication and thus the most common form of communication between *monarchs regarding themselves as equals ('*Monsieur mon frère*', or '*cousin*', or '*ma soeur*', etc.). It is also written on smaller paper and by no means always countersigned by a government minister. It could serve many purposes, including provision of the *credentials of a *diplomatic agent, recall of the agent, the expression of condolences on a death, and so on.

lettre de chancellerie. The most ceremonious form in which a communication from a monarch could be presented, resplendent with the titles of the sending sovereign and other regal flourishes. Normally countersigned by the *foreign minister (sense 1), the *lettre de *chancellerie* could serve a variety of purposes, including provision of the *credentials of a *diplomatic agent, recall of the agent, and so on. Never common, it was a form used more when there was a discrepancy in rank between sender and receiver, and typically when the monarch was communicating with the president of a republic. *See also lettre de cabinet.*

lettre de part. *See* diplomatic courier.

lettre de récréance. *See* recredential.

Levant Consular Service. One of several specialized sections of the British network of *consuls in the nineteenth and early twentieth centuries, the Levant Service covered the Ottoman Empire and its fringes, or what today is called the Balkans, Turkey and the Middle East. It grew out of the consular posts inherited from the Levant Company in 1825, though it was not formally constituted as a reformed separate service employing natural-born British subjects until 1877. With heavy (especially judicial) responsibilities under the *capitulations and mounting political tasks as Anglo-Russian rivalry increased, the Levant Service was exceptionally large, elaborate and expensive; its consuls also had a higher status than those in the general service and by the First

World War had replaced the China Service, the other main specialized service, as the most prestigious element in the whole consular establishment. Because of the ending of the capitulations, among other reasons, the independent Levant Consular Service was amalgamated with the General Consular Service in 1934.

levee. (1) Originally a seventeenth century term meaning a morning assembly or reception of visitors (including diplomatic envoys) held by a prince on rising from his bed (from the French '*se lever*', to rise or get up). (2) Levee, or *levée*, subsequently came to mean a reception of visitors by a prince or president, or the representative of either, at any time of day.

liaison office. *See* representative office.

lieger. Late medieval/early modern usage for an *ordinary, resident envoy, as in the term 'lieger ambassador'. Sometimes spelled 'ledger' or 'ligier' (for example by *Hotman), it derives from 'ledger' meaning a book that lies *permanently* in some place.

limited sovereignty. *See* Brezhnev Doctrine.

line ministry. Alternatively 'line department', any ministry other than the foreign ministry.

linkage. So called by Henry *Kissinger, the simultaneous negotiation of two or more unrelated issues, with agreement on one being made conditional on agreement on the other. This approach is deeply offensive to those who believe that all issues should be treated 'on their merits'. A classic case was provided by the negotiations in the 1980s which linked the South African presence in Namibia to the Cuban presence in Angola. South Africa eventually withdrew from Namibia not because it acknowledged a legal obligation to do so but because – among other reasons – it was offered the Cuban withdrawal from Angola *in exchange*. *See also* Homans's theorem; package deal.

listening device. One used by a *receiving state, contrary to international law, to overhear conversation within a diplomatic mission or to intercept its messages. Also known as a 'bug', such devices have sometimes (especially during the *Cold War) been implanted in *diplomatic premises during the course of their construction. *See also* bubble; freedom of communication.

listening post. A diplomatic or consular mission which gives particular emphasis to, and is of unusual importance for, gathering information. The missions of some states at the UN in New York are sometimes described in this way, though it is more usual to come across the term in connection with missions located adjacently to territories into which access is difficult if not impossible. Such was the case with the US legation in Riga, Latvia, in regard to American information-gathering on the Soviet Union in the 1920s and early 1930s, and also with the US consulate-general in Hong Kong in regard to mainland China prior to the Sino-American rapprochement in the early 1970s. *See also* China Watchers; Henderson.

lobbying. Applying pressure on those with legislative or executive authority to obtain a decision favourable to one's cause. Deriving from the habit of those petitioners who sought to catch British legislators outside the chamber of the House of Commons, that is to say in the lobby, lobbying is usually a major preoccupation of *diplomatic missions.

local diplomatic rank. *See* diplomatic rank.

localitis. The adoption by diplomats of the point of view of the government of the *receiving state, traditionally assumed to be the result of having been posted there for too long. Sometimes known as 'going native', this is the chief reason why diplomats now tend, at some cost in the waste of acquired expertise, to be rotated between different regions and not spend longer than three or four years at the same *post. Another reason for short terms of duty in some posts is 'anti-localitis', the opposite of localitis. This is the adoption by diplomats of an attitude of undiscriminating hostility to the interests and policies of the host state, caused by unfriendly treatment or harsh or primitive conditions of life in the state concerned. *See also* hardship post.

locally engaged staff. Normally, members of the staff of a *diplomatic mission or *consular post who are nationals of or permanently resident in the *receiving state. However, this category may also include those employed by a mission who are spouses of members of the *diplomatic staff or, for example, spouses of businessmen or women from the sending state who are doing a limited tour of duty in the country concerned. Although, with the consent of the receiving state, its citizens may be employed as *diplomatic agents, this is rare. Hence, the vast majority of locally engaged staff are to be found among the ranks of the *administrative and technical and the *service staff, and among the ranks of any private servants. *See also* dragoman; honorary consular officer; *proxenos*; Wicquefort.

Locarno, spirit of. An atmosphere of reconciliation and *détente. It derives from the Pact of Locarno, which comprised a whole series of interlocking treaties *initialled in the Swiss town of Locarno in 1925 (and *signed in London shortly afterwards). The Pact brought Germany out of the purdah to which she had been consigned following the First World War, and was hailed as 'the real dividing line between the years of war and the years of peace'. In 1953 Winston Churchill, as his last prime ministerial years were coming to an end, unsuccessfully sought high-level East–West talks in the hope that the spirit of Locarno might thereby be regenerated.

Lomé Convention (1975). So called because signed in Lomé, the capital of Togo, this is a comprehensive trade and aid agreement between the *European Union states and 71 developing countries in Africa, the Caribbean and the Pacific.

London Gazette. *See* gazette.

Luxembourg compromise (1966). The understanding arrived at by the six member states of the *European Economic Community that each could *veto any key decision of the *Council of Ministers. This ended the crisis of the previous year provoked by the French government's decision to boycott all meetings of the Council in protest at the prospect of a shift to majority voting in January 1966.

M

Maastricht, Treaty of (1992). The Treaty on European Union (TEU), as it is formally styled, was finally settled at a *European Council meeting in Maastricht in the Netherlands in December 1991. It was then *signed on 7 February 1992 and *entered into force in November 1993. It marked the largest advance in European integration since the foundation of the *Common Market, providing for both Economic and Monetary Union (EMU) and the creation of the *European Union via addition of two new '*pillars' of policy cooperation to the existing economic one (Pillar One): *Common Foreign and Security Policy (Pillar Two), and Justice and Home Affairs (Pillar Three).

Machiavelli, Niccolò (1469–1527). A Florentine diplomat, civil servant, playwright, and political and military theorist. Machiavelli is now best known for his short book *The Prince*, which analysed the political world as it was rather than as it ought to be. It thus scandalized the Church, and his name became a byword for cunning, deceit and ruthlessness. His most important work, however, is to be found in the *Discourses on the First Ten Books of Titus Livy*, where he uses the Roman historian as a foil to advance his own political theory. Machiavelli's diplomatic *despatches to the Florentine *signoria* from other Italian city states and from France and Germany, together with the *instructions with which he was supplied, are to be found in two of the four volumes of his works translated into English in the late nineteenth century under the title *The Historical, Political, and Diplomatic Writings of Niccolo Machiavelli*, vols III and IV ('The Missions'). More interested in military than diplomatic technique, Machiavelli's only explicit reflection on the last (and that entirely conventional) is to be found in his letter of 1522 which was subsequently entitled 'Advice to Raffaello Girolami when he went as Ambassador to the Emperor'.

Nevertheless, Machiavelli is important for students of diplomacy because not only was he the first of the *realists (sense 1) but, as Meinecke points out, 'the first person to discover the real nature of *raison d'état'. *See also* Guicciardini.

major power. A convenient term now sometimes used to describe the half-dozen or so most powerful states in the contemporary world. It does not carry the historical baggage of the term *great power, while its vagueness permits it to embrace the one remaining *superpower – the United States – and its nearest rivals, together with powerful states who do not have permanent seats on the UN *Security Council as well as those that do. In effect, if 'superpower' is regarded as a synonym for 'great power', the category of 'major power' covers both the great powers and the upper *middle powers. *See also* permanent members.

Malmesbury, First Earl of. *See* Harris, Sir James.

mandates. Territories placed under the *mandates system.

mandates system. At the end of the First World War the defeated states were stripped of their *colonies and imperial territories. But, in a departure from previous practice, the victorious powers did not feel able straightforwardly to *annex those of them whose peoples were, in the words of the *Covenant of the League of Nations, 'not yet able to stand by themselves under the strenuous conditions of the modern world'. Their well-being was stated to be 'a sacred trust of civilization', and was to be placed in the hands of certain 'advanced' (and victorious) states who would govern on the basis of a mandate formally granted by the Council of the League, but in the drafting of which the prospective mandatory had a large hand.

The mandatories were obliged to report annually to the League, which established the Permanent Mandates Commission to examine the reports on its behalf and advise it on the execution of the mandates. The Commission was composed of independent experts, with nationals of non-mandatories in the majority. It was not, however, a very intrusive form of international supervision, and one well-placed observer (Salvador de Madariaga, a former member of the League's Secretariat) said of the system that 'the old hag of colonialism puts on a fig leaf and calls herself mandate'.

By the time the League was wound up in 1946 a few mandates had become *sovereign states. Those that remained were transferred to the UN *trusteeship system, other than South West Africa, as South Africa (the mandatory power) would not agree to this.

manual of military law. *See* military manual.

marshal of the diplomatic corps. The British official who oversees ceremonial occasions which involve both the state and members of the London *diplomatic corps. Thus, for example, the marshal organizes and is in attendance at the *presentation of letters of credence. Traditionally a retired armed services officer, he is a member of that part of the Royal Household which is called the Lord Chamberlain's office. However, it should be noted that the day-to-day functions of the marshal are performed by the *Protocol Department of the *Foreign and Commonwealth Office under the supervision of a director (formerly assistant under-secretary), who also has the title 'vice-marshal of the diplomatic corps'.

mediation. (1) The active search for a negotiated settlement to an international or intrastate conflict by an impartial *third party. The search is 'active' in the sense that the work of the intermediary may go so far as to involve drawing up the *agenda, calling and chairing negotiating sessions, proposing solutions, and employing threats and promises towards the rivals. It is now a matter of controversy whether the mediator need be impartial prior to the start of negotiations but there is still general agreement on its necessity once they have commenced. (To suggest that partisanship for one side in a conflict is a necessary or at least advantageous attribute of a mediator – as some do – is to commit a category error. A so-called 'mediator' who adopts a partisan attitude succeeds merely in rendering the negotiation an exercise in ordinary *multilateral diplomacy.) Not to be confused with *conciliation or *good offices, this strict concept of mediation is the older – and still a very common – usage. (2) On a more recent and looser usage, any diplomatic activity by an intermediary, of whatever quality or degree, which is designed to promote a negotiated settlement to a conflict. *See also* venue.

medium power. *See* middle power.

megaphone diplomacy. A term applied to the style of public exchanges in the early 1980s between the Soviet Union on the one hand and the United States and the United Kingdom on the other. The low-point of all this was probably President Reagan's speech before the British House of Commons in June 1982 which referred to the Soviet Union as an 'Evil Empire'. *See also* propaganda; public diplomacy.

mémoire. *See aide-mémoire.*

memorandum. *See aide-mémoire.*

memorandum of understanding (MOU). A document which sets out an understanding reached between two states as to their international commitments regarding some matter, but which does so in a way which indicates that the understanding is not legally *binding. In other words, it is not a *treaty – although, confusingly, some treaties are called memoranda of understanding. Like a treaty, an MOU may be given a name other than that. An MOU can take the form either of a single document or of an exchange of *notes (sense 2).

memorial. An older term for a *note or memorandum.

Mendoza, Don Bernadino de. *See* Gentili.

messenger. *See* diplomatic courier; herald; Queen's Messenger.

Metternich, Prince Klemens von (1773–1859). A diplomat and statesman of the Austrian Empire. Metternich's ambassadorships included Paris, where he obtained a close view of Napoleon. In 1809 he was appointed foreign minister and in 1821 chancellor, and held both posts until driven into exile in 1848. Deeply conservative in his views, Metternich presided over the Congress of *Vienna in 1815 and was without doubt one of the great architects of the restoration of the international order which had been mangled so effectively in the French revolutionary wars. This impressed Henry *Kissinger, who made him the central figure in his Harvard doctorate. *See also* Talleyrand.

MFA. *See* foreign affairs, ministry of.

MI5. The popular name for the Security Service, Britain's *counter-intelligence and counter-terrorism agency.

MI6. *See* Secret Intelligence Service (SIS).

micro-mission. A term sometimes used to describe a very small mission or office established by the sending state in the receiving state, consisting of perhaps just one or two *diplomatic service personnel and a few *locally engaged staff. It may be a *resident diplomatic mission with an ambassadorial head, a *satellite office, or a *consular post.

micro-state. Often understood to mean a state with under one million inhabitants. A term with a roughly similar meaning is 'mini-state'.

middle power. Sometimes known as a 'medium power', a state which is regarded as being in the second rank after the *great powers/*super-powers but has sufficient weight within its own region to be considered a 'regional great power'. A good example is South Africa in southern Africa. The status of middle power was implicitly recognized by the creation of semi-permanent seats on the Council of the *League of Nations in 1926, though the subsequent efforts of Canada and Australia (sometimes described as 'the original middle powers') to have priority given to this class of states in elections to non-permanent seats on the UN *Security Council did not prove successful. The interesting theory has been advanced that middle powers are predisposed to exceptional international virtue since they have insufficient power to foster 'imperialist' policies but enough to make them good soldiers on behalf of the UN.

military adviser. *See* military attaché.

military attaché. Usually an army officer temporarily attached to a *diplomatic mission, although an individual listed as 'Naval and Military Attaché', for example, could be a naval officer assigned the task of representing the army as well; known in the US Foreign Service as an 'army attaché' and in at least one other diplomatic service as an 'army adviser'. As between member states of the *Commonwealth, the equivalent individual is designated as a 'military adviser'. *See also* service attaché.

military manual. The volume containing a state's instructions to its senior military personnel on the conduct of *war or *armed conflict in accordance with *international humanitarian law.

military observer. A member of a *military observer group.

military observer group. A group of military officers charged with monitoring a *ceasefire or an *armistice. They are usually from the army and of middling rank, and seconded on an individual basis. Used by the UN in relation to a number of disputes, the almost invariable practice is for the officers to be unarmed. *See also* chief military observer; observer mission; peacekeeping; special representative.

Military Staff Committee. The body provided for by the UN *Charter to assist the *Security Council in matters relating to *collective security. In practice the committee has not yet been called upon so to act.

millet. In the Ottoman Empire, a group granted extensive self-government under a religious leader in return for its support of the sultan. Orthodox Christians, Armenians, Jews and the other major non-Muslim minorities benefited under the *millet* system. It was of diplomatic significance because the sultan's government tended to think of the European trading communities and their diplomatic heads, starting with the Venetians and their *baillo, as 'millets'. *See also* capitulations.

minder. A colloquial expression for a person employed in certain countries to subject a diplomat's movements outside embassy premises to 'visual surveillance'.

mini-state. *See* micro-state.

minister. (1) The abbreviated title of the head of a *legation. The full title is *envoy extraordinary and minister plenipotentiary. (2) In *diplomatic ranks, that which lies below *ambassador (sense 1) and above *counsellor (or, where it is used, above *minister-counsellor). (3) A member of a government. A minister in this sense is therefore a politician and not an *official. *See also* public minister.

minister-counsellor. In the *diplomatic ranks (sense 1) of some states, a position which lies beneath that of *minister (sense 2) and above that of *counsellor.

minister-in-attendance. A *minister (sense 3) accompanying a *head of state on a *state visit.

minister plenipotentiary. A lesser *diplomatic rank (sense 1) used in the seventeenth and eighteenth centuries, but now obsolete.

minister resident. A term for *heads of mission of the third *diplomatic class agreed by the powers at the Congress of Aix-la-Chapelle in 1818. In direct line of descent from the *resident, the minister resident was still noted in the early editions of *Satow's Guide* but had disappeared by the time of the Vienna Convention on Diplomatic Relations (1961). *See also* Regulation of Vienna (1815).

ministry of foreign affairs (MFA). *See* foreign affairs, ministry of.

minorities treaties. The term given to a number of special *treaties, special chapters inserted in treaties, and *declarations (sense 3) made shortly after the ending of the First World War, in which certain (chiefly central and east European) states undertook obligations in respect of their nationals belonging to racial, religious, and linguistic minorities, and which conferred on the *League of Nations the right to engage in some protective measures in respect of the implementation of those obligations. The League set up a system of committees to examine petitions alleging breaches of the treaties, and gave publicity to those complaints which were deemed to be justified. The obligations had been more or less exacted from the states concerned, and with the passage of time were increasingly resented. For their part, the minorities often complained about the insufficiency of the protection. In the 1920s it is likely that the system helped to protect minorities against some graver forms of injustice. But with the subsequent decline of the League the system became increasingly irrelevant.

When the *United Nations was established, no attempt was made to revive the system for the protection of minorities, this being virtually the only aspect of the League's work which found no reflection in the structure of the UN. In part this was because the Second World War did not result in the creation of new states, from which such undertakings could be demanded; in part because of the general unpopularity of restrictions being placed upon *domestic jurisdiction. Moreover, on this last matter the new states which later emerged from the breakdown of colonialism were particularly sensitive. Nonetheless, the UN's increasing emphasis on the protection of *human rights has helped to provide a little protection for some minorities. The *Organization for Security and Cooperation in Europe has established the post of High Commissioner on National Minorities to identify and promote the resolution of ethnic tension which might endanger peace and stability. And in 1999 *NATO went to great lengths to protect the Kosovan minority in Serbia. Minorities have not, therefore, been wholly forgotten.

minute. In British Diplomatic Service usage, any kind of written communication between officers within the *Foreign and Commonwealth Office or between officers within the same mission. What in a business corporation or other kind of organization is normally now called a 'memo' (internal memorandum), the minute may be either formal or informal, and is used even to designate something as small as a one-line observation on an incoming *telegram.

minutes. (1) A record of the proceedings of a meeting or conference, with any decisions highlighted; thus sometimes known as 'conclusions'. In French the term is *procès-verbal*. Minutes usually provide a summary of the proceedings but occasionally these are recorded *verbatim* (word for word). It is customary for an official of the party acting as host formally to record the minutes and circulate a draft after the meeting for the approval of the other participants. Agreed minutes may constitute a *treaty if this is the intention of the parties. (2) The plural of *minute: 'The minutes on the jacket containing the last despatch from Rome suggest a clear division of opinion within the Office!'

mise en demeure [*de faire quelque chose*]. A formal demand made of a government to do something, usually to agree to a proposal without conditions or make a plain statement of its intentions. Harold *Nicolson, who includes the term in the glossary of his book on *Diplomacy*, says that the tone of such a demand is 'curt'.

mission. (1) Sometimes 'overseas mission', a generic term usually restricted to resident *diplomatic missions and *consular posts but including those of a less conventional nature as well, such as *interests sections and *representative offices. *See also* permanent mission; special mission. (2) In American usage, the term is also employed to signify the complete roster of personnel – military as well as civilian – supervised by the US *head of mission accredited to a particular state.

modus vivendi. A temporary or provisional agreement, this is an older term for what is now more usually styled an *interim agreement.

monarchy. That system of government in which supreme authority is vested by the state's constitution in a single and usually hereditary figure, such as a king or queen. Once the common form of government, monarchies are now relatively rare; and the authority vested in the monarch is almost invariably of a formal kind only.

monitors. *See* election monitoring; observer mission.

Monroe Doctrine. The doctrine (as it later became known) enunciated in 1823 by President James Monroe of the United States in which that state's opposition to European encroachment in the Western Hemisphere was proclaimed. *See also* sphere of influence.

Montevideo Convention on the Rights and Duties of States (1933). A *treaty signed by the United States and certain Latin American states. It was preceded and has been followed by other such attempts to

define its stated subject matter, none of which has ever commanded general assent. Partly this is because some such alleged rights and duties are virtually self-evident; and partly – and more importantly – because of the difficulty of getting wide agreement on what rights and duties are basic.

The Convention is, however, often quoted for its statement that for a territorial entity to be an *international person it needs a permanent population, a defined territory, a government, and the capacity to enter into relations with other states. This last requirement, of course, is another way of referring to *sovereignty (sense 1).

most favoured nation clause (mfn). A feature of commercial treaties, this is a clause which amounts to an undertaking made by one party to a second that any more favourable trade concession which it might make in the future to a third would automatically apply to it as well. This grew in importance in the period between the First and Second World Wars and its general application became the principle on which the General Agreement on Tariffs and Trade, now superseded by the *World Trade Organization, operated.

multilateral diplomacy. Diplomacy conducted via conferences attended by three or more states, as distinct from *bilateral diplomacy (both senses). Multilateral conferences vary enormously in size, level of attendance, longevity, and extent of bureaucratization, from small ad hoc conferences to huge ones with a wide-ranging agenda, such as the annual sessions of the UN *General Assembly. *See also* open diplomacy; parliamentary diplomacy.

multinational corporation (MNC). A business corporation which has a visible and significant wealth-generating presence in more than one state or, in other words, engages to a significant degree in direct (as opposed to indirect or portfolio) foreign investment. The term 'multinational' may suggest that the directors and senior managers of these companies are representative of the countries in which they operate, whereas in fact they still tend to be dominated by personnel from the MNC's country of origin. It is to avoid this misleading impression that some, including the UN, prefer the term 'transnational corporation' (TNC).

multiple accreditation. (1) The accrediting of a diplomat to two or more states or *international organizations. In the usual case, an ambassador is resident in the capital of one of the states to which he or she is accredited, while the other(s) are in the same region. If the capital is host to an international organization he or she may well be accredited to this as well. Expressly sanctioned by the Vienna Convention on *Diplomatic Relations, multiple accreditation of this kind has always been popular with smaller states because of the cost-savings which it permits but in recent years has been resorted to by larger states as well. (2) The accrediting of the same person by two or more states as head of mission to another state. Because of the great confidence and unanimity of outlook which must obtain between states before they can embark on this course, this is rare. There are some signs, however, that the *European Union may experiment with this procedure. *See also* cut-price diplomacy.

multitrack diplomacy. One negotiation pursued along several different tracks. This includes most characteristically the efforts of private individuals, churches and other *non-governmental organizations, banks and *multinational corporations. It might be said that the agreement which ended the war in Kosovo in 1999 was a product of multitrack diplomacy, not least because of the key role believed to have been played in securing it by a Swedish-born financier and investment banker whose company was based in London. *See also* mediation.

Munich agreement. The agreement between Britain, France, Germany and Italy in September 1938 which approved Germany's plan to *annex certain areas of Czechoslovakia. It led to 'Munich' (the city in which the agreement was signed) becoming almost a synonym for *appeasement.

municipal law. That system of law which operates within a *state. It is sometimes spoken of as domestic law. *See also* international law and municipal law.

N

name of a state. In the normal way it is entirely up to each *state to determine its own name and titles, and international *comity suggests that other states respect that choice. However, problems sometimes arise when the chosen name is in a form which another state finds repugnant because, for example, it appears to conflict with that state's own constitutional or political claims, or conflicts with its view of the legitimacy of a specific situation. The areas in which problems may express themselves include: the *accreditation of *heads of mission, the making of *treaties, and the name whereby a state is known in an *international organization. If, for example, a state's purported *annexation of a territory is not recognized by another state, the second state will not be able to include the name of the territory in the titles of the first state when accrediting a new head of mission; and the *receiving state may refuse to accept the new head without the inclusion in his *letters of credence of that name. It may therefore be necessary for the *sending state to make do, *ad interim, with the despatch of a *chargé d'affaires en titre, whose *credentials, being addressed to the *foreign minister and not the *head of state, do not need to recite the state's full titles. This situation arose with regard to Italy after its claim, in 1936, to have annexed Abyssinia. Rather similarly, Ireland's insistence after 1937 that its name was simply that ('Ireland') led to difficulties with those *Commonwealth states whose head of state assertedly was sovereign of, inter alia, the United Kingdom of Great Britain and Northern Ireland. The credentials issue was resolved, but for a number of years Britain's head of mission to Ireland had to be known there as the British Representative. In a rather different sphere, the claim of the former Yugoslav province of Macedonia, after it had become sovereign in 1991, to the name, simply, of Macedonia, gave great offence to Greece, on both historical and political grounds. The issue held up the state's membership of the UN, and when she was admitted in 1993 it was by the name which other states have since generally used: the Former Yugoslav Republic of Macedonia. It also delayed the conclusion of a *status of forces agreement in respect of the UN's Preventive Deployment operation in Macedonia.

A state's *diplomatic mission, *permanent mission, or *delegation will in the normal way bear the state's official name, as in 'Embassy of France'. But occasionally another, easily recognizable, name may be used. Thus at the 1907 *Hague Conference, which was attended by many Latin American states (at that time an unusual event), the United States decided that its name (in French, the *diplomatic language [sense 1] of the day) did not begin with *États-Unis* but with *Amerique*, so giving it a higher place at the conference table than such states as Argentina, Brazil, and Chile. During the early 1960s Britain – which is formally, in shortened form, the 'United Kingdom' – decided, first in respect of its *Commonwealth posts and later in respect of its embassies and consulates, that 'Britain' and 'British' would be substituted for the use of the United Kingdom as both a noun and an adjective (other than in formal legal documents where the full title was required), notwithstanding the fact that strictly speaking Northern Ireland is not part of Britain. But an exception was made in respect of permanent missions to international organizations and delegations to conferences, so as not to lose the advantage in such contexts of the British representative sitting next to the representative of the United States (or, sometimes, almost next, Tanzania having since inconveniently called itself the 'United Republic of Tanzania'). Thus, while a capital city may have a 'British Embassy' or a 'British High Commission', Britain's permanent mission to the UN is that of the 'United Kingdom'.

See also alphabetical seating; colony.

nation. (1) An aggregation of people who, as the result of having certain important phenomena in common – such as descent, language, history, culture, or simply feeling – assert that collectively they constitute a *national (sense 1) unit. *See also* self-determination. (2) A popular synonym for *sovereign state (sometimes extended to 'nation-state').

national. (1) The adjectival form of *nation (sense 1). (2) A subject or citizen of a particular *state.

national day. The annual occasion when a *head of mission holds a reception to celebrate a date of great national significance. This is usually independence day, the birthday of a monarch, or the anniversary of the revolution which brought the government to power. Ireland celebrates St Patrick's Day. To these occasions it is normal to invite members of the *receiving state's government and other local dignitaries, other heads of mission, and the local *expatriate community.

National day celebrations can present problems for heads of missions. Invitations to opposition leaders in some countries can lead to threats to boycott the occasion by the receiving state, while the need to employ a selective guest list where the entire expatriate community is too large to accommodate at the function can generate ferocious ill will on the part of those left out – and little good will on the part of those included, since they expect to be there as of right. As for the national day parties of other ambassadors, attendance at these has become more and more exhausting as the number of states has increased.

national interest. That which is deemed by a particular state to be a vital or desirable goal in its *international relations (sense 1).

nationalism. (1) The doctrine that *nations (sense 1) should constitute sovereign states. (2) Chauvinistic attitudes and behaviour on the part of nations (sense 2). (3) Pride in one's nationhood (sense 1), more particularly in its non-political achievements and in what are deemed to be its distinctive characteristics. Also called cultural nationalism.

nationality. (1) The *national (sense 1) collectivity to which a person claims to belong. (2) The state of which a person is a citizen or subject.

national judge. A judge appointed by a party to a contentious case at the *International Court of Justice when the bench of the Court does not include a judge of that *state's *nationality (sense 2). Thus, when neither party has a judge of its nationality on the bench, each may appoint a national judge. Such a judge does not necessarily have to be (but in fact generally is) of the same nationality as the appointing party. This arrangement is a concession to the fact that, although all judges on the Court sit as independent individuals and not as the representatives of their states, in practice the judges tend to espouse the *claims presented by their own states – and national judges do so almost invariably.

National Reconnaissance Office. The American *intelligence organization for satellite *imagery collection. Though established in 1960, the NRO was not exposed until 1973 and not officially acknowledged until September 1992.

national security advisor. In the United States, a White House officer who is the president's personal assistant on national security affairs. The holder of this position has easy access to the president and a sizeable staff. When the president is distrustful of the *State Department and the national security advisor is a potent figure, he or she can have much more influence over American foreign policy than the *secretary of state, even though the post does not usually carry a cabinet seat. *See also* Kissinger; National Security Council (NSC).

National Security Agency (NSA). The *sigint arm of the US *intelligence community.

National Security Council (NSC). In the United States, the body which under the same act of 1947 that created the *CIA is designed to 'advise the president with respect to the integration of domestic, foreign, and military policies relating to the national security ...'. Its statutory membership consists of the president (who chairs its meetings), the vice president, the secretaries of state and defense, the director of the CIA, and the chairman of the Joint Chiefs of Staff. In addition to these, the president can invite anyone he likes, for example his personal *national security advisor. Though limited by statute to an advisory role, 'co-ordination is predominance', as Zbigniew Brzezinski, National Security Advisor to President Carter, points out in his memoirs. As a result, a tussle for control over foreign policy between the NSC and the *State Department, as well as other executive branch agencies,

has been a much noted feature of Washington politics since the first half of the 1960s.

national self-determination. *See* self-determination.

NATO. The North Atlantic Treaty Organization is a military *alliance created by the North Atlantic Treaty signed by 12 states in Washington on 4 April 1949. The key article included the statement that 'an armed attack against one or more of [the parties] in Europe or North America shall be considered an attack against them all'. Conceived as an anti-Soviet alliance under American leadership, NATO became the major safeguard of the West during the *Cold War. Four more European states acceded to the Treaty between 1952 and 1982 (with appropriate extensions of the Treaty's area of responsibility), to be followed in 1999 – to the disquiet of Russia – by three states which, in whole or in part, had been members of the former *Warsaw Pact: the Czech Republic, Hungary and Poland. In 2002 seven more states (Bulgaria, Estonia, Latvia, Lithuania, Romania, Slovakia, and Slovenia) were invited to begin accession talks and are expected to join in 2004. The supreme body within NATO is the *North Atlantic Council; its headquarters is located in Brussels.

Since the end of the Cold War NATO has been used as a vehicle for coordinating the response of its members to 'out-of-area' threats, notably in Iraq and in the former Yugoslavia. In the case of the latter, NATO is playing a prominent role, and is currently in effect administering the Serbian province of Kosovo. However, in respect of Iraq, the attempt of the United States and Britain to enlist NATO support for their *intervention in early 2003 did not succeed. *See also* Partnership for Peace; silence procedure.

naval adviser. *See* naval attaché.

naval attaché. Usually a naval officer temporarily attached to a *diplomatic mission, although an individual listed as 'Naval and Military Attaché', for example, could be an army officer assigned the task of representing the navy as well. As between members of the *Commonwealth, the equivalent individual is designated as a naval adviser. *See also* service attaché.

necessity. The doctrine that a breach of *international law is justified if it is imperative to ensure self-preservation, defend a *vital interest, or prevent a humanitarian catastrophe. States are reluctant to endorse the doctrine in general terms, but are not averse to invoking it in particular cases. *See also* intervention.

negative vetting. *See* positive vetting.

negotiation. (1) Discussion, or 'talks', between the representatives of two or more states designed to produce an *agreement on a point which is either of shared concern or at issue between them. The characteristic method of achieving success in a negotiation is for the parties to exchange concessions. On this narrow, traditional conception, negotiation proceeds through three stages: *prenegotiations, the *formula stage, and the details stage (where the skeletal formula is fleshed out). The last two stages are sometimes known as 'negotiations proper' or 'around-the-table' negotiations. *See also* back channel; bargaining; consensus decision-making; endgame; full powers; Homans's theorem; interim agreement; linkage; mediation; open diplomacy; playing it long; precondition; proximity talks; ratification; ripe moment; salami tactics; secret diplomacy; step-by-step diplomacy; stopping the clock; tabled offers; unanimity rule; weighted voting. (2) Communication by any means designed to achieve the purpose indicated in this entry's sense 1.

neutral. A state which has declared its *neutrality.

neutralism. A term that was used in the early post-1945 period to describe *non-alignment. *See also* Non-Aligned Movement.

neutrality. A legal status assumed unilaterally by a state during a time of *war, indicative of its intention of staying out of the war. The status involves rights and duties on the part of both the neutral state and the *belligerents (sense 1). The neutral must not, by acts of either commission or omission, assist any belligerent, and must allow the belligerents to treat the commerce of its *nationals (sense 2) in accordance with the *laws of war. For their part the belligerents must not infringe the neutrality of the neutral state, and must allow it to act towards their nationals in accordance with the laws of war. The practice of neutrality has often been far less clear cut than the rules of neutrality would suggest, for political and/or military reasons. Politically, a neutral may wish to display benevolent neutrality towards one side; and the proximity of a powerful belligerent may also incline a neutral away from a strictly neutral path, so as to stave off the danger of its neutrality being violated. In general, that is perhaps least likely to occur in wars which are limited in both scope and aim. However, the first half of the twentieth century was marked by total war, and in its second half the UN Charter posed a potential question about the relevance of the concept of neutrality – one made pertinent by the Security Council's post-Cold War *peace enforcement activity. Accordingly, neutrality is now much less heard about than it used to be – although circumstances continue to arise in which states are anxious to keep out of the armed conflicts of others. Neutrality is to be distinguished from *neutralism and *non-alignment. *See also* neutral; Non-Aligned Movement; permanent neutrality; perpetual neutrality.

neutralization. A formal collective act by which a lesser state gives an undertaking, *guaranteed by a group of greater powers, that it will not involve itself in *war (except in *self-defence) and will take great care not to give political offence in any quarter. In the past neutralization has been used in an attempt to protect small states against powerful neighbours and, more particularly, to maintain the *independence (sense 1) of *buffer states. During the *Cold War Austria (1955) and Laos (1962) were neutralized but, for the reasons given in the entry on buffer states, the device has since the middle of the twentieth century lost most of its relevance. *See also* neutrality; non-alignment; permanent neutrality.

neutral state. One which in respect of a *war assumes the status of *neutrality.

new diplomacy. The latest fashion in diplomatic method: *resident missions in the late fifteenth century, and parliamentary-style debate between the official representatives of states after the First World War.

Newly Industrialized Country (NIC). A country in the so-called

*Third World which has achieved very rapid growth in its manufacturing sector and become an important exporter of manufactures.

newsletter. In the early modern period, a handwritten but unsigned circular employed by governments to keep their foreign missions abreast of developments at home and elsewhere. In Italy they were known as *foglietti* and in France as *gazettes à la main*. Newsletters containing important information were also produced by private enterprise, a notable example being that produced by the Fugger family of Augsburg, the great mining, commercial and banking dynasty usually described as the financiers of the Habsburgs. *See also* gazettes.

news management. The manipulation by government departments (including ministries of *foreign affairs) of independent media organizations to support a particular line of policy. Unnecessary in totalitarian states (where such organizations do not exist), advisable in authoritarian ones (where they are sometimes tolerated provided that they behave), and indispensable in liberal democracies (where they are the 'fourth estate'), this is normally achieved by the selective briefing of journalists and sometimes by the 'leaking' of official documents.*International organizations also engage in news management, though they are reputed to be less good at it.

niche functions. A way of referring to the limited tasks often performed by a *satellite office of a diplomatic mission, as when its responsibilities concern, for example, only commercial matters or the administration of an aid programme. *See also* non-resident mission.

Nicolson, Harold (1886–1968). British diplomat, politician, journalist, broadcaster and author. His diplomatic career started in 1909 and ended with his resignation 20 years later at the rank of *counsellor. Its high points were his membership of the British delegation to the Paris peace conference in 1919, and his work as secretary to the British foreign secretary, Lord Curzon, at the Lausanne conference in 1922–23. After his resignation he devoted himself to writing and politics (from 1935 to 1945 he was National Labour MP for West Leicester). For students of diplomacy, his most important books are the 'Studies in Modern Diplomacy' trilogy, which included a biography of his father (who was *Permanent Under-Secretary at the Foreign Office during the First World War), an examination of the Paris peace conference, and an account of Curzon as foreign secretary. He also published a valuable study of the Congress of Vienna (1815). It was in 1939, ironically enough, that he published the first of his two general works on diplomacy, which was entitled simply *Diplomacy* (subsequently revised in 1950 and 1963) and had been foreshadowed by the 'Terminal Essay' in *Curzon: The Last Phase*. The second, called *The Evolution of Diplomatic Method*, appeared in 1954. Much of Nicolson's writing on diplomacy turns on the distinction between the *old and the *new diplomacy. On the former, which he strongly prefers, he is persuasive if hardly original; on the latter, while often acute, his sureness of touch is not so obvious. Nevertheless, he is always a pleasure to read, and his *Diaries* are justly famous.

nine/eleven. '9/11' is shorthand for 11 September 2001, the day of the *terrorist attacks by al-Qaeda on the World Trade Center (the 'Twin Towers') in New York and the Pentagon in Washington.

Nobel Peace Prize. A prestigious prize awarded annually by a five-member committee appointed by the Norwegian parliament from funds left in his will by Alfred Bernhard Nobel (1833–96), the Swedish industrialist who invented dynamite and became one of the wealthiest men in Europe. In his will, Nobel stated that prizes should be given to those who, during the preceding year, 'shall have conferred the greatest benefit on mankind' and that one part be given to the person who 'shall have done the most or the best work for fraternity between nations, for the abolition or reduction of standing armies and for the holding and promotion of

peace congresses'. Statesmen, *international organizations, and *non-governmental organizations have thus been strong contenders – and very prominent among the winners. The first (in 1901, with one other) was Henri Dunant, founder of the *International Committee of the Red Cross. In 2002 the prize was awarded to former US president, Jimmy Carter.

NO DIS. A US Foreign Service abbreviation employed by ambassadors on *telegrams to Washington when they want to get a wide hearing for their views. It stands for 'No Distribution', and thereby guarantees that everyone will want to see it!

Non-Aligned Movement (NAM). The movement consisting for the most part of *Third World states which had as its rationale a determination to resist pressure to abandon their *non-aligned stance. Its origins are to be found in a *summit meeting held in Bandung in Indonesia in April 1955, though it was not formally launched (in Belgrade, Yugoslavia) until 1961. Since the Lusaka summit in 1970, summit meetings of members have been held triennially.

non-alignment. The policy of refusing to join either of the military *alliance systems which were a key feature of the *Cold War.

non-diplomatic agent. An *agent (sense 3) who enjoys neither *diplomatic status nor *consular status. In the case of such agents who are posted at a capital city, their lack of diplomatic or consular status may be because their work is either insufficiently interstate in character (a tourist information officer, perhaps) or because it involves business activity. In the case of those outside the capital, diplomatic status is ordinarily unavailable, and while consular status might be appropriate (for a trade promotion officer, perhaps), it requires the existence of a *consular post in the city in question. If neither status is available or appropriate, it may be that the *receiving state will, by special arrangement or as a matter of courtesy, afford such agents certain limited privileges and immunities.

A state or territory which lacks *sovereignty (sense 1) may also, by agreement, appoint non-diplomatic agents to a foreign capital city or to a city which is not the capital. Palestine, for example (in the shape of the Palestinian Authority), has appointed a number of *'general delegations', each led by a *delegate-general (although the latter are often called ambassadors by the Authority). *See also* agent-general.

non-diplomatic relations. Relations and contacts (of a non-military kind) which occur between states in the absence of *diplomatic relations (sense 1). They may occur through a *protecting power or an *interests section, through *consular posts, or through ad hoc diplomatic encounters.

non-governmental organization (NGO). Though sometimes held to subsume the *multinational corporation, the usual connotation of this term is a private, non-profit-making body which has an international membership. Such bodies, especially when granted *observer status, are often active in *international organizations and major conferences. In order to distinguish them from national non-governmental organizations (a phrase sometimes heard in *International Relations (sense 3) circles but unknown in Political Science), NGOs are sometimes referred to as *international* non-governmental organizations (INGOs). Very roughly speaking, NGOs are to the *international society what pressure groups are to the state; hence the vogue for using the term 'civil society' (in its Hegelian sense) to refer to the sphere of free association in which they operate. A good example of an NGO is the International Committee of the Red Cross.

non-justiciable dispute. A dispute which is not considered by the parties to be capable of settlement by *adjudication. Such a view is not a reflection of the technical unsuitability of some disputes for adjudication as, formally speaking, any dispute can be settled by this means. But if the heart of the dispute is not about the application or interpretation of existing *international law, but is indicative of dissatisfaction with that law, adjudication will not provide a genuine settlement. It may therefore be more profitable to proceed by way of bilateral *negotiation, or by involving a third party – as in the use of *mediation, *conciliation, *good offices, or *inquiry. Non-justiciable disputes are sometimes called political disputes. *See also* justiciable dispute.

non-intervention. The doctrine that *intervention is improper. *See also Panch Schila.*

non liquet. The statement by an adjudicatory body that it is unable to decide a case because of the absence of relevant legal rules. It is thought to be a highly unlikely situation, as if the plaintiff's case is ill-founded, the court or tribunal would find in favour of the respondent. *See also* justiciable dispute; non-justiciable dispute.

non-paper. A near descendant of the *bout de papier* of traditional bilateral diplomacy, this term is now used, particularly in such bodies as the UN and the EU, to describe an authoritative but unofficial document circulated either by a member or by one of the organs of the organization. It is usually focused on a controversial question where the author either has not formulated an official position, or has but does not yet wish to imply commitment to it. The purpose of the non-paper is to test the reaction of the other members and hopefully to generate movement in *negotiations on the subject. Being unofficial, it can easily be abandoned if it should arouse strong opposition. Variations on the non-paper include the 'non-plan' and the 'non-map'. A non-map showing a suggested redrawing of the boundary between the Turkish and Greek zones of Cyprus was produced by the UN Secretary-General, Boutros Boutros-Ghali, in the early 1990s. *See also* flying a kite.

non-party. *See* third party.

non-resident mission. A diplomatic mission, the head and members of which are accredited to the *receiving state but are ordinarily resident in another state (possibly, even, their home state, or perhaps dispersed among several resident missions) from which, from time to time, they visit the receiving state. However, it is possible that one or more of its members may be permanently based at an outpost, or what may be referred to as a *satellite office, of the mission in the receiving state. Such an outpost may be staffed by junior officers, or meant to deal with non-political matters (sometimes called *'niche functions'). As such it is unlikely to be regarded as a diplomatic mission in its own right. Therefore, at its local address it may be called something like 'The Office of the Ruritanian

Embassy', with the address of the embassy being that of its non-resident head; and the outpost's head may be called 'the officer in charge', who will be responsible to the non-resident head of mission. Such arrangements seem to be becoming more common – and must be distinguished from ones (which appear to be less common) where the head of mission is non-resident but a diplomatic mission from the *sending state, called its 'Embassy' and headed by a *chargé d'affaires *ad interim*, is resident in the receiving state. *See also* multiple accreditation; resident mission.

non-self-governing territory. A *dependent territory, that is, one which does not enjoy *sovereignty (sense 1). *See also* colony; Committee of 24; Declaration on the Granting of Independence to Colonial Countries and Peoples.

non-state actor. An entity or group which seeks to have an impact on the internationally related decisions or policy of one or more states. Thus such an actor might be an *international organization, a *non-governmental organization, a *multinational corporation, armed elements seeking to free their territory from external rule, or a *terrorist group. A non-state actor may also be an individual.

non-tariff barrier. An obstacle to trade other than a tariff, such as an import quota or measures against dumping.

Nordic Council. An assembly of parliamentary delegates from Denmark, Finland, Iceland, Norway, and Sweden which advises the Nordic Council of Ministers on cooperation between these states in areas other than defence and foreign affairs. The Council's secretariat is in Stockholm, Sweden; that of the Council of Ministers in Copenhagen, Denmark. *See also* parliamentary assembly.

Nordic states. A common way of referring to the states whose parliamentarians are represented in the *Nordic Council.

normalization. (1) The restoration of *diplomatic relations (sense 1). (2) The restoration of diplomatic relations, plus a growth in trade, cultural exchanges, tourism, and other such indications of a close relationship.

This term has become an issue in Arab–Israeli negotiations, Arabs favouring the former definition, Israelis the latter.

North Atlantic Council. The governing body of *NATO. Chaired by the NATO Secretary-General, it is composed of *permanent representatives of ambassadorial rank of all alliance members and meets at least once a week. At least twice a year the Council also meets at foreign minister level, and it meets at the *summit as well when the occasion demands it. Nevertheless the Council's decisions have the same authority at whatever level they are taken. These decisions are arrived at on the basis of *'unanimity and common accord'. Many subsidiary bodies now exist to support the work of the Council.

note. (1) A strictly formal, third person, no-frills communication which is sometimes known as a *note verbale*. This is the customary mode of written communication between an embassy and a ministry of foreign affairs. A note is generally rubber-stamped at the bottom and initialled by the person authorizing its issue. Notes are generally numbered in sequence, starting again each year. (2) A note as in sense (1), except that it is couched in the first person singular (and hence is called a first person note). British requests for *agrément* are so sought (by the incumbent *head of mission in the state concerned). (3) A strictly formal communication from one state to another setting out the proposed terms of an *agreement or understanding between them. With a confirmatory reply an exchange of notes is thereby constituted, so establishing a *treaty or a *memorandum of understanding.

note verbale. See note.

nul et non avenu. Literally, null and void; traditionally the phrase used in refusing to accept an offensive message and returning it to the sender.

nunciature. A *diplomatic mission of the *Holy See. *See also* nuncio (sense 2).

nuncio. (1) In Europe in the middle ages, a *messenger or 'living letter'. (2) Since the sixteenth century, a resident representative of the *Holy See with the same *rank as an *ambassador. Accredited to the civil authorities, the nuncio – unlike the *apostolic delegate – has a political ('external') as well as religious ('internal') commission from the pope. At the Congress of Vienna in 1815 it was agreed that the papal nuncio would always be the *dean of the *diplomatic corps (and there is an echo of this in the Vienna Convention on *Diplomatic Relations). However, a predictable dispute subsequently arose as to whether the Regulation agreed at Vienna meant that any nuncio, wherever he was accredited, would head the local order of diplomatic *precedence, or whether he would only enjoy this in capitals where a nuncio was to be found in 1815. Today, it is only common to find the nuncio automatically made dean of the diplomatic corps in Roman Catholic countries. *See also* internuncio; nunciature; pro-nuncio; Regulation of Vienna; Vatican City State.

O

obedience, embassy of. *See* embassy of obedience.

object of international law. A real or notional person who, lacking *international personality, does not possess rights and duties under *international law. Although individuals are generally in this position, exceptions to it are made in respect of some matters which fall within *international criminal law.

observer mission. A mission with this function. In addition to *military observer groups and *permanent observer missions, such a mission may be established in relation to an individual event or proceeding of a domestic kind. Thus since the late 1980s the UN and other *international organizations have created numerous missions to engage in *election monitoring, the members of which tend to include election officers, area specialists, lawyers, and parliamentarians. Controversial trials are among other events which attract observer mis-

sions. All such missions can only operate with the consent of the *host state (sense 2). *See also* election assistance.

observer status. The status granted by an *international organization or conference to another international organization, *non-governmental organization, or state which is not a member of or participant in the organization or conference in question. The representative of such a body has no entitlement to take part in any vote or – in contrast to one enjoying *consultative status (sense 1) – to participate in formal discussions, although he or she may be invited so to do. Official observers are normally granted automatic access to *plenary sessions and may also be admitted to closed sessions of special interest to them; they are also usually provided with all non-confidential documents. The observing entity may try to use its position to influence informally some of the proceedings or, more generally, the attitude of the member or participating states towards it. For many years observer status was enjoyed at the headquarters of the *United Nations by certain states who did not wish to join or who could not obtain membership. The *Holy See still has a *permanent observer there. Non-governmental organizations and international organizations have greatly swollen the ranks of observers. It is not uncommon for hundreds of NGOs to have observer status at an international organization. *See also* permanent observer mission.

October War. The armed attempt by Egypt and Syria in 1973 to reclaim Sinai and the Golan Heights from Israel. Militarily it had little success; but politically it marked a turning point in favour of the Arab states. This was initially reflected in some subsequent Israeli disengagement from Arab occupied territory, engineered through the *shuttle diplomacy of Henry *Kissinger.

Since the Arab attack was launched on 6 October, that year's Israeli religious holiday of Yom Kippur – the Jewish Day of Atonement – the War is often referred to in Israel as the Yom Kippur War. In the Arab world it is known as the War of Ramadan, because it broke out during that year's month of Muslim fasting in daylight hours.

See also Six-Day War.

office of the deputy high commissioner. In a small number of *Commonwealth states, an office established outside the capital city by a *high commission to engage in *consular functions. Its head is designated a *deputy high commissioner (sense 2).

officer. A common term used within *diplomatic services today for any of their members.

officer-in-charge. The sort of title given to the head of a *satellite office of a *non-resident mission. As such an office is not, formally speaking, a *diplomatic mission of the *sending state in the *receiving state but an outpost of the sending state's non-resident mission to that state, its head cannot be given one of the titles by which heads of diplomatic missions are known.

official. A member of a state's civil or diplomatic service or of an *international organization's *secretariat. An official is therefore to be distinguished from a *minister (sense 3). *See also* international civil service.

official spokesman/woman. The official with the duty of making statements to the press on behalf of a ministry or delegation; in French *porte-parole*.

official visit (of head of state). *See* state visit.

old diplomacy. The essentially European diplomatic system which prevailed until the First World

War. It relied heavily on secret negotiations by professional diplomats based chiefly in resident embassies. Invented in Renaissance Italy, it was refined by *Richelieu, theorized by *Callières and provided with its manual by *Satow. While admitting its defects, Harold *Nicolson was among the more prominent of its defenders in the twentieth century. Oddly enough, while there are several *new diplomacies there appears to be only one old diplomacy.

open diplomacy. A rather loose phrase encapsulating the democratic doctrine that both in the making of foreign policy and the *negotiation and *ratification of agreements in its pursuit, the public – universally peace-loving – should be as fully involved as possible. Though the doctrine itself has been traced to Kant, the slogan is associated especially with the name of US president, Woodrow *Wilson, who led the American delegation at the Paris Peace Conference at the end of the First World War. It is to be found in the first of his famous Fourteen Points, which had been presented to Congress on 8 January 1918 as a propaganda counter-offensive to the recent Bolshevik revelation of the secret treaties negotiated during the conflict. Here, Wilson stated his belief that the programme for world peace must include 'Open covenants of peace, openly arrived at, after which there shall be no private international understandings of any kind but diplomacy shall proceed always frankly and in the public view'.

There is no doubt that Wilson, formerly an academician, was temperamentally as well as morally uncomfortable with diplomacy conceived as negotiation, and that it is right to regard him as the prophet of 'open diplomacy'. It is worth noting, however, that Wilson was not so naive as to believe that all negotiations could be successfully conducted under comprehensive and intimate public scrutiny (nor did he try to do this in Paris). Though the statement that covenants should be 'openly arrived at' certainly fostered this interpretation, it was an exaggeration for propaganda purposes which was soon corrected, though neither quickly nor publicly. On 12 March 1918, in a letter written to his secretary of state, Robert Lansing, Wilson stated that 'when I pronounced for open diplomacy I meant not that there should be no private discussions of delicate matters, but that no secret agreement of any sort should be entered into and that all international relations, when fixed, should be open, aboveboard, and explicit'. This was transmitted to Congress and included in the *Congressional Record* for 12 June. The same correction was included in the commentary on the Fourteen Points drafted by Frank Cobb and Walter Lippmann, approved by Wilson, and presented to the Allied Supreme War Council by Colonel House, the president's highly influential personal emissary, in October 1918. It was repeated by Wilson himself at a secret session of the Council of Ten on 13 January 1919. *See also* parliamentary diplomacy; secret diplomacy.

opinio iuris. *See* customary international law.

Oppenheim's International Law. A classic twentieth-century English-language work which is described by its current editors as a 'practitioner's book'. Lassa Oppenheim (1858–1919) was of German origin, but came to Britain towards the end of the century and was appointed a professor at Cambridge in 1908. He wrote the Introduction to the first edition of *Satow's Guide to Diplomatic Practice*. 'Oppenheim', as it became known, first appeared during the period 1905–6, and over the next 50 years, latterly revised by other hands, went through a number of editions – eight for Volume I on Peace and seven for Volume II on War. Hersch Lauterpacht had prepared the 5th, 6th, 7th and 8th editions and was working on the 9th when he died in 1960. After an interval of almost 40 years since its last revision, Volume I appeared in a 9th edition in 1992, edited by Judge Sir Robert Jennings and Sir Arthur Watts.

optional clause. The name given to Article 36(2) of the Statute of the *International Court of Justice, under which any party to the Statute may, in relation to any other state accepting the same obligation, become subject to the *compulsory jurisdiction of the Court. States are not on the whole very keen to do this. And such acceptances of the optional clause as have been made tend to be for a specific period of time, and to have reservations attached to them – which are sometimes far reaching. Thus the network of compulsory jurisdiction which exists is not extensive.

orator. (1) A professional speech-maker or teacher of speech-making. Orators were often employed on diplomatic missions in ancient Greece and in the fifteenth and sixteenth centuries were still employed by *envoys solely for the purpose of making an oration. *Wicquefort says of the *embassy of obedience that 'an orator, hired for that purpose, pronounces the harangue in the presence of the pope, and of the college of cardinals'. (2) In echo of this ancient usage, 'orator' was also a term commonly employed in this later period as a synonym for the envoy himself, reflecting as it did the importance attached at this period to the oration delivered by a special ambassador – usually in classical Latin – at his reception.

order of precedence. *See* precedence.

ordinaries. A diplomat's salary, as opposed to his *extraordinaries. Now historical.

ordre international public. Principles of international public policy; to all intents and purposes, a synonym for *ius cogens.*

Organization for Economic Cooperation and Development (OECD). Founded in 1961 to replace the Organization for European Economic Cooperation, it is a forum for the industrialized states to discuss and attempt to coordinate their economic and social policies. Its headquarters is in Paris, France.

Organization for Security and Cooperation in Europe (OSCE). This body is the successor to the Conference on Security and Cooperation in Europe, a *standing conference (also known as the Helsinki conference after the city in which the original agreement was signed) which served as a multilateral forum for dialogue and cooperation between East and West from 1975 onwards. With the end of the *Cold War in the early 1990s, the Conference became increasingly institutionalized and in 1995 was transformed into the OSCE. The aims of this organization are to prevent local conflicts, bolster European security, and build peaceful and democratic societies. The *heads of state or government of its 55 members (which include Canada and the United States) meet every other year; its Ministerial Council meets at least annually; and there is a Permanent Council responsible for routine operational tasks, composed of the members' *permanent representatives. The OSCE also has a *Parliamentary Assembly, a High Commissioner on National Minorities, and an Office for Democratic Institutions and Human Rights. It establishes ad hoc missions to serve as instruments of conflict prevention and *crisis management.

The Organization's headquarters is in Vienna, Austria. The OSCE is a testimony to the remarkable breaking down of barriers in Europe during the 1990s. It has no executive authority over its members, but does useful work, as in Kosovo, where it had 1400 observers until the start of the NATO bombing in March 1999 forced their withdrawal.

Organization of African Unity (OAU). *See* African Union.

Organization of American States (OAS). Founded in 1948, the OAS nevertheless has roots going back to the late nineteenth century. It aims to assist in the maintenance of peace on the American continent, has programmes to promote economic and social development, and latterly has put a good deal of emphasis on the promotion of democracy. For many years it was composed of the United States and the Latin American states, but now includes Canada and the non-Latin states of the Caribbean. The General Assembly of the OAS meets annually; a Meeting of Consultation of Ministers of Foreign Affairs is called whenever an urgent issue arises; and its Permanent Council meets on a permanent basis at the Organization's headquarters in Washington, DC, USA. The OAS also has a Juridical Committee to advise on such matters, and a Commission on Human Rights to watch over their observance. The Latin American states' reservations about some aspects of United States' activity on the continent (exemplified in the Organization's emphasis on *non-intervention) has sometimes manifested itself in the work of the OAS. But as these states are all committed to the maintenance of existing borders and, generally, to the *pacific settlement of disputes, the members have from time to time been able to work usefully together in this area.

Organization of the Islamic Conference (OIC). Founded in 1971 to promote solidarity and cooperation between Islamic countries, it has (at February 2003) 57 members and three states with *observer status. Its supreme organ is the Conference of the Heads of State, which meets every three years, and its Conference of Foreign Ministers meets annually. Its headquarters is in Jeddah, Saudi Arabia (the state which provides most of the OIC's funding, and therefore wields considerable influence within the Organization). Various of the OIC's members often find themselves at odds with each other, sometimes seriously, which obstructs much by way of common action. However, some observers have detected somewhat greater cohesion within the Organization during the 1990s.

oriental attaché. *See* dragoman.

oriental counsellor. *See* oriental secretary.

oriental secretary. A British subject proficient in local languages who held the rank of *secretary or *counsellor at British diplomatic and consular missions in the Near East (including Persia) in the nineteenth century and first half of the twentieth. (Oriental counsellors sometimes held the rank of counsellor only *locally.) Similar posts, also employed by the US Diplomatic Service at this time, were designated 'Chinese secretary' in Peking and 'Japanese secretary' in Tokyo. (French diplomacy employed a *secrétaire d'Orient* in the Near East and a *secrétaire d'Extrême-Orient* in the Far East.) The oriental secretary was one of the products of the strong nineteenth century reaction against the long-standing dependence of British diplomacy on the *dragomans of the Ottoman Empire, who had come to be widely distrusted for the most confidential work. Ronald Storrs, who held the post of oriental secretary at the British Agency and *Consulate-General in Cairo from 1909 to 1914, said that he was 'the eyes, ears, interpretation and

Intelligence (in the military sense) of his Chief, and might become much more'. Nevertheless, where an oriental secretary was posted at a major embassy, as for example in Istanbul, he was always subordinate to the *secretary of embassy.

Ottoman diplomacy. *See* dragoman; hostage; *sefaretname*.

outreach. As now used by *diplomats (sense 1), a broad and rather vague term signifying either *lobbying, networking, or *public diplomacy – or all three. *See also* diplomat-in-residence.

overseas mission. *See* mission.

overseas territory. *See* colony.

P

P5. *See* permanent members.

P-8. The 'Political 8'. This term was coined to describe meetings of the G7 group of Western industrialized states plus Russia in the period between 1994, when Russia attended a post-summit meeting with the G7, and 1998, when it became a full member, thus giving birth to the *Group of Eight. Until 1998, discussions involving Russia concentrated on political and security questions, to the exclusion of financial and most economic issues.

Pacific Community. Formerly known as the South Pacific Commission, this international body assists small island states and territories in the Pacific with the exploitation of their land, marine, and social resources.

pacific settlement. The process of trying to solve disputes by such means as *negotiation, *inquiry, *mediation, *conciliation, *good offices, *arbitration, *judicial set-tlement, and resort to regional agencies.

package deal. An agreement produced by exchanging concessions across a broad range of issues. *See also* Homans's theorem; linkage.

pacta sunt servanda. The principle that *treaties are *binding on the parties to them.

pacta tertiis nec nocent nec prosunt. The principle that *treaties do not impose any obligations, nor confer any rights, on third states.

Palácio das Necessidades. The Portuguese foreign ministry, so called because it has been based in the building bearing that name since 1911.

Panch Schila. The five principles of *peaceful coexistence attached to the Chinese-Indian Commercial Treaty of April 1954 (by which India recognized Chinese *suzerainty over Tibet): mutual respect

198

for sovereignty and territorial integrity, non-aggression, non-interference in domestic affairs, equality and mutual benefit, and peaceful coexistence.

paradiplomacy. International activity (typically *lobbying) by regional governments such as that of Quebec, and stateless nations such as that of the Kurds.

parallel reciprocity. A condition in which the parties to a conflict foster an atmosphere conducive to negotiations by simultaneous adoption of unilateral *confidence-building measures. The key point is that their actions should be simultaneous, thereby avoiding the risk of making the first conciliatory gesture and exposing themselves to charges of weakness or betrayal by hardliners. This term came to prominence during the period at the beginning of the 1990s when the United States was trying to persuade the Arabs (including Palestinians) and Israelis to attend a peace conference.

paraphe. *Initialling a document, either at the end or in the margin of each page. From the French *parapher*, to initial.

parking offences. *See* diplomatic privileges and immunities.

parliamentary assembly. In international relations (sense 2), an organ of or one related to an *international organization consisting of parliamentarians nominated by the member states. Parliamentary assemblies are therefore unelected, even though their members are elected representatives in their national parliaments. The *Council of Europe, *NATO, the *Nordic Council, and the *Western European Union all have parliamentary assemblies. The nominal purpose of such bodies is to bring a modicum of democratic accountability into intergovernmental organizations. Appointments to these bodies are also a useful source of government patronage.

parliamentary diplomacy. (1) *Multilateral diplomacy which takes place in public in the organs of an *international organization. A *parliamentary assembly does *not* engage in parliamentary diplomacy, such assemblies not being diplomatic organs. *See also* open diplomacy; propaganda. (2) Dialogue between the parliamentarians of different states. This is fostered by the Inter-Parliamentary Union, the Geneva-based world organization founded in 1889 and currently having as members over 100 national parliaments, and by regional inter-parliamentary organizations.

Partnership for Peace (PfP). The *NATO body designed to create an *entente-style relationship between NATO members themselves and like-minded non-member countries in Europe and Central Asia, notably those which emerged from the former Soviet Union or were part of the Soviet bloc.

party. (1) A *state which has adhered to a *treaty. (2) A state which is involved in legal proceedings and, by analogy, one involved in an international conflict.

passport. *See* ask for passports; diplomatic passport; handed his/her passports.

peace. In international legal terms, the absence of *war or *armed conflict.

peacebuilding. *See* peacemaking.

peace dividend. The great surge in funds which was supposed to become available for non-military spending in the West as military budgets were cut back in Europe and North America with the ending of the *Cold War at the beginning of the 1990s.

peace enforcement. The currently favoured name for action on the basis of *collective security. However, whereas collective security envisaged armed action against cross-border *aggression, peace enforcement also refers to such action taken within a state against internal disturbers of the peace.

peaceful coexistence. A Soviet foreign policy slogan during the *Cold War which usually meant conducting the struggle of

Communism against the capitalist world with sufficient restraint to avoid the risk of general war, i.e. mutual nuclear annihilation. It did *not* mean (as some in the West believed) 'live and let live'. It had its origins in the ideological convolutions of the Bolshevik leadership in the aftermath of the October Revolution of 1917. *See also* appeasement; Cuban Missile Crisis; *Panch Schila*.

peacekeeping. Impartial and non-threatening third-party activity taken at the request or with the consent of disputants who wish, at least for the time being, to live in peace. It may be embarked upon with a view to containing a *crisis, maintaining stability along a line of international division (perhaps in a *buffer zone), or resolving a dispute. Such activity was periodically taken throughout most of the twentieth century. But its distinctive characteristics were not delineated and conceptualized as 'peacekeeping' until the late 1950s and the early 1960s. This was a result of the pacifying role of the *United Nations in the *Suez crisis of 1956, which led to peacekeeping being seen by some as a specifically UN province. But that was a mistake: peacekeeping can be undertaken by any *international organization, group of states, or even by an individual state in which the disputants have confidence.

Typically, until the approach of the 1990s, peacekeeping was conducted by a small *international force made up of battalions seconded from suitable states, or by a group of *military observers made available on an individual basis by their states. Instances of current peacekeeping operations of this type include the UN Truce Supervision Organization (UNTSO) on Arab–Israeli borders; the UN Peacekeeping Force in Cyprus (UNFICYP), where it operates along the dividing line between Turkish-held northern Cyprus and the rest of the state; and the Multinational Force and Observers (MFO) – a non-UN body – in Sinai between Egypt and Israel.

Such operations are tending to become known as traditional peacekeeping, to distinguish them from the operations established in the 1990s – called, by some, second generation peacekeeping – which often included substantial civilian as well as military elements, and which sometimes were markedly more abrasive and less impartial than the earlier sort. This last type of activity, however, had by the end of the decade tended to develop into clear-cut *peace enforcement. In conceptual terms this is a good thing, since as a practical matter there is no real half-way station between (traditional) peacekeeping and activity which is willing to threaten and take armed action against one of the disputants. *See also* chief military observer; commander; contributor state; special representative (sense 1).

peacemaking. A term which encompasses the processes of *pacific settlement. But it may also go beyond them to refer to the creation of those attitudes, political arrangements, and underlying social and economic conditions which are sometimes thought to provide the only lasting basis for secure international and domestic peace. Such an approach is also known as peacebuilding.

peace process. A popular synonym for *negotiation or *diplomacy (sense 3) which aims at the resolution of a major conflict. It became current during the successful Egyptian–Israeli negotiations promoted by US President Jimmy Carter in the late 1970s. Subsequently it has been applied to much longer and less promising negotiations, more in the hope that peace may eventuate than on the basis of real progress in that direction. In such circumstances, use of the term – though well intentioned – is ill-advised since it may encourage the belief that peace is being made when in fact it is not.

peace support operation. A generic term used nowadays to refer to any *peacekeeping, *peacemaking, or *peace enforcement operation.

peace treaty. A *treaty which brings a *war to a conclusion.

Pentagon. A popular way of referring to the United States Department of

Defense, after the shape of the building in which it is located.

people's bureau. The name given by the Libyan government in 1979 to its *diplomatic missions abroad.

Permanent Court of Arbitration (PCA). Established by the *Hague Conferences of 1899 and 1907 the PCA is, as has often been said, neither permanent nor a court. Rather, it consists of a list of arbitrators (nominated by the parties to one or other of the Hague conventions regarding the PCA). When a dispute is submitted to it, each of the parties selects two arbitrators from the list (only one of whom may be its own *national (sense 2) or from the arbitrators it placed on the list), and they select a fifth. The award is given by majority vote. The PCA has not been much used since about 1930, but its Bureau has been active in facilitating ad hoc *arbitration.

Permanent Court of International Justice (PCIJ). Set up in 1921 and superseded in 1946 by the *International Court of Justice, which is in all essential respects similar to the PCIJ.

permanent delegate. A member of a *permanent delegation. This was the original title of *permanent representatives at the UN.

permanent delegation. The usual term for the *permanent missions which a number of members of the *League of Nations established to maintain contact with it. They were not necessarily resident in Geneva (the League's headquarters and meeting place); but the members of those *delegations that were came to receive certain privileges and immunities, and in time they were constituted as a formal *diplomatic corps. The members of the delegations were known as permanent delegates.

permanent diplomatic mission. Another name for a *diplomatic mission. *See also* permanent mission.

permanent members. The five states with permanent seats on the UN *Security Council – the P5 as they are often known: Britain, China, France, Russia, and the United States. Each of them enjoys the right of *veto. The Western permanent members are known as the P3. Since the early 1990s there has been much discussion about the enlargement of the Security Council and, in particular, about possible changes to the states entitled to permanent membership (which has remained unchanged throughout the UN's life). However, agreement on this matter has not yet emerged.

permanent mission. (1) The name given to a mission of permanent character sent to the headquarters of an *international organization by a member state. The mission represents the state at the organization;

maintains liaison between it and the *sending state; negotiates with and within the organization; reports on its activities; protects the sending state's interests in relation to the organization; and ensures the participation of the sending state in its activities (ordinarily it is the mission's personnel who participate on behalf of their state in the meetings of the organization's organs and committees). The *head of mission is called the state's *permanent representative to the organization.

If an organization is of particular significance for a state, and its degree of activity justifies such action, the state is likely to accredit a permanent mission to it. Virtually all members of the *United Nations, for example, maintain missions in New York, and the headship of such missions is one of the most important overseas appointments in their diplomatic services. However, there is no question of *agrément being required from the organization or from the head of its secretariat for the head of such a mission. This is because the organization is quite unlike an individual state, being instead a collectivity of states; nor is the *presentation of credentials by the *head of mission to the head of the organization's *secretariat attended by the formality which customarily and the pomp which occasionally marks the equivalent visit of an incoming head of mission to the receiving state's *head of state. Furthermore, the cre-

dentials with which the head of a British permanent mission is furnished are not called letters of credence but a *letter of introduction.

On the other hand, these procedural differences can once in a while eventuate in controversy over a head of mission's credentials. As these do not have to be cleared in advance, a civil conflict within a state can result in two claimants to a state's seat turning up at the organization, which then has to decide between them, or postpone the decision. Such matters are, of course, rarely subject to detached appraisal, but are determined by the political considerations involved and the relative number of votes that can be mustered by the backers of each claimant.

The members of a permanent mission (and also the officials of the organization to which they are accredited) are not hugely less in need of legal *privileges and immunities than the members of a diplomatic mission accredited to a foreign state. In immediate terms, this is a matter for the *host state (sense 2), which can be expected to attend to it by obtaining the necessary legislation. (If it did not wish to do so, it would hardly have agreed to play host to the organization, nor would the latter's members have settled on that location.) Generally, such privileges and immunities are not as extensive as those given to the members of embassies, but are reasonably liberal and sufficient for the missions' needs.

The Vienna Convention on the *Representation of States in their Relations with International Organizations of a Universal Character (1975) sets out one possible form of such privileges and immunities, but the Convention has not been widely accepted, let alone embodied by host states in their municipal law. The absence of *reciprocity in this matter means that it is difficult to bring effective pressure on hosts to accept what others judge to be a desirable international standard. (2) Sometimes 'permanent mission' is used as a synonym for a diplomatic mission accredited to a foreign state, more especially a *resident mission.

permanent neutrality. The position of those states which not only remain *neutral during all wars between third parties but accept no commitments in peacetime (*alliances or military base agreements, for example) which might lead them into *belligerency in some future contingency. This peacetime aloofness from military commitments might, as in the case of Sweden, be based on a purely unilateral political position which can, as a result, be changed unilaterally. Alternatively, it can derive from an international obligation. The paradigm case of this kind of permanent neutrality, sometimes regarded as the only true version, is Switzerland, at least since the Congress of *Vienna in 1815. Here it was declared that 'The neutrality and integrity of Switzerland and her independence from any foreign influence are in the interest of European politics as a whole'. Switzerland did not join the UN until September 2002. Austria also, by treaty, became a permanent neutral in 1955, but nonetheless decided to join the UN in the same year.

permanent observer. The head of a *permanent observer mission. *See also* observer status.

permanent observer mission. A mission, office, or *delegation headed by a permanent observer. States now tend to use the term 'mission' as the collective term for their observers, whereas *international organizations usually call it an 'office', but occasionally a 'delegation'. At the conference held in Vienna in 1975 on the *Representation of States in their Relations with International Organizations of a Universal Character, an argument arose as to whether such missions should be permitted 'representative', i.e. *diplomatic, functions. Successfully supporting this position were those – notably Switzerland and the *Holy See – who for political or religious reasons were unable to attain membership of an international organization but wished nevertheless to be as closely associated with it as possible. *See also* observer mission; observer status.

permanent representative. The head of a *permanent mission (sense 1). Although such officials are almost invariably given the personal title and status of ambassador, and are so spoken of, formally speaking they are not ambassadors to the international organization in question, as an ambassador is traditionally the representative of one head of state to another. *See also* permanent delegate.

permanent under-secretary of state (PUS). The title of the *official at the head of Britain's *Foreign and Commonwealth Office, who is also head of the *Diplomatic Service. In other words, Britain's senior *diplomat. The PUS is, of course, subordinate to the FCO's *ministers (sense 3).

perpetual neutrality. Another term for *permanent neutrality. By a *treaty of 1839 Belgium was declared to be perpetually neutral.

personal diplomacy. Activity of a diplomatic kind conducted by someone who is not a *diplomatic agent and may be acting without formal authorization or even encouragement, but whose personal standing ensures that he or she will be heard. A *head of state without executive power may engage in such activity, an instance being the role sometimes played by Britain's Edward VII (who reigned from 1901 to 1910). *See also* personal representative; track-two diplomacy,

personal envoy. *See* personal representative; special representative.

personal rank. Occasionally a diplomatic or consular officer has been permitted, for personal reasons, to use a diplomatic designation which is unrelated to his or her current responsibilities. Thus, an officer who has served as an ambassador or minister (sense 1) and then become a consul-general, may (as a matter of courtesy) possibly retain the former designation. Although this will probably be referred to as a personal rank, it is really not that but a personal title. *See also* career ambassador; career minister.

personal representative. A term which may be used for an individual charged with a specific diplomatic task by his or her *head of state or government. US presidents have often used personal representatives – or 'personal envoys' – to minimize congressional interference in their conduct of foreign policy. (Under the constitution the president can only appoint *special envoys as officers of the government with the prior 'advice and consent of the Senate'.) Such agents are usually not, therefore, 'personal' in the sense of being chosen because of any intimate personal relationship which they have with him, though they may be. US presidents can give any rank or title to a personal representative or, as with Harry Hopkins, who was employed in highly sensitive matters by President Roosevelt during the Second World War and was his intimate, none at all. The UN Secretary-General may also appoint a personal representative, perhaps to observe a critical situation, to assist in the attempt at its alleviation, or to head a *peacekeeping operation or a *peacemaking mission. Such an individual is likely, in UN terms, to be less senior than a *special representative (sense 1), but senior to a *representative. *See also* roving ambassador; special mission.

personal standard. The flag flown by a *head of mission on his or her means of transport. It may be a slightly altered national flag, such as the sending state's *diplomatic flag. For security reasons, such personal standards are sometimes not flown.

personal union. A term used prior to the early part of the twentieth century to describe the rare case of two *sovereign states that happened to have the same *head of state but nothing else in common.

***persona non grata* (png)**. The term used by a *receiving state to indicate that a *diplomatic agent or a *consular officer is no longer acceptable as such. Anyone so designated must be recalled by the *sending state. Other members of a *diplomatic mission or of a *consular post may also be declared unacceptable – but in their case the Latin expression is not used. They too must then be recalled or their functions with the mission or post terminated. A

receiving state is not obliged to explain its reasons for declaring persons *personae non gratae* or unacceptable. However, it is well understood that such reasons may include the belief that the individuals in question are engaged in *espionage, connected with terrorism or subversive activity, or have committed some other breach of the receiving state's criminal law. *See also* handed his/her passports; tit-for-tat expulsions.

piece of paper. *See bout de papier*.

pillar. A *European Union metaphor signifying one of the three areas of cooperation which it is hoped will eventually support a fully or at least more united Europe. These 'pillars' are the supranational institutions and policies of the Community ('first pillar'); the *Common Foreign and Security Policy ('second pillar'); and Police and Judicial Cooperation in Criminal Matters ('third pillar').

placement. *See* seating arrangements.

playing it long. A British diplomatic term, now somewhat dated, for procrastinating in a *negotiation in the expectation that future circumstances will put the other side in a weaker position, lead it to drop the issue altogether or see it disappear into political oblivion. The Florentines, who were also keen on this tactic, called it 'enjoying the benefit of time'. *See also* Guicciardini.

plebiscite. A vote by the electorate of a state or territory on a question of major importance, such as union with another state or (as for instance in a number of post-First World War plebiscites) which state the territory should join. Also called referendum.

plenary. The meetings of an international conference or organization which are empowered to take final decisions on the business in hand. All member states are entitled to attend plenary meetings (whereas some committees or working groups may have a limited membership), and are likely to be represented by the heads of their *delegations or missions.

plenipotentiary. A diplomat possessing *full powers (i.e. to sign a treaty). In the medieval period such an official was usually known as a 'procurator'.

plural accreditation. *See* multiple accreditation.

policy planning department. The department in the ministries of *foreign affairs of some states charged with engaging in medium- or even long-term foreign policy planning. To be able to do this, the planners are ideally given freedom from current operational preoccupations and permitted to work directly under the executive head of the MFA. A product of the period since the Second World War, policy planning departments were inspired in part by the model of the planning staffs long employed by military chiefs of staff. The EU has a similar department. Known as the 'Planning and Early Warning Unit', this operates under the *High Representative for CFSP.

political agent. *See* political resident.

political appointee. A *diplomat appointed from outside the ranks of the career *diplomatic service. Political appointments, which are normally made at *ambassador level in return for services rendered to the government (including financial campaign contributions), are much commoner in some countries than others. In the West, the United States is best known for this practice, and a law passed in 1980 which prohibited ambassadorial nominations as a reward for campaign contributions has had little effect. In British practice political appointments are remarkably rare. Even Mrs Thatcher, who was well known for her suspicion of the *Foreign and Commonwealth Office and British diplomats in general, made only one – and that was a recently retired former career diplomat. Political appointments, it need hardly be said, cause considerable resentment among the professionals.

political director. A common title for one of the most senior *officials, if not the most senior of all officials, in a ministry of *foreign affairs. The post normally carries with it direct responsibility for political – as opposed to commercial, consular and cultural – affairs. Regular meetings of the political directors of the MFAs of the EU's member states play a key role in its *Common Foreign and Security Policy.

political dispute. *See* non-justiciable dispute.

political officer. A common term for a post in the political section of an embassy, including a US embassy. The political officer, who especially in 'hard language' countries is a language and area specialist, deals with a wide range of subjects beyond the local power structure. Today, human rights is often part of the brief. *See also* chancery.

political reporting. Reporting from a *diplomatic mission to the ministry of foreign affairs on the local political scene which is not related to a specific *negotiation. Once one of the chief diplomatic (and often consular) tasks, political reporting came under attack with the late-twentieth-century explosion in the number and speed of alternative sources of information on world events, including most recently the internet. Nevertheless, states need political information on subjects which may not attract media attention or which are not penetrable by the media; they also need information presented in the context of specific policy analysis or recommendations – and they need to be certain that all of the information which they receive, including that on subjects which *does* attract media attention, is *accurate*. As a result, political reporting by embassies and consulates continues to be of considerable value and is unlikely to disappear.

political representative. *See* representative.

political resident. Also known simply as 'resident', the title used for the head of the British mission to the seven Trucial States of the (Persian) Gulf until their formal dependence on Britain was ended in 1971. This unusual term was employed because these entities (also known as the Gulf Sheikdoms) were 'British *protected states', for the conduct of whose foreign relations Britain was responsible under special treaty relations dating from the early nineteenth century. The head of the British mission was thus something more than an ordinary *ambassador. Based in Bahrain, the political resident's senior representatives in Abu Dhabi, Bahrain, Dubai, and Qatar were known as 'political agents', as was his subordinate officer in Kuwait (a protected but not a Trucial state). The term 'Trucial' arose from the assurances which used to be sought each year by Britain from the several rulers that they would observe a 'truce' – that is, would abstain from piracy.

polpred. The English representation of the term used by the Soviet Union in its early days to designate its *heads of mission, the traditional diplomatic titles being deemed bourgeois. The alternative Soviet term indicated, roughly speaking, that the person concerned was a representative of the people. Unfortunately for the Soviets, polpred was not a recognized diplomatic *class, with the consequence that its holders necessarily found themselves at the end of the line on any occasion on which diplomats were ranked according to *precedence. The traditional usage was soon resumed!

Ponsonby Rule. In British constitutional law, foreign policy, and hence the making and *ratification of *treaties, is the prerogative of the Crown. Some treaties, however, have always required parliamentary assent to take effect: for example, those ceding British territory, involving financial obligations, or requiring the modification of municipal law. Those apart, however, the government (acting in this area for the Crown) could, in theory, make what treaties it liked, and had no obligation to publicize this activity.

During the interwar period, the Labour government of 1924 intro-duced the rule that before a treaty was ratified it would be laid before both Houses of Parliament for 21 sitting days, thus allowing members of the legislature to comment. The junior *minister (sense 3) involved was called Ponsonby. The succeeding Conservative government abandoned the practice, but it was reinstituted when Labour was returned to power in 1929, and has since been followed.

Porte. *See* Sublime Porte.

porte-parole. *See* official spokesman/woman.

positive vetting (pv). A British term for the careful and 'proactive' investigation into the background not only of members of, or candidates for, the *intelligence services but also of anyone needing access to highly classified information, including – as and when the need arose – members of the *Diplomatic Service. Introduced in the 1950s following the discovery that the *KGB had recruited people while still at university who subsequently rose to senior positions, 'pv-ing' focused on detecting any association with extremist political organizations and any evidence of behaviour likely to render an *officer vulnerable to blackmail. ('Negative vetting' involves only checking to see if information in existing records has adverse security implications.) This procedure has now been replaced by 'developed vetting', a more flexible system by means of which the rigour of the investigation is varied according to (a) the degree of sensitivity of the information to which access is sought and (b) the extent to which the individual's security may be at risk.

post. The city or state where a *mission (sense 1) is located.

post differential. *See* hardship post.

pourparlers. *Negotiations.

pour presenter (cards). Cards which used to be left by diplomats making formal calls on fellow diplomats soon after their arrival in a capital. The practice seems now to have been discontinued, not least because of the great increase in the size of the average *diplomatic corps.

power politics. A loose term, generally used to express the belief that in the relations of states, power – especially military power – is crucial. However, its users tend to ascribe too sweeping a significance to military power; to suggest that power is sought by states as an end, whereas it is almost always wanted as a means to achieve certain ends; to give inadequate weight to the huge importance for states of cooperative activity; and to mislead by suggesting that power (of the appropriate kinds) is absent from domestic politics. *See also* realism (sense 3); *Realpolitik*.

precautionary principle. The assertion that, to safeguard the environment, all states have a duty to take precautionary action against possible dangers to the environment. It appears in some environmental *instruments, but is not (yet) a principle of *customary international law – and were it to become so its imprecision might lessen its utility. *See also* common but differentiated responsibility, principle of.

precedence. The order in which *diplomatic agents, when present in that capacity, are ranked. Until the early nineteenth century it often gave rise to considerable discord, as states sought the ranking for their diplomats which matched their own conception of their importance. An agreed solution to this problem was reached at the Congress of *Vienna (1815) in the shape of the *Regulation of Vienna, which received general acceptance. It has been echoed in the Vienna Convention on *Diplomatic Relations (1961). The position is now:

(a) As among *heads of diplomatic missions* in a particular capital, the order of precedence is divided into three classes, on the basis of the three *diplomatic classes into which heads of mission fall. Within each class, heads take precedence in accordance with the date and time at which they took up their functions. This is determined either on the basis of the presentation of their *letters of credence or *letters of commission to the *head of state or the presentation of a *working copy of them to the foreign ministry. Each *receiving state must determine which of these practices it adopts, apply it uniformly, and arrange for credentials to be presented in the order in which heads of mission arrive. (Equivalent arrangements must be made by Commonwealth states of the *Queen's Realms in respect of the presentation of *letters of introduction.) Thus the ambassador or high commissioner who has been longest in a particular capital will be at the front of the precedence line.

(b) The *head of a *special mission* to a particular state normally takes the same precedence as the head of his or her state's diplomatic mission to that state.

(c) The *heads of *permanent missions to the UN* have a different order of precedence each year, in accordance with the arrangements for the order of seating and *roll-call voting in the *General Assembly. This is decided at the start of each annual Assembly, when a member state is chosen by lot to take the first seat to the left in the front row, and the other members follow in English alphabetical order from left to right in each row of seats. *See also* alphabetical seating.

(d) As among the *staff of a state's diplomatic or permanent mission*, precedence among *diplomats reflects their *diplomatic rank (sense 1) and their seniority within that rank; as among *temporary diplomats, precedence is determined by the sending state. There are occasions when a *sending state may wish to obscure the significance of an individual's role within a mission, so that, e.g., a senior intelligence officer may be 'buried' well down the list.

(e) *Heads of *consular posts* rank within each class of head according to the date of the grant of the *exequatur, or the date of their provisional admission to the exercise of consular functions when it precedes the *exequatur*.

(f) *Honorary consular officers* who are heads of consular posts rank in each class after career heads, on the same basis as such heads.

(g) As among *consular officers at a state's consular post*, precedence is determined by the state in question.

A state's Order of Precedence refers to many other dignitaries besides diplomats.

precondition. A concession required of one party by another before agreeing to enter around-the-table *negotiations with it. More often a feature of adversarial relationships, insistence on preconditions is a common tactic of those who are least attracted to negotiations, either because they feel that time is on their side or because they fear that otherwise their supporters would suspect their real intentions. *See also* prenegotiations.

pre-emptive attack. *See* self-defence.

preferential trading agreement. One which involves discriminatory tariff barriers, and hence runs counter to the *most-favoured-nation principle.

prendre acte. To declare that note has been taken of a statement made by another party and that this may be brought up against it in the future.

prenegotiations. The first stage of a *negotiation, or that which precedes the formal 'around-the-table' stage. Prenegotiations are usually concerned with three questions: whether or not negotiations are a good idea; if so, what the *agenda should be; and how any formal negotiations should be conducted – that is, questions of procedure. Prenegotiations, especially where the agenda and composition of *delegations are concerned, are often thinly disguised talks of a substantive nature.

presentation of credentials. Inasmuch as, formally speaking, an *ambassador (sense 1) is the representative of the *sending state's *head of state accredited to the *receiving state's head of state, it is natural that his or her *letters of credence should be delivered personally to the latter. At one time this was of real significance, because of the political importance of *monarchs. Now it is, in its essence, a ceremonial occasion only. Indeed, it is no longer an essential prerequisite for an ambassador's *tour of duty formally to begin. And if some such

ceremony is still required, there appears to be no reason why it should not be conducted by a head of state's deputy, or some other appropriate personage – as has occasionally been considered or suggested in cases where the head of state is also *head of government, and therefore extremely busy. But there have been cogent objections to this idea: sending states would not like it, and the receiving state might also suffer some disadvantage, with the result that it has only rarely been adopted. Generally, therefore, the traditional ceremony continues, and often with some colour and pomp. Furthermore, the event can have some political value, especially for the sending state, inasmuch as it may afford an opportunity for a helpful private discussion between the newly accredited *head of mission and the head of state.

In most states the ceremony tends to conform to a similar pattern, but there are minor differences in the degree of formality and form of dress, and the personal style and temperament of the head of state may also affect the detailed procedure at the ceremony. Typically, the head of mission is escorted by the head of the foreign ministry's *protocol department or, in the case of Britain, by the *Marshal of the Diplomatic Corps, and perhaps by a senior *official or a *minister (sense 3). After the ambassador's introduction, short speeches are made (but in the United States the speeches are exchanged in written form), some light discussion ensues, and then a few members of the ambassador's mission and his or her spouse may be introduced. The ceremony is similar for a *high commissioner who is presenting *letters of commission to a head of state. But in Britain, whereas an ambassador is conveyed in a cotton-lined landau pulled by two horses, a high commissioner's coach is silk-lined and pulled by four (one of which is ridden by a postilion).

In respect of a high commissioner from one of the *Queen's Realms to another, credentials take the form of a letter of introduction from the sending state's prime minister to that of the receiving state, and are presented to the prime minister very informally. However, in London this last aspect of the procedure has recently been abandoned, because sometimes it was not possible to arrange an appointment for the new high commissioner to call on the prime minister for some considerable time. Instead, the letter of introduction is now delivered to the Foreign and Commonwealth Office in the same way as ambassadors and non-Realm high commissioners deliver *working copies of their letters of credentials and letters of commission. In consequence of the use of letters of introduction, high commissioners to Britain from one of the Queens (other) Realms do not meet the Queen at a credentials ceremony soon after their arrival. So that such diplomats do not feel left out, a special audience of the Queen is arranged for them shortly after they have taken up their position – but, as this is not a ceremonial occasion, they have to make do with travelling to it by their own car (which is often a matter of regret!).

presents. *See* decorations.

presidential statement. One made by the president of the UN *Security Council on behalf of all its members.

prestige. Reputation for power.

prevailing language. An additional language in which some treaties are drawn up and which prevails in the event of any divergence of interpretation of a point between the versions cast in the languages of the parties. The Egyptian–Israeli Peace Treaty concluded with the following statement: 'Done at Washington, D.C. this 26th day of March, 1979, in triplicate in the English, Arabic, and Hebrew languages, each text being equally authentic. In case of any divergence of interpretation, the English text shall prevail.'

Prevention and Punishment of Crimes against Internationally Protected Persons, including Diplomatic Agents, Convention on. Adopted by the UN General Assembly in 1973, the Convention came into force in 1977, and as of late 2002 has 121 *parties. Each of them is obliged to take appropriate measures, including ones of co-operation with other states, to ensure that the purposes of the Convention are achieved.

preventive diplomacy. A term used by the UN's second *Secretary-General, Dag Hammarskjöld, to refer both to his *'quiet diplomacy' and to *peacekeeping operations. It then fell into disuse. But in 1992 the then Secretary-General, Boutros Boutros-Ghali, called for more 'preventive diplomacy', by which he meant not just his personal diplomatic activity but also fact-finding and the 'preventive deployment' of 'peacekeeping' missions within and between states, the latter not necessarily with the agreement of both sides. A mission with this term in its title operated on the Macedonian border with Yugoslavia and Albania from 1995 to 1999. The variety of activities that the term has been used to designate makes it an unsatisfactory one.

principal. A *delegation leader of high political standing, typically a *head of state or government or a government *minister.

privileges and immunities. *See* consular privileges and immunities; diplomatic privileges and immunities; permanent mission.

Privileges and Immunities of the Specialized Agencies, Convention on. A convention approved by the

UN General Assembly in 1947. Rather more than half the world's states have become *parties to it.

Privileges and Immunities of the United Nations, General Convention on. Adopted by the *General Assembly in 1946, the Convention has been accepted by three-quarters of the UN's members. It provides for the UN's immunity from jurisdiction, the inviolability of its premises and papers, certain currency and fiscal privileges, and *freedom of communication. It also entails full 'diplomatic' immunity for the UN's senior personnel, and immunity in respect of the official acts of lesser officials. However, even for those states which have become parties to this Convention, national legislation will normally be required for the UN's privileges and immunities to be recognized within the legal system of any particular state. (One well-known derogation from the position set out in the General Convention is that the United States refuses to exempt from US taxation those of its nationals who are members of the UN *Secretariat.) *See also the entry which begins* Headquarters of the United Nations.

prize court. *See* blockade.

procès-verbal. *See* minutes.

proconsul. A term frequently applied with rhetorical flourish to a grand and senior figure in the administration of an empire, particularly a colonial governor, in the age of European imperialism. ('Proconsul' was the title given to the commanders of armies or governors of provinces of the Roman Empire.) The *Viceroy of India was typically seen as a proconsul, though he would have resisted most strenuously the suggestion that he was a mere colonial governor.

pro-consul. A rank sometimes given to *consular officers who come immediately below vice-consul. For many years it was British practice to employ pro-consuls for the purpose of administering oaths, taking affidavits or affirmations, and performing notarial acts. The rank is not widely used.

procurator. See plenipotentiary.

progressive development. The alteration of or the settling of apparent inconsistencies in *international law. See also codification; International Law Commission.

pro-memoria. See aide-mémoire.

pro-nuncio. The title preferred to *nuncio for the *Holy See's diplomatic representative of *ambassadorial rank in states which refuse automatically to permit this envoy to be *dean of the *diplomatic corps. If there is no 'nuncio', the question of his *precedence provided for under the terms of the *Regulation of Vienna of 1815

cannot arise. See also apostolic delegate; internuncio; nunciature; Vatican City State.

propaganda. The use of mass communications to reinforce or change public opinion, domestic or foreign. If the source is openly admitted it is known as 'white' propaganda; if concealed or misrepresented, as 'black' propaganda. Traditionally regarded in International Relations (sense 3) as the antithesis of *diplomacy (sense 1) because of its noise, tendency to mendacity, and design to appeal to the people over the head of the government, propaganda is not necessarily anti-diplomatic; it all depends on its content. For example, propaganda may be used to help break an *impasse in negotiations by testing the water with new ideas, or to sustain the momentum of faltering talks by 'talking them up'. See also megaphone diplomacy.

protected state. (1) A *sovereign state which, by *treaty, has placed itself under the general protection of another. This almost always involves the conduct by the stronger state of the foreign relations and defence of the weaker one. The terminological expression of this status – and, indeed, the status itself – was deeply out of step with the ethos of the later twentieth century, so that all treaties of protection appear to have been brought to an end by 1971. However, much of the substance of the status has been incorporated in the Compacts of Free Association made since the mid-1980s between the Marshall Islands, Micronesia, and Palau on the one hand and the United States on the other, whereby the latter has full responsibility for the defence – but not for the foreign relations – of these very small sovereign states. *See also* associated state; political resident; protectorate. (2) A state whose interests in a second state are protected by the diplomatic mission of a third. *See also* interests section; protecting power.

protecting power. (1) A state which is in that relationship to a *protected state (sense 1). (2) A state which undertakes to protect the interests of a second state in the territory of a third. This important diplomatic institution originated in the sixteenth century in the right asserted by the French court – for reasons of prestige and economic gain – to protect the interests of any Christians whose business or pleasure took them to the Ottoman Empire and found themselves without the protection of diplomats from their own state. The responsibility was discharged, in the face of increasing competition from other European powers, by the French *embassy (sense 3) in Istanbul and its outlying *consulates. Protecting powers are still employed by states which feel that their interests in another do not justify the expense of a mission but today they come into

play chiefly as a result of a breach in *diplomatic relations (sense 1). For example, following the breach between Iran and the USA in 1979, Switzerland became the protecting power for the United States in Tehran, while Algeria assumed the same role for Iran in Washington. The institution is enshrined in the Vienna Convention on *Diplomatic Relations (1961). *See also* interests section.

protectorate. (1) In much international terminology, a synonym for *protected state (sense 1). (2) In the 1990s the term was used (as in reference to the Serbian Province of Kosovo) to refer to that part of a *sovereign state over which a group of third states or an *international organization exercises effective authority. (3) In British constitutional terminology, a territorial entity which, while not formally a part of the monarch's dominions, is treated as if it were. To all intents and purposes, therefore, British protectorates were in the position of *colonies. None of Britain's remaining *dependent territories enjoys this status.

protest. A formal expression of one state's strong dissatisfaction with an aspect of the policy of another. Depending on the importance of the issue, it may be personally delivered to the head of the offending state's *diplomatic mission by the *foreign minister of the protesting state or by one of its *officials, and/or by *note (sense 1). *See also* *démarche.*

protocol. (1) Rules of diplomatic procedure, notably those designed to accord to the representatives of *sovereign states and others, as well as different *classes of officers within them, the treatment in all official dealings to which their recognized status entitles them. Public occasions present the most testing times for such rules, and it is for this reason that a state's chief of protocol has in the past sometimes been known as its 'master of ceremonies'. (2) An annex to a *treaty. (3) An agreement of a less formal kind than is usually connoted by the word 'treaty'. (4) The *minutes of a conference or a formal record of what has happened, e.g. a protocol of deposit of an instrument of *ratification. (5) A treaty signed in order to elaborate a *framework treaty.

provisional entry into force of treaties. *See* entry into force.

proxenos. In ancient Greece, a citizen appointed by a foreign government to defend its interests in his own state, as Cimon the Athenian statesman was appointed by Sparta to look after Spartan interests in Athens. The *proxenoi* were usually leading political and social figures who were glad to have this public testimony that their reputations extended beyond the borders of their own states. Appointments were often made hereditary. Resembling the modern day *honorary consular officer, the *proxenos* – citizenship only excepted – was the forerunner of the *resident ambassador created in Italy during the late fifteenth century.

proximity talks. *Negotiations conducted between hostile parties via an intermediary, usually at the same *venue but without face-to-face contact between the adversaries. Commonly occasioned by the refusal of one party to recognize the legitimacy of the other, their physical proximity at least makes the intermediary's task of communication somewhat easier, and also has *propaganda advantages for both parties: to the one refusing *recognition, that of *signalling to the outside world that this obstacle will not be allowed to stand in the way of peace; to the one anxious to obtain it, that of suggesting that recognition is no longer so far off. The UN-brokered negotiations on the Greek island of Rhodes during 1949, which led to armistice agreements between Israel and her four Arab neighbours, were something in the nature of proximity talks. Such talks under UN *mediators were also employed at the *Palais des Nations* in Geneva in the mid-1980s to produce a settlement between Afghanistan's Soviet-backed regime and Pakistan, as the latter refused to recognize the former. They were also employed by the United States at the talks held in 1995 in Dayton,

Ohio (at an air force base) with a view to generating a breakthrough on the problem of Bosnia. *See also* contact group.

proxy. This term is a contraction of 'procuracy' and has two closely related meanings relevant to diplomacy: (1) Acting via another, as in negotiating, fighting, or voting 'by proxy'. (2) One who acts on behalf of another. *See also* plenipotentiary; representative; representative character.

public diplomacy. Not to be confused with *open or *parliamentary diplomacy, a late-twentieth-century term for *propaganda conducted by *diplomats.

publicist. A learned writer on *international law.

public minister. Sometimes also *'foreign minister', the term for a *diplomatic agent of any class before the word *'diplomat' came into common usage, though the term *ministres publics* remained current in French diplomacy until well into the twentieth century. In 1758 *Vattel said that 'This expression, in its most general sense, is used of every person intrusted with the management of public affairs, but it is particularly applied to those who are appointed to fulfil such duties at a foreign court.'

puppet state. A *sovereign state which appears to move not just at the will of a stronger state (which is not unusual internationally) but only at its will. It is an imprecise term, but is probably best used to refer to a less independent situation than that indicated by the terms *dependent state or *satellite state. *See also* sphere of influence; vassal state.

pursuivant. In medieval diplomacy, a *herald's assistant.

Q

Quai d'Orsay. The French Ministry of Foreign Affairs, which settled in the purpose-built palace on the *quai d'Orsay* (no. 37) in Paris in 1853.

qualified majority voting (QMV). The term for the system of *weighted voting employed by the EU's *Council of Ministers. The weighting of each member state's votes is based on population, though the system has always favoured the smaller states. (In practice, most decisions in the Council are still reached on the basis of *consensus.) *See also* constructive abstention; unanimity.

Queen's Commissioner. A term employed in the mid-nineteenth century by the British to describe what soon came to be known instead as a military, and subsequently as a *service, attaché.

Queen's Messenger. 'King's Messenger' when a king is on the throne, a full-time British *diplomatic courier. The origins of the King's Messengers have been traced to the late twelfth century but it seems to have been Henry VIII, not least because he saw advantage in employing them in a quasi-police role as well, who first gave real impetus to their development. In 1547, the last year of his reign, he decided that the King's Messengers – at that time 40 strong – should be formed into a Corps of King's Messengers and placed under the control of the Lord Chamberlain. Further regularization occurred in 1772, but it was 1824 before the King's Messengers were constituted on the basis which still obtains today. In that year, at the instigation of the Foreign Secretary, George Canning, and with the willing assent of George IV, the *Foreign Office took over their financing and control. Henceforward, the 'King's Foreign Messenger Corps' became the overseas messenger service for the whole of the government (including the royal household). Previous abuses were also addressed, notably by tightening up conditions of entry. From this time onward, King's Messengers had to be British subjects, preferably former officers in the armed services, under thirty-five on the date of their appointment, adept in foreign languages and unlikely to fall off a galloping horse. These conditions were never substantially modified, the preference for former serving officers remaining particularly marked. Of all possible candidates, such men were thought most likely to be loyal, resourceful, and disinclined to be meek in asserting their legal rights of immunity in the face of ignorant or truculent border officials. In the period between the great improvement in roads in the later eighteenth century and the solid advance of the railways by the middle of the nineteenth, King's Messengers maintained their own carriages at Dover, which had seats which could be turned into beds. Always likely to be attacked for the large sums of money which they had to carry to meet their heavy expenses as well as for the secrets contained in their *despatches, their carriages also had racks for arms, at a minimum two pistols and a sword. East of Berlin or south of Vienna they were generally forced onto horseback again, and had to be accompanied by a guide and two guards – or even, over certain stages, by a troop of cavalry loaned to them by the King of Prussia or Habsburg Emperor.

Today, the Queen's Messengers, whose work remains important, are more likely to be found in a plane than on the back of a horse, and each flies on average 250,000 miles a year on duty (since the late 1980s, 'club' class rather than first class). Until 1960, teams of messengers were stationed abroad in good centres for civil airline connections, and by 1945 there were ten such teams. However, the vast improvements in international air transport over the past five decades have made it possible for all journeys to start and finish in London, and the system of stationing Queen's Messengers abroad was ended. The strength of the corps fluctuated between 40 and 50 over the 1945–80 period but since then has declined steadily, most recently because the end of the *Cold War reduced the number of classified documents to be carried and the frequency with which diplomatic missions had to be visited. The establishment is now 15 and, as far as despatches are concerned, only those classified as 'secret' or above are carried. (Commercial organizations now carry most mail classified as 'confidential' or below.) The badge of office of the Queen's Messengers remains the *silver greyhound. *See also* casual courier; diplomatic bag; express; freedom of communication.

Queen's Realms. *Sovereign states whose *head of state is The Queen of, among other states, the United Kingdom of Great Britain and Northern Ireland. *See also* Commonwealth; high commissioner.

quid pro quo. In *negotiation, something given in return. *See also* concession (sense 1).

quiet diplomacy. The conduct of business in the style of *bilateral diplomacy (both senses) by someone who is not a *diplomatic agent and whose public manner of doing things is usually different. The term was notably associated with the UN's second Secretary-General, Dag Hammarskjöld.

R

raison d'état. Shorthand for the doctrine that the moral codes generally prevailing in relations between individuals may be ignored by government agencies if the security of the *state is in jeopardy. In other words, it is the doctrine that governments may do anything, such as breaking promises, ordering assassinations, or making alliances with heretics and infidels, if they believe such actions are necessary to preserve the state. Originating in the thought and practice of Renaissance Italy, where it was first labelled *ragione di stato*, *Richelieu was perhaps its most celebrated practitioner. *See also* Barbaro; Guicciardini; Machiavelli.

Ramadan, War of. The Arab states' term for the *October War (1973).

rapid reaction embassy. (1) Equipment held on standby for the emergency despatch of a *diplomatic mission. Such a need might arise in respect of a state which has been subject to such internal tribulation that the *sending state's previous *embassy (sense 1) is either destroyed or without the means necessary for the staff to be self-sufficient; or in respect of a state in which the sending state has not hitherto had a *resident mission but to which the despatch of such a mission is now deemed to be very urgent. Modelled on army mobile field headquarters, a rapid reaction embassy typically consists of large containers holding essential equipment (notably for satellite communications, encryption, computing, and power generation) and prefabricated accommodation if necessary. Also called a flat-pack embassy. (2) A colloquial way of referring to an embassy which has been so established.

rapporteur. At a conference, the person chosen to draft a report on the work of a committee or working group and, when it is agreed, present it to the *plenary body on the committee's behalf. Since the report will usually contain proposals and the reasons for them, the opportunity to produce the first draft provides the *rapporteur* with a position of some influence.

rapprochement. An overcoming or putting aside of previous difficulties in *diplomatic relations (sense 2), a reconciliation and growth in intimacy. The term was commonly employed to describe the improvement in relations – at first cautious and slow, then dramatic and rapid – between the United States and the People's Republic of China at the beginning of the 1970s: 'the Sino-American rapprochement'.

ratification. The formal act whereby a state consents to be bound by a *treaty which it has already *signed. Some treaties, in accordance with their terms, become operative as from signature – in which case the signature is referred to as 'definitive'; but others require ratification for them to become *binding on a signatory. Some states use the terms 'acceptance' or 'approval' to express their ratification of a treaty, and *international organizations expressing their consent to be bound by a treaty tend to describe this consent as an 'act of formal confirmation'.

The practice of ratification was institutionalized at a time when poor communications made it difficult if not impossible for there to be any certainty that negotiators had not exceeded their *instructions, or that their masters had not changed their minds altogether since despatching them. It is a procedure still valued for the opportunity for second thoughts which it provides and the greater authority which it lends to treaties. Furthermore, the constitutions of some states require that treaties, or certain kinds of treaties, must have the approval of a body such as parliament, in which case it is clearly necessary – from a domestic point of view – that the treaties signed by these states should be subject to ratification. One well-known instance of this is the need for treaties to which the United States becomes *party to have received the approval of its Senate. By contrast, there is no equivalent requirement in Britain, although it is customary to seek specific parliamentary approval for very important treaties. Another reason for the requirement of ratification is that all states will in respect of some treaties need to pass domestic legislation for the treaties to take effect.

As to the form ratification takes, usually it is an act of the *head of state, but in some cases it may be an act of the government or of the foreign minister. For the ratification to be effective in establishing the state's consent to be bound, it must then be directly passed to the other signatories or lodged with the *depositary nominated by the treaty. It must be remembered that ratification does not necessarily result in the treaty's immediate *entry into force. *See also* executive agreement; Ponsonby Rule.

realism. In the study of *International Relations, a label either for (1) views or policies which pay more respect to what is achievable in practice than what might be ideal – first strong in the work of *Machiavelli and influenced by a low view of human nature; (2) the doctrine that the focus of the subject should be the interplay of states, in which case 'Realism' is usually written thus, i.e. with a capital letter; or (3) the position of those scholars who believe, generally in conjunction with the preceding sense, that states aim primarily at dominance over other states, in this event the label also being normally employed with a capital letter. *See also* idealism; power politics; *Realpolitik*.

Realpolitik. The German term for political *realism (sense 1), attributed to Ludwig von Rochau, who published *Grundsätze der Realpolitik* in 1853. It is now usually contrasted with '*Idealpolitik*' or *idealism.

rebus sic stantibus. *See clausula rebus sic stantibus*.

recall. (1) The temporary or permanent withdrawal of a *diplomatic mission. The latter eventuality, it should be noted, does not necessarily entail the breach of *diplomatic relations (sense 1). (2) The temporary or permanent recall of a *head of mission. A temporary withdrawal often indicates the *sending state's displeasure with some act of the *receiving state. A permanent recall generally indicates that the head of mission's *tour of duty is being brought to a normal end. *See also* letters of recall.

receiving line. A device for the efficient welcoming of guests, at an embassy reception this is a line generally composed of ambassador and spouse together with any guest of honour. (At a big reception, selected senior diplomatic staff may also stand in the line.) As host, the ambassador will head the line, though a butler or other aide will sometimes stand in front to elicit and announce accurately the names of the guests, who then proceed down the line. Hosts normally 'receive' in this way for about half an hour after the time stated for the reception on the invitation. However, at a *national day reception, for example, standing in line to welcome late arrivals may well merge into bidding goodbye to early departers, thus occupying virtually the whole period of the function.

receiving state. The state which agrees to receive a *diplomatic or a *special mission from another state. It is also sometimes spoken of as the *host state.

reception. The formal welcome extended by the *receiving state to a new *head of mission. Unless it happens that *presentation of credentials is to take place very soon after the new head's arrival, the reception is likely to take the shape of an audience with the minister of foreign affairs. A reception will also be arranged for a *special mission.

reciprocity. The principle stipulating that if one state acts in a certain way towards a second, the latter is very likely (provided it is practical for it to do so) to claim the right to reply in kind. Very influential, this principle underlies much state behaviour, diplomatic intercourse not least, and thus contributes to ensuring the observance of legal obligations. *See also* bilateral diplomacy; diplomatic privileges and immunities; diplomatic representation; international law; tit-for-tat expulsions.

recognition. A state's acknowledgement of a situation, with the intention of admitting its legal implications.

recognition of a government. The *recognition by one state of a new government in another, especially one which has come to power by unorthodox means. During the past two decades many states have abandoned the practice. This policy has the advantage both of avoiding the accusation that recognition of a government implies approval, or non-recognition disapproval; and in a civil war of easing the establishment of diplomatic contacts with rebel groups with a view to protecting the interests of the *sending state. *See also de facto* recognition; *de jure* recognition; Estrada doctrine.

recognition of a state. The *recognition by one state of another, extended either explicitly or implicitly. It is often said that this should be granted if the aspirant state meets the conditions stipulated in the *Montevideo Convention (1933). However, in practice the decision whether or not to grant recognition of a state (and also *recognition of a government) is often a political act. Recognition of a state is distinguishable from and a prerequisite for the establishment of *diplomatic relations (sense 1). However, unlike the latter, recognition is a unilateral act. A breach of *diplomatic relations (sense 1) does not imply a withdrawal of recognition. Indeed, if the facts remain the same, recognition cannot be withdrawn. *See also de facto* recognition; *de jure* recognition.

recredential. In French a *lettre de récréance*, this is a letter of acknowledgement written by the head of a *receiving state to the head of a *sending state on receipt from the latter of *letters of recall of his or her ambassador. Usually formulaic, it expresses satisfaction at the agent's conduct and regret at his or her departure.

Redcliffe, Lord Stratford de. *See* Canning, Stratford.

Red Cross. *See* International Committee of the Red Cross.

Red Cross Conventions. The chief embodiments of *international humanitarian law, these are the four conventions, alternatively known as the 'Geneva Conventions', which were agreed at Geneva in 1949 and are still in force today. They deal respectively with (i) the care of the wounded and sick members of armed forces in the field; (ii) the care of the wounded, sick and ship-wrecked members of armed forces at sea; (iii) the treatment of prisoners of war; and (iv) the protection of civilian persons in time of war. Almost all states are party to these important and – at least in the last regard – innovative Conventions. Nevertheless, post-1949 changes in methods of warfare, among other things, required greater attention to be given to the protection of the civilian population against the direct effects of hostilities. As a result, in 1977 two new treaties of international humanitarian law were adopted: the 'Protocols additional to the Geneva Conventions'. A clear majority of states are today bound by at least one of these. *See also* International Committee of the Red Cross.

red line. Another term for a *fallback position.

red memo. A message of rebuke sent to one of its diplomats by a ministry of *foreign affairs.

referendum. *See* plebiscite.

Refugees, Convention Relating to the Status of. Signed at a UN conference held at Geneva in 1951, it *entered into force in 1954, and has been *ratified by about three-quarters of the world's states. Broadened by a 1967 Protocol, the Convention confers refugee status on those who find themselves in a member state and are deemed by the latter to satisfy the Convention's requirements.

regime. *See* international regime.

regional customary international law. *See* special customary international law.

regional organization. An *international organization whose members are restricted to a region (loosely interpreted), such as the *African Union or the *League of Arab States.

registry. The section of a ministry of foreign affairs or of a diplomatic mission in which mail is handled and documents are – or should be – registered, filed, and indexed by archivists. *See also* chancelier; diplomatic archives.

Regulation of Vienna (1815). A landmark in the development of diplomatic procedure which was agreed at the Congress of *Vienna. The Regulation divided *heads of mission into three classes: (i) *ambassadors, *legates or *nuncios (who alone had the *representative character); (ii) *envoys, ministers or others, accredited to sovereigns; and (iii) *chargés d'affaires, who were accredited only to the minister for foreign affairs. (This was modified at the Congress of Aix-la-Chapelle in 1818 by the insertion of another class – minister *resident – between envoys and chargés d'affaires, thereby making four classes in all.) However, the radical development came in article 4, under which it was agreed that, henceforward, within each class heads of mission would take *precedence according to the date of the official notification of their arrival at their posting. See also diplomatic classes; presentation of credentials.

reis effendi. A high official of the Ottoman government directly subordinate to the *grand vizier. Originally head of the chancery of the sultan's *divan* (council), he later came to act as secretary of state and minister of foreign affairs.

relation. An early modern term for a detailed report from a diplomat or consul on a particular subject, usually attached to a *despatch. 'I have bene large in this subject [Barbary pirates] in former relations', Sir Thomas Roe, English Ambassador in Istanbul, informed King James I in March 1621. Such reports did not compare with the quite unique Venetian *relazioni*.

relazione. A detailed account of the political, military, economic and social conditions within a state produced by the *Venetian diplomats who had served there. Dating from the second half of the thirteenth century though not achieving its final form until the sixteenth, the *relazione* was much fuller than a *despatch and was updated by each successive ambassador and solemnly read to the senate on his return. The Venetian *relazioni* were unique and acquired great fame; as a result, copies were bought both by governments and collectors. They were not, however, universally admired. *Torcy, the bustling foreign minister of Louis XIV, who required a written *mémoire* or final report from his own envoys on their return from abroad, noted tersely that the Venetian style contained 'beaucoup de paroles, nulle conclusion'. See also sefaretname.

RELEX. From *Relations Extérieure*, a common abbreviation for directorates-general of the *European Union dealing with *Common Foreign and Security Policy, trade, development, and enlargement.

reparation. (1) The redress of an illegal act. See also damages. (2) Compensation exacted for an act which is deemed to have been politically or morally improper (usually both). Victors in *war have sometimes exacted reparations from the defeated states – as instanced notably in the 1919 Treaty of Versailles made at the conclusion of the First World War.

representation. (1) A synonym for *diplomacy (sense 1). See also diplomatic functions; representations. (2) The ceremonial and social – and often extremely tedious – side of the work of a diplomatic agent, especially an ambassador. Apart from entertaining and attendance at state ceremonial occasions, 'representational duties' include such chores as standing in line at the airport with the rest of the *diplomatic corps to welcome some foreign dignitary to the country. (3) The permanent mission abroad of a body such as the *European Commission. The Commission has 'Representations' in all of the member states of the *European Union. (4) In the plural, an umbrella term for diplomatic missions *and* consular posts. *See also* representative character.

Representation of States in their Relations with International Organizations of a Universal Character, Vienna Convention on (1975). This deals with the position (including the privileges and immunities) of *permanent missions, *permanent observer missions, and of *delegations to organs of *international organizations and to conferences convened by and under the auspices of international organizations. As of October 2002 it remained five *ratifications short of the 35 needed for it to *enter into force, *host states (sense 2) in particular being unhappy at the extent of the privileges and immunities which it proposes. Meanwhile, the position of missions and delegations is regulated by specific agreements

between individual host states and the organization concerned.

representations. Diplomatic language for a mild, or at least relatively mild, protest: 'I have been making representations to the MFA about their disregard of the German Ambassador's privileges and immunities.'

representative. All heads of mission represent their states, but the term representative does not usually appear in the formal titles which indicate their *diplomatic rank (sense 1). However, if (as sometimes happens) a difficulty occurs over the use of such a title, the states concerned may agree to resort to the generic term 'representative', or the *sending state may unilaterally adopt that designation. The two states may also, in these circumstances, agree on the *diplomatic class into which the representative falls; alternatively, the *receiving state will make its own determination on the matter.

Such a case arose in respect of British–Irish representation during the Second World War (at which time there was a difference of opinion as to whether Ireland was a *dominion). Britain refused to agree to Ireland's wish that the representative of each of them should have a diplomatic rank and title. It was therefore agreed that their representatives should be so called. However, a further problem arose as Ireland refused to use the name

'United Kingdom', as its full version included the words 'and Northern Ireland'. Thus while Britain called her representative in Dublin the 'Representative of the United Kingdom', Ireland called him the 'British Representative'.

The title of representative may also be given to an individual appointed by the UN to support the *Secretary-General's efforts in the field of peace and security. *See also* accredited diplomatic representative; accredited representative; diplomatic representative; personal representative; polpred; representative character; representative office; special envoy; special representative.

representative character. The representation of the person of the sending sovereign. This idea used to be employed to justify *diplomatic privileges and immunities, and the related right to demand direct access to the receiving sovereign, which according to Article 2 of the *Regulation of Vienna (1815) was considered exclusive to *diplomatic agents of the first class (*ambassadors, *legates and *nuncios). This generally gave ambassadors no more than a negotiating point on top-level access, although it could sometimes be used to great advantage. The disappearance of *monarchical regimes and the political emasculation of those which remained, together with the practical obstacles to effecting this doctrine, saw the importance attached to it diminish during the course of the nineteenth century. Even the early editions of *Satow's Guide*, published shortly after the First World War, regarded the 'representative character' of the ambassador as little more than an historical curiosity. Nevertheless, many diplomats from all sorts of states remain deeply conscious of representing the person of their *head of state. *See also* exterritoriality; functional approach; representation.

representative functions. A synonym for *diplomatic functions.

representative office. Sometimes known as a 'liaison office', a mission other than a *consular post or an *interests section which represents one state in another in the absence of *diplomatic relations (sense 1) between them. In these circumstances, typically where one party refuses to *recognize the government or state of the other but both are keen to promote contacts, representative offices are a favoured solution to the problem of resident representation. In effect informal embassies, they were employed in Japan's relations with certain states prior to the ending of the occupation regime in 1952 (though foreign 'liaison missions' in Japan were formally accredited to the Supreme Command of the Allied Powers). They were also exchanged between the United States and the People's Republic of China in the interval between the *rapprochement between them in the early 1970s and US recognition of the PRC in 1979. And they are currently popular with Taiwan and the Turkish Republic of Northern Cyprus.

reprisal. An act which is illegal in itself but which is allegedly justified as a means of retaliation for an illegal act by another state. During the second half of the twentieth century the issue of reprisals, especially where they involved the use of force, became highly controversial. In consequence, the concept of lawful defence has sometimes been stretched to cover acts which once would straightforwardly have been called reprisals. *See also* countermeasures; reciprocity; retorsion; sanctions.

republic. A state in which the *head of state is elected by the people or a representative body, as distinct from a *monarchy where the headship devolves (generally) on the basis of heredity.

reservation. A qualification made by a party to a *treaty, *resolution, or *consensus statement purporting to exclude itself from the operation of a particular provision of the treaty. In principle, the validity of a reservation depends on the consent of the other parties. But in practice the situation often becomes less than entirely clear. Nor is clarity in this area helped by the recent practice of *ratifications and *accessions being accompanied by interpretative declarations, which are not meant to have the legal effect of reservations but which sometimes seem, in the effect they are intended to have, to be little different from reservations.

residence. The home of the *head of mission while in the country of his or her accreditation when distinct, as is now commonly the case, from the *chancery or *embassy (sense 1); it might be anything from a hotel room to a mansion. Sometimes described as the 'private residence', it was expressly included within the definition of the 'premises of the mission' in the Vienna Convention on *Diplomatic Relations (1961) and is entitled to exactly the same inviolability and protection as the chancery or embassy proper. The physical separation of the residence from the chancery can have advantages for diplomacy. When the US *Army Attaché in Paris, Major General Vernon A. Walters, was instructed by the White House in 1970 to make secret contact with the Chinese Ambassador, he decided, according to his memoirs, 'that the way to do this was to go and see him at the residence in the Neuilly suburban district of Paris, rather than to attempt to go to the Chinese chancery downtown. This would draw a lot of attention'. *See also* diplomatic premises; *hôtel de l'ambassadeur*.

resident. (1) In early modern European diplomacy, a *public minister (including an ambassador) who was permanently resident in the state of his accreditation. (2) Later, the term was used to describe a minister of the third class, that is, one below an *envoy but above a *secretary of embassy. By the end of the eighteenth century the term had dropped out of use, though it re-emerged as 'minister resident' as the title for the third class of diplomatic agent provided for in the addition to the famous *Regulation of Vienna (1815) at the Congress of Aix-la-Chapelle in 1818. *See also* Barbaro; political resident.

resident clerk. *See* duty officer.

resident mission. A *diplomatic mission the head of which is resident in the *receiving state. Generally, its other members will also be resident there, but occasionally some or even most of them will be resident at a mission in another state, or dispersed among several other missions. Sometimes (although it seems less common than it used to be) a resident mission will have a non-resident head, with the mission in the receiving state being headed by a *chargé d'affaires *ad interim*. *See also* multiple accreditation; non-resident mission; satellite office.

residual mission. The term by which the British mission in Rhodesia was known after the latter's unilateral declaration of independence in 1965. (Before that the mission had been called a *High Commission, even though Rhodesia had not been a *sovereign state. This terminology had been used to reflect the territory's special position in the *Commonwealth.)

resolution. The standard form in which UN bodies, and other *international organizations, record their decisions, which may or may not be *binding. The resolution begins with a preamble which rehearses the background to the subject in question and then proceeds to the operative paragraphs. *See also* General Assembly; Security Council.

res nullius. *See terra nullius*.

retorsion. Retaliatory acts which are legal in all circumstances. *See also* reprisals.

retreat. The session of a *summit meeting where the heads of state and government meet strictly on their own and usually in a quiet location away from the main venue. Traditionally associated with *Commonwealth Heads of Government Meetings, retreats, which typically last for a day or a day and a half, are now a feature of certain other serial summits as well. *See also* Camp David.

review meeting. A conference held periodically to review the operation of and if necessary revise a *treaty. For example, the *Conference on Security and Cooperation in Europe

(CSCE), which was launched by the Helsinki Final Act (1975), operated chiefly through meetings of this kind held every three or four years.

Richelieu, Cardinal (1585–1642). Armand Jean du Plessis, Cardinal and Duke of Richelieu, was chief minister to King Louis XIII of France from 1624 until his death shortly before the end of the Thirty Years' War. To students of diplomacy Richelieu is best known for being the first prominent figure to insist on the importance to a community of states of *continuous* negotiation between them, the first to create (in 1626) a ministry of *foreign affairs, and – despite being a pious Catholic – one of the most successful statesmen in modern European history to apply the doctrine signified by the phrase *raison d'état*. The Cardinal's *Testament Politique*, which was written shortly before his death for the private guidance of Louis XIII and did not see the light of day until 1688, contains a succinct distillation of his political and diplomatic wisdom. At one time thought to be a forgery, it is now accepted by historians to be substantially authentic.

right of legation (*ius legationis*). It was long claimed that states had a right to despatch *ambassadors (sense 1) or *ministers (sense 1) to foreign states. However, the alleged right was largely without substance, as there was little point in acting on it if the *receiving state was not agreeable. And it is now universally accepted that *diplomatic missions are established on the basis of the receiving states' consent.

right of transit. Known earlier as the right of innocent passage, the alleged right of *diplomatic agents, and members of their *families (sense 1), to pass freely through third states on their way to and from a diplomatic post. Strictly speaking, however, diplomats have no greater rights in this regard than their fellow citizens. Thus, if a visa is ordinarily required for people of their nationality, they must obtain one. Nevertheless, diplomatic agents (and their families) passing legitimately through a third state on the way to or from their posts are entitled to such immunities as are necessary to ensure their passage. *See also* safe conduct.

rights and duties of states. *See* Montevideo Convention.

Rio Branco, Baron of. José Maria da Silva Paranhos Junior, Baron of Rio Branco (1845–1912), among other things consul (in Liverpool), and foreign minister of Brazil. He is generally credited with the major role in delimiting Brazil's national frontiers, promoting the policy of *rapprochement with the United States, and being the founder of the Brazilian diplomatic service. The Brazilian diplomatic academy, founded in 1945 (the centenary of his birth), is named after him.

Rio Branco Institute. *See* Rio Branco, Baron of.

ripe moment. The juncture in a dispute when the parties are most inclined (perhaps out of exhaustion) to make a settlement and when, therefore, it is best to start a *negotiation or force the pace of an existing one. It is, of course, allied to the concept of 'premature negotiation'. Sometimes presented as a twentieth-century insight, the doctrine of the ripe moment, or 'ripeness', was discussed at some length by *Guicciardini in the early sixteenth century; he called it the 'right season'.

rogatory letter. A letter or commission requesting that a judicial authority in one state obtain evidence, serve process, or serve a summons on behalf of a judicial authority in another. Consuls play a prominent role in delivering such letters and in some circumstances may assist in their execution. The US State Department believes that the use of such letters is a time-consuming, cumbersome, and costly process and should only be used as a last resort.

Rogers Act (1924). *See* Foreign Service, US.

rollback. A provision in an agreement whereby the parties undertake to dismantle all of their existing policies that are inconsistent with it. *Standstill agreements often have a rollback element.

roll-call voting. A method of voting used in *international organizations and conferences in which an officer calls the roll of member states, whose representatives then answer 'Yes', 'No' or 'Abstain' as the names are called. Latterly it has often been replaced by electronic voting. *See also* precedence.

Rosier, Bernard du (?–1475). Provost and later archbishop of Toulouse, Rosier also knew the world of diplomacy and has been authoritatively credited with writing the first textbook on the subject in Western Europe. Completed at the end of 1436, this was called *Ambaxiator Brevilogus* or 'Short Treatise about Ambassadors'. His book was also remarkable for its preference for the word *'ambassador' as the title for the most important envoys several centuries before this became routine.

round (of negotiations). A series of negotiating sessions. While a session normally lasts for hours, a round can last for weeks, months or even years.

round-table conference. A conference presented by its prime-movers as one at which all *delegations are, as conferees, of equal status and there are no opposing sides – however much these claims are belied by reality. Round-table conferences are typically employed in an effort to ease the prickly relations between delegations representing *sovereign states and those representing *non-governmental organizations and armed factions. The term is generally employed as a metaphor for the round table of medieval legend at which King Arthur is said to have sat with his knights to reinforce feelings of equality and harmony within his court. (Rectangular tables, of course, have sides and – if oblong – may be presented as having a 'head' and a 'foot' as well.) Occasionally, however, a real round table may be employed at an international conference, as at the Bonn talks on Afghanistan in November 2001.

roving ambassador. A *special envoy with the task of visiting a number of countries, usually although not necessarily within the same region. In the past roving ambassadors were usually employed to explain its policies by a new government suspicious of the loyalties of the resident ambassadors which it had inherited, and it would be surprising if they were not still occasionally used for this purpose. Today, however, they are more visible as a feature of the diplomacy of a major power which wants to promote a settlement of a regional conflict. Roving ambassadors are normally people of great experience and seniority.

rules of procedure. Rules agreed by a decision-making body to govern its proceedings. In international relations a well-known instance is to be found in the Provisional Rules of Procedure of the UN *Security Council (as amended on 21 December 1982), which deal with the calling of meetings, production of the agenda, representation and credentials, the presidency, the role of the secretariat, conduct of business (including use of *rapporteurs), voting, official and working languages, publicity of meetings and records, admission of new members, and relations with other UN organs, non-governmental organizations, and private individuals.

S

safe-conduct. Sometimes loosely described as a *laisser passer* (in German, *Passierschein*), this was an official permit for a diplomat or any other individual to enter and travel 'without let or hindrance' through a specified state, usually one with which his or her country was at *war. However, until *international law began to give relatively uniform protection to diplomatic envoys in the country of their accreditation after the sixteenth century, it was customary for safe-conducts to be required by diplomats even in *receiving – as well as transit – states, and securing them was a task for intrepid *messengers. Of course, a number of developments have dramatically reduced the problems which traditionally led diplomats to seek safe-conducts, especially in transit states. Among these are air travel and the emergence of the customary rule (since codified in the Vienna Convention on *Diplomatic Relations 1961), that a diplomat admitted to a third country in the course of a journey to or from his or her post, is entitled to personal inviolability and 'such other immunities as may be required to ensure his transit or return'. As a result, safe-conducts fell into disuse in the twentieth century. *See also* right of transit; visa.

salami tactics. A term used by Henry *Kissinger for an approach to *negotiations which, when on the receiving end, he did not favour: extracting small concessions one after another as if they were thin slices cut one after another from a long and apparently inexhaustible sausage.

salute. *See* gun salute.

sanctions. The means adopted to enforce a legal obligation. They may be utilized on an individual or a collective basis. Under the UN Charter the *Security Council has the right to take or authorize measures, including armed measures, in face of any threat to or breach of the peace; and in so doing it may intervene in matters which are essentially within a state's *domestic jurisdiction. Given, on the one hand, the disposition of UN members to favour a broad interpretation of the term 'threat to the peace' and, on the other, the ending of the *Cold War, the way was opened for the Council to engage in or empower the taking of a variety of measures against those whom it deemed to be lawbreakers. Hence during the last decade of the twentieth century there was a noticeable increase in the number of cases of UN-sponsored collective sanctions. Prominent among them were those directed against Iraq, Libya, and the Federal Republic of Yugoslavia (Serbia and Montenegro).

San Francisco Conference. The 1945 conference at which the UN *Charter was concluded.

satellite office. A term sometimes used to describe a (generally small) office of a diplomatic or consular character which does not have the status of a *diplomatic mission or *consular post in its own right (although its members will enjoy *diplomatic or *consular status). This is because it is only an outpost in the *receiving state of a diplomatic mission or consular post accredited to that state. Accordingly, the senior member of the satellite office cannot be given a typically head-of-mission title, such as ambassador; instead some such title as 'officer in charge' is likely to

be used. The person to whom it is given will be responsible for the conduct of the office to the *head of the mission. Satellite offices, sometimes known simply as 'offices', are commonly employed by certain states to handle trade, aid, and immigration questions.

satellite state. A state which is or tends to be habitually subservient to another in respect of an important area or areas of policy. During the *Cold War it was widely applied in the West to the East European associates of the Soviet Union. It has some affinity with the concept of a *vassal state. *See also* bloc; Brezhnev Doctrine; dependent state; puppet state; sphere of influence.

Satow, Sir Ernest (1843–1929). Born of an English mother and a Swedish father, Satow was a British scholar-diplomat whose most significant postings were in the Far East. These culminated in China, to which he was posted as Envoy Extraordinary and High Commissioner shortly after the relief of the siege of the *legation quarter in Peking in 1900. Satow received much of the credit for the agreement subsequently negotiated between China and the other powers, and remained in Peking until 1906. If students of the Far East now remember Satow for his profound scholarship on this region, by diplomats he is recalled chiefly for his authorship of what is now called *Satow's Guide to

Diplomatic Practice, which is in its fifth edition and is indisputably *the* English-language manual of the profession. It is a shame, however, that this still holds to the merely technical truth that Satow 'never married'. In fact, he had a 'common law' Japanese wife called Kane who bore him two sons, one of whom worked subsequently as a botanist at Kew Gardens in London. It has been alleged – though this is disputed – that, although he was knighted and made a privy councillor, it is for this reason that the Foreign Office never promoted him to ambassador. In Japan Satow remains a celebrity to this day.

Satow's Guide to Diplomatic Practice. The highly technical manual on *diplomacy (sense 1) first written by Sir Ernest *Satow and published by Longmans, Green and Company of London in 1917 under the title *A Guide to Diplomatic Practice*. In 1922 he published a second edition to make corrections to the first and bring the work up to date. However, Satow died in 1929 and the three subsequent editions to appear were each revised by different persons recently retired from the *Foreign Office. The third edition (1932) was produced by Hugh Ritchie, formerly a technical assistant in the Treaty Department; the fourth (1957) by Sir Nevile Bland, whose last post was ambassador at The Hague; and the fifth (1979) was revised by Lord Gore-Booth, who was *permanent under-secretary at the Foreign Office in the second half of the 1960s. For students of Satow, therefore, the most valuable edition is the second, while for professional diplomats the best one is obviously the most recent, that is the fifth, which has also been translated into Japanese and Chinese. However, two points need to be made about the current edition, the first to bear the title *Satow's Guide to Diplomatic Practice*: (a) the information on which it is based is now at least a quarter of a century old; and (b) while there is still a family resemblance to the early editions written by Satow himself, the massive alterations and the inclusion of whole chapters on institutions and processes which did not even exist in Satow's lifetime (such as the UN) make the appropriateness of continuing to attach Satow's name to this *Guide* at least questionable. Though not an official document, and published commercially, it is in effect the British Foreign and Commonwealth Office's 'Guide to Diplomatic Practice'.

saving. A British Diplomatic Service term for a relatively low priority message sent telegraphically, rather than by the less economical *diplomatic bag.

savingram. A half-way house between a letter and a *telegram in that it is a message in the same form as an *unofficial letter but sent *saving.

schutzbrief. *See* letter of protection (sense 1).

seal. (1) An emblematic figure or design pressed into a piece of wax as a means of authenticating either the document so marked or the signature on it. (2) An engraved tool or 'stamp' employed for making such markings on wax. States customarily have a seal of this kind for use on papers of the highest importance, such as *treaties. In Britain this seal is called the Great Seal of the Realm. (3) A piece of wax or similar substance which overlaps a fold in a letter or document, thereby making it impossible (or at least very difficult) to open it and then 're-seal' it without detection.

seating arrangements. At official and social functions in a *receiving state, the rules of *precedence apply to the seating of *heads of mission, and their position as a class is determined by the receiving state's domestic order of precedence. Other *diplomatic agents are seated on the basis of their diplomatic rank and the time they have served in that rank in the receiving state (their position as a class again being determined by the receiving state's order of precedence). *Temporary diplomats are placed in the light of their precedence within their mission. Precedence at table is widely known by the French word, *placement.*

However, the application of these principles can, in respect of individual functions, often give rise to difficulty, in the solution of which the *protocol (sense 1) department of the receiving state is likely to provide valuable assistance. But it remains that diplomatic feathers will sometimes be ruffled. The traditional form of protest at a host's failure to recognize a guest's proper seniority as revealed by the *placement* is for the insulted guest to turn his or her soup bowl upside down on the table, after the soup has been served but before it is eaten, and to depart in silence. Happily, this rarely happens.

At international political meetings the representatives of participating states may be seated on any basis which is mutually agreed – resort to an *alphabetical basis often being found convenient. But difficulties can arise when the participating states are not in *diplomatic relations (sense 1) or do not even *recognize each other, or when *non-state actors are involved. Ad hoc solutions are then required, which (provided the parties agree to meet in the same room) may include the use of separate or *round tables. *International organizations have their own arrangements for their meetings, which will carry through to social functions. Those utilized at the UN are indicated in the entry on precedence (c); those of the Commonwealth in the entry on that body.

second-generation peacekeeping. *See* peacekeeping.

secondment. The temporary attachment of a government *official to a department which is not his or her own, or of a non-official to a government department. When such an arrangement results in the individual serving in a *diplomatic mission, he or she may usefully be thought of as a *temporary diplomat. *See also* attaché.

second secretary. In *diplomatic ranks, that which lies beneath *first secretary and above *third secretary. *See also* secretary of embassy/legation.

secret agent. A person employed by an agency of secret *intelligence (sense 2) chiefly to supply *intelligence (sense 1) – one engaged in *espionage. There are three main types: the traditional spy, working temporarily and by stealth; the agent who has been 'planted' on a long-term basis in a sensitive target; and – most useful – the *agent in place. The distinction between the last two is usually their nationality.

secretariat. The collectivity of officials responsible for the administration of a body such as an *international organization. *See also* international civil servant.

secretary. A term in varying use to designate anyone from a lowly clerical official to the *ministerial (sense 3) or *official head of a government department. *See also* secretary of embassy/legation.

secretary-general. A term sometimes used to designate an organization's chief administrative *official – as, for example, in the case of the UN and in some foreign ministries, for example the *Quai d'Orsay. In the UN *specialized agencies, the term director-general is often preferred.

secretary of embassy/legation. In the diplomatic services of the modern period, especially its later part, a *diplomatic agent of the lowest rank. Nevertheless, in many embassies and legations the secretary was the only other diplomatic agent after the *head of mission and was thus often *chargé d'affaires in the former's absence, which was frequently prolonged. *Torcy created the French Political Academy to train secretaries of embassy.

secretary of state. In the United States, the *ministerial (sense 3) head of the *State Department. In the United Kingdom, the title given, in conjunction with the name of their department, to most senior ministers (sense 3). One such is 'Secretary of State for Foreign and Commonwealth Affairs'.

secretary of state's certificate. *See* Foreign Office Certificate.

secret diplomacy. *Negotiations in regard to which any number of the following are kept secret: (1) the content of the negotiations; (2) the fact that negotiations are going on;

(3) the content of any agreement successfully negotiated; or (4) the fact that any agreement has been successfully negotiated. If secret diplomacy is defined as in sense 1, this is nothing more than a pleonasm since serious negotiation is secret by definition. The attack on 'secret diplomacy' during and after the First World War chiefly had in mind senses 2 and 3. *See also* open diplomacy; Wilson, Woodrow.

secret intelligence. *See* intelligence.

Secret Intelligence Service (SIS). The British *intelligence agency (sense 2) for collecting *foreign intelligence other than by means of *sigint, which is the responsibility of *Government Communications Headquarters. It was formed, under this name, in 1921 and is responsible to the *Foreign and Commonwealth Office. Sometimes known as MI6. *See also* intelligence community; Joint Intelligence Committee.

Security Council. The *United Nations organ with primary responsibility for the maintenance of international peace and security. It was established in 1945 with 11 members, five of whom were *permanent members: Britain, China, France, the Union of Soviet Socialist Republics (with the breakdown of the USSR in 1991 Russia inherited this seat), and the United States. As from 1966 the Council's membership was increased to 15 by raising the number of non-permanent members

from six to ten. These members are elected by the *General Assembly for two-year terms.

Any decision of the Council (which votes by *show of hands) has since 1966 required nine votes; before that date the required number of votes was seven. On a non-procedural matter it is also necessary that none of the permanent members casts a negative vote. (This represents a very early *de facto* amendment of the UN *Charter, which specifies that non-procedural draft resolutions require the concurring votes of the permanent members to pass.) Any such vote on a non-procedural draft resolution which would otherwise have been passed (because it received the requisite number of positive votes) is informally called a *veto, in that it prevents the adoption of the resolution. In the UN's early years the phenomenon of the double-veto was also encountered. Where there was disagreement over whether a proposal was procedural, that question would first be voted on, and was treated as non-procedural; thus a permanent member could first veto the claim that a draft resolution was procedural, and then veto the substantive resolution – hence the 'double-veto'.

The UN Charter made provision for the Security Council to have armed forces at its disposal so that it could take enforcement measures in support of the principle of *collective security and, in the event of such forces being used, for them to be controlled by the Council's Military Staff Committee. However, member states declined to place any forces in the Council's hands, so this whole scheme for the implementation of collective security foundered. Instead, what the Council has occasionally done in response to *aggression (where the political circumstances have also been appropriate) is either to invite states to place forces under its command or to authorize certain states to take action on its behalf. (In practice there has been little difference between these two modes of action.)

During the *Cold War the division between East and West resulted in the Council rarely acting in the manner which the Charter anticipated, and vetoes abounded. However, it did utilize and extend the device of *peacekeeping. Since the end of the Cold War the Council has become much more involved in both peacekeeping and *peace-enforcement – a consequence of the greater political harmony in the Council and the concomitant sharp decline in the use of the veto. But it should not be assumed that this pattern is now fixed. The Council's effectiveness is chiefly a function of relations between its permanent members. Any general deterioration in those relations will be reflected in the Council's activity. *See also* informal consultations.

security intelligence. (1) Information on 'internal' threats to a state or its government, which is sought abroad as well as at home. (2) The agencies involved in the collection of this kind of information. In Britain this is *MI5 (or the 'Security Service'), in the United States the 'Intelligence Division' of the Federal Bureau of Investigation (FBI), in France the *Direction de la Surveillance du Territoire (DST)*, and in Germany the *Bundesamt für Verfassungsschutz (BfV)*.

Security Service. *See* MI5.

sefaretname. A general report on his mission submitted by an Ottoman envoy on his return to Istanbul, perhaps modelled on the Venetian *relazione*. They were rare before the late seventeenth century. Such reports (alternatively known as *sefaret takriri*) were required more insistently during the eighteenth century as the *Porte became anxious for intelligence on developments in Europe, especially in the spheres of military and naval technology, science, and industry. About 50 *sefaretnames* survive, though all are in Ottoman Turkish save for the one in French written by Mahmoud Raif Efendi, chief secretary of the first permanent Ottoman ambassador to Britain, who was appointed by Selim III in 1793.

self-defence. The inherent right of states, either on their own or with the assistance of their friends and associates, to use force to protect their political independence and territorial integrity. According to the UN *Charter, the right of self-defence may be exercised only following an armed attack and until the *Security Council has taken the measures necessary to maintain international peace and security. However, the speed and destructive capacity of weapons have increased greatly since the Charter was written. As a result, sometimes acts said to be in self-defence are taken pre-emptively, so as to prevent an anticipated attack by orthodox means, or one by a *terrorist group. It should be noted that while the Charter does not authorize states to take pre-emptive action in self-defence, it undoubtedly empowers the Security Council itself to take or authorize such action following a determination by the Council that there exists a 'threat' to international peace and security. *See also* intervention.

self-determination. Often prefixed by the term 'national', this is a doctrine which postulates the right of *national (sense 1) groups to determine their political condition for themselves, and more particularly whether they should constitute *sovereign states. The doctrine's espousal by President Woodrow *Wilson had some impact on the emergence of new states in central and eastern Europe after the First World War; and its wide popularity after the Second World War contributed to the rapid ending of the overseas empires of the West European colonial powers. *See also* colonialism; Declaration on the Granting of Independence to Colonial Countries and Peoples; General Assembly.

sending state. The state which sends a *diplomatic or a *special mission to another state.

senior foreign service. The current term for the small group of officers in the US *Foreign Service who fill its most demanding and sensitive positions. *See also* career ambassador.

senior member. Where the *trade representatives in a national capital form, or are believed to form, a distinct body, this is the term sometimes used to describe the person who plays in it a role analogous to that of *dean. The person concerned may be responsible, among other things, for publishing a list of its members.

separate opinion. The opinion which may be delivered by a judge of the *International Court of Justice who concurs in the judgment or opinion of the Court but does so, at least in part, on the basis of different reasoning from that expressed by the majority.

serial summit. *See* summitry.

serious consequences. A euphemism for the threat or use of armed force.

service adviser. In a Commonwealth *high commission, the equivalent to a *service attaché.

service attaché. A generic term for any officer in the armed forces (air force, army or navy) temporarily attached to a *diplomatic mission. The term 'defence attaché' is also sometimes used for this group as a whole though the British, French, and Americans now usually reserve this title for the *senior* service attaché at a diplomatic mission, irrespective of that person's own branch of the armed forces. (To make things a little clearer, the title indicating service affiliation is usually added, in the British case for example: 'defence and air attaché'.) In French diplomacy the term *Attaché militaire* denotes seniority. At *high commissions in the *Commonwealth the word 'adviser' is substituted wherever 'attaché' appears in the above titles.

The duties of service attachés, or as they are known in the US Foreign Service 'armed forces attachés', invariably involve acquiring information on the armed forces of the country in which they are based. Where relations are close this will not be difficult and, in such circumstances, an important part of their duties is also to organize collaboration between the two countries' armed forces – examples of which are joint training exercises, officer exchanges, harmonization of weapons systems, defence sales and after-sales services and training,

naval ship visits, and visits in both directions by senior and other officers and units.

It has been well said that service attachés stand at the interface between secret *intelligence and *diplomacy (sense 1), and this sometimes gets them into trouble, especially when they find themselves in unfriendly states. In the first place, there is always the risk that they will find themselves having to serve different – and sometimes competing – masters: the ambassador, the defence ministry, the secret service. In the second place, they are always liable to be declared *persona non grata* by a *receiving state on grounds of *espionage. It is because of the sensitivity of their work that, apart from the *head of mission (where *agrément* is mandatory), the service attaché is the only member of the staff of a diplomatic mission whose name *may*, if the receiving state so requires, need to be submitted for approval prior to appointment. (In practice, receiving states almost always do so require.) Under the Vienna Convention on *Diplomatic Relations a receiving state can also refuse to accept service attachés altogether, or certain kinds of service attaché.

Persons faintly resembling service attachés had begun to appear in early modern Europe and in 1681 *Wicquefort argued for their introduction, not least to spare the ambassador himself the inconvenience and possible embarrassment of being obliged to accompany an importunate prince on campaign. (It could be especially embarrassing for a Christian ambassador required to accompany the Ottoman sultan or his *grand vizier on campaign against fellow Christians.) However, it was not until the nineteenth century that the habit of appointing recognizably modern military and naval attachés became common in Europe. Air attachés, of course, were an innovation that had to await the interlude between the First and Second World Wars of the twentieth century.

service staff. The domestic service of a diplomatic mission: drivers, cooks, gardeners and cleaners, for example. Traditionally, they only enjoyed immunity from the jurisdiction of the *receiving state if that state had specifically granted it. But under the Vienna Convention on *Diplomatic Relations, such staff enjoy immunity in respect of their official acts, provided they are not *nationals of or permanently resident in the receiving state. *See also* GlavUpDK.

servitude. A right of an absolute character which one state enjoys in the territory of another. Such rights exist not infrequently – such as those relating to military *bases, tracking stations, and pipelines. But as the term 'servitude' has semantic and historical connotations of a large power imbalance between the two states concerned, it has fallen out of favour. *See also* capitulations.

Seventh Floor. The policy-makers in the *State Department in Washington, this being the level of the building occupied by the *secretary of state and the under-secretaries of state.

Sheriffs' List. The list provided for under section 5 of the *Act of Anne, 1708, naming the individuals attached to *diplomatic missions (including personal servants of the ambassador) on whom it was a criminal offence to attempt to initiate legal proceedings, typically for debt. It was known as 'the Sheriffs' List' because although compiled in the office of one of the principal secretaries of state it then had to be 'transmitted to the sheriffs of London and Middlesex for the time being, or their under sheriffs or deputies, who shall, upon the receipt thereof, hang up the same in some publick place in their offices, whereto all persons may resort, and take copies thereof, without fee or reward'. The Sheriffs' List was thus the original London *Diplomatic List, and this List still carried this eighteenth century title until the early 1960s, even though it was by this time generally referred to orally as 'the London Diplomatic List'. The offence created by the Act of Anne was abolished by the Diplomatic Privileges Act passed by the United Kingdom parliament in 1964, and in the same year the Sheriffs' List was formally restyled 'The London Diplomatic List'.

sherpa. A senior official who is responsible, in collaboration with counterparts from other states, for preparing the ground for a *summit. In the case of *Group of Eight summits, this work includes drafting the final *communiqué as well as agreeing the agenda, and is supported by separate meetings between 'sous-sherpas' (one specialist in foreign affairs and one in finance under each sherpa) and *political directors from foreign ministries.

show of hands voting. Indication of a voting decision by the raising of the hand, as for example in the UN *Security Council.

shuttle diplomacy. A term owing its origin to the frenetic diplomatic style of Henry *Kissinger following the *October War of 1973. Urgently seeking to promote the disengagement of Israeli forces from Egyptian and Syrian territory, the number of flights between the capitals of the parties which he made during two periods over the next seven months in pursuit of such a limited objective was probably unprecedented for anyone of his seniority in the government of a major power. The term 'shuttle', once applied to this activity by the *New York Times* in January 1974, seemed to fit it to perfection and it stuck. It has also been retrospectively applied to the urgent (and successful) efforts of the American mediator Cyrus Vance, in respect of the 1967 crisis over Cyprus that almost brought Greece and Turkey to war.

side accreditation. *See* multiple accreditation.

side letter. A letter accompanying a broader agreement. Side letters typically cover either a point regarded as too sensitive to be given the prominence of inclusion in the main body of a *treaty or contain undertakings by the signatories to a *third party, or vice versa, which are essential to its fulfilment. Side letters of both kinds accompanied the main Camp David Accords of September 1978 and the Egypt–Israel Peace Treaty to which the Accords led in the following March.

sigint. 'Signals intelligence' is the *intelligence activity which involves interception and decrypting of communications plus interpretation of the significance of emissions from such sources as radar installations. The former division of sigint is usually known as 'communications intelligence' and the latter as 'electronic intelligence'. In Britain, Government Communications Headquarters (GCHQ) specializes in sigint; in the United States the task is performed by the National Security Agency (NSA). Sigint facilities are not unknown within *diplomatic missions, while the communications of these missions have for long been a major target of sigint attack themselves.

See also bubble; Echelon; freedom of communication; listening device.

signalling. The attempt to communicate intentions by non-verbal means, for example by the timing and *venue of a *summit.

signature. The formal signing of the text of a *treaty, usually by the heads of the *delegations who have been entrusted with its *negotiation. Treaties are often signed subject to *ratification; but if the need for that procedure is not stated in the treaty, it may be assumed that the treaty becomes operative immediately, or as from the date specified in the treaty – in which case the signature is termed definitive. A treaty may also be signed *ad referendum*. *See also* adoption; full powers; initialling; plenipotentiary.

silence procedure. A device of *consensus decision-making in *multilateral diplomacy, the rule that a proposal with strong support is deemed to have been agreed unless any party raises an objection to it before a specified deadline. In other words, silence signifies assent – or at least acquiescence. It may be used either as in effect a form of *ratification by governments when their permanent missions have already reached a consensus, or as a form of pressure on the reluctant minority when they have not. The silence procedure, so-called, is employed in bodies such as *NATO,

the *European Union (for example in the framework of its *Common Foreign and Security Policy via *COREU), and the *Organization for Security and Cooperation in Europe.

silent procedure. *See* silence procedure.

silver car pass. Originally called a 'carriage pass', this item was introduced in Britain in the mid-nineteenth century to ensure that the carriage of Queen Victoria's mistress of the robes was given such assistance by the police as would enable it to proceed without interruption. The pass was soon also given to *ambassadors (sense 1). From time to time the design was changed, and in the 1930s it was decided to make it in silver. In the late 1970s the high price of that metal resulted in the pass being made of red leather, but it is still called a 'silver' pass. It is issued on the authority of the Commissioner of the Metropolitan Police Service and, other than in respect of members of the Royal Family, to the post rather than the post-holder. Besides ambassadors and *high commissioners, such a pass is carried by members of the government, ex-prime ministers, and other specifically designated 'special people'.

silver greyhound. The badge of office of the Corps of *Queen's Messengers. A badge of office was granted by Charles II to the (then) King's Messengers at the Restoration of the monarchy in 1660. This was in recognition of their loyalty to the royalist cause during the English civil war and subsequent 'commonwealth' period. However, until the first King's Messengers' passports were issued in 1900, this badge also served to identify them as British *diplomatic couriers when on their travels abroad. Until 1714 the badge was embroidered onto the tunics worn by the messengers but thereafter it was made of metal and worn about the neck in the manner of a senior decoration, as it still is today. It consists of a garter blue ribbon with a royal coat of arms pendant and beneath it a silver greyhound. (Both the shape of the royal coat of arms and the cypher on it vary with each new monarch, thereby underlining the fact that the messenger's loyalty has been transferred to the current sovereign.) The greyhound, of course, symbolizes 'despatch'.

single mission principle. The rule for long adopted by the Swiss authorities that *sending states could maintain in Switzerland only one mission accredited to the UN and the other *international organizations with headquarters in the country. However, in 1994 this principle was abandoned, enabling sending states who wished to do so to establish separate missions to the UN's European Headquarters, to individual *specialized agencies, and to the Conference on Disarmament, and the General Agreement on Tariffs and Trade

(subsequently the *World Trade Organization).

single negotiating text. A technique employed in *multilateral diplomacy by a 'coordinator' or by a mediator in *proximity talks. Following consultation with each of the parties, a single text is drawn up and submitted to them for consideration. The text is then amended in light of this second round of consultations and re-submitted. The process is repeated as many times as needed to reach agreement.

sitrep. A situation report provided by a diplomatic mission. It is also widely used in a military context.

Six-Day War. The brief and hugely successful Israeli campaign of June 1967 against Egypt, Jordan, and Syria, in which the Gaza Strip and the Sinai Desert, the west bank of the River Jordan (including East Jerusalem), and the Golan Heights were all taken. *See also* October War.

size of diplomatic mission. *See* diplomatic mission.

small post. A term used in some foreign services to categorize a post which, in terms of size, falls below a certain level.

sous-**sherpa.** *See* sherpa.

sovereign immunity. Another, generally less formal, way of referring to *state immunity.

sovereign rights. Usually, the basic legal powers which are necessary for a *state to act independently, including its actions on the international stage. See also sovereignty (sense 2).

sovereign state. A territorial entity which enjoys *sovereignty (sense 1).

sovereignty. A term which is used in a number of different ways, often causing confusion due to a failure to distinguish between these distinct usages.

(1) The condition which makes a territorial entity eligible to participate fully in *international relations (sense 2). It consists of constitutional independence; that is to say, the situation which exists when an entity's constitution is not contained, however loosely, within a wider constitutional scheme, but stands apart and alone. Thus the constituent states of a *federal state do not enjoy this sort of sovereignty, no matter how large or powerful they are; nor does an internally self-governing *colony. Sovereignty in this sense is a legal status which derives from the constitutional position of the entity concerned, and is both absolute (in that it is either possessed or not) and unitary (in that its internal and external implications are inextricably connected). Externally, sovereignty in this sense makes an entity eligible to participate in international relations, but the extent to which it does so depends upon its own inclinations and the extent to which other sovereign states are willing to have dealings with it. Thus, this sense of sovereignty is utterly basic for the practice and study of international relations in that it serves to identify the territorially based *international actors, and hence the entities which engage in *diplomacy (sense 1). See also equality of states.

(2) The ensemble of legal rights which are central to a *sovereign state's external and internal activity. Often called its *sovereign rights, *international law either (in respect of the state's external activity) bestows them on a state, or (in respect of the state's internal activity) places an obligation on other states not to *intervene in the state's domestic affairs. Sovereign rights include (subject to any specific obligations the state has accepted to the contrary) the right to exercise jurisdiction throughout its territory, on its *territorial sea, and in its *air space (these matters often being referred to simply as the right of *domestic jurisdiction); the right to *self-defence; the capacity to enter into *diplomatic relations (sense 1); and the capacity to make *treaties. Sovereignty in this second sense is a consequence of sovereignty in the first, in that sovereign rights attach to those entities which enjoy sovereign status. The infringement of a sovereign right, however, has no bearing on the sovereign status of the entity concerned.

(3) The extent to which a sovereign state is under no specific or general international obligations regarding its internal behaviour and decision making. In this sense its sovereignty consists of the degree to which it is legally free to conduct itself as it sees fit. Thus this concept of sovereignty is relative in nature. Sometimes it is called legal sovereignty. It is enormously difficult to measure; but it easily permits the comment that a state's sovereignty has been diminished by its acceptance of a specific obligation. Such an act has, of course, no effect on a state's sovereignty in the first sense. Indeed, such acts are a run-of-the-mill activity for sovereign states.

(4) The extent to which a sovereign state is under no external pressures regarding any aspect of its behaviour. This concept also, therefore, is a relative one. Sometimes it is known as political sovereignty. As all states, large and small, are constantly aware of the factor of political constraint, all of them enjoy a less-than-full measure of this kind of sovereignty. But this in no way undermines state sovereignty in the first sense. For sovereign states the lack of complete political freedom is simply a fact of international life.

(5) The power exercised by those who control a state's decision-making processes. Thus it might be said that a state's sovereignty is in the hands of the people, the cabinet, the supreme leader, or whoever – or, perhaps more accurately, some mixture of such elements. But *who* exercises sovereignty is quite distinct from whether or not an entity enjoys sovereignty (senses 1 and 2), or the extent to which an entity is sovereign (senses 3 and 4).

Soviet bloc. *See* Eastern bloc.

special agreement. *See compromis*.

special ambassador. *See* special mission.

special customary international law. Rules of *customary international law which apply among (and only as among) limited numbers of states, often as exceptions to rules of general customary international law. Such law is sometimes referred to as 'regional customary international law' because it often develops among states in one region. *See also* diplomatic asylum.

special envoy. The way in which reference is sometimes made to an individual who is charged by his or her state, or by an *international organization, with a specific mission, often of a *mediatory kind. Alternatively, such a person may be called a *special representative (sense 2). These terms were, for example, used in the late 1990s to refer to the United States and British representatives who, among others, were asked to seek a solution to the Cyprus problem. *See also* personal representative; roving ambassador; special mission.

specialized agencies. Those multi-member international organizations having responsibility for economic, social, cultural, educational, health, and related matters, which have been linked to the UN through special agreements. The UN *Economic and Social Council has responsibility for trying to coordinate their work on the basis of consultation and recommendation. But each of the 14 specialized agencies is an independent body, with its own membership, budget, deliberative and governing organs, secretariat, and headquarters. The full current list is as follows: the Food and Agriculture Organization, the International Bank for Reconstruction and Development (widely known as the World Bank), the International Civil Aviation Association, the International Fund for Agricultural Development, the International Labour Organization, the International Maritime Organization, the International Monetary Fund, the *International Telecommunication Union, the United Nations Educational, Scientific and Cultural Organization, the United Nations Industrial Development Organization, the Universal Postal Union, the World Health Organization, the World Intellectual Property Organization, and the World Meteorological Organization. *See also* Privileges and Immunities of the Specialized Agencies, Convention on.

special mission. A temporary mission, consisting of either an individual or a group, which is sent by one state to another (with the latter's agreement) for the purpose of dealing with it on specific questions or of performing in relation to it a specific task. The head of such a mission may be called a special ambassador or a special envoy. However, the *credentials of a special mission will refer to the mission as a whole (unlike the always-personal form of those issued to the head of a *diplomatic mission). If a special mission is given *full powers, they too may relate to all the mission's members; but alternatively they may empower specified members of the mission or just its head. The functions of a special mission generally begin when it arrives in the receiving state's territory.

Before the establishment of permanent embassies with general functions all diplomatic missions were special missions. If the *sending state already has a resident mission in the capital of the state concerned, that mission may resent the arrival of the special mission, seeing it as suggesting that the resident mission cannot competently handle the issue which has prompted the despatch of the special mission. However, in the event of the *receiving state reacting badly to the work of the special mission, its use may protect the interests of the resident mission – and the special mission may in fact have been employed with that in mind. *See also* embassy of obedience; Special Missions, Convention on (1969).

Special Missions, Convention on (1969). The Convention *entered into force in 1985, but has been *ratified by only 32 states. Many of its provisions for the treatment of the members of *special missions are similar if not identical to the equivalent ones in the Vienna Convention on *Diplomatic Relations (1961) and reflect the same *functional theory. Under the Convention, the existence of neither *diplomatic nor *consular relations is necessary for the sending or reception of a special mission; nor does the severance of either diplomatic or consular relations of itself terminate any current special mission.

special passport. A document which is more than an ordinary passport but less than a *diplomatic passport. It may be supplied to the representatives of a state who serve abroad but do not enjoy *diplomatic status. *See also* Queen's Messenger.

special relationship. One between two states which is sufficiently intimate to result in each doing more for the other than it would do for a third party. However, it is not always the case that one state's belief that a relationship is special is reciprocated by the other. And even where both deem their relationship to be special, its actual impact on behaviour may be difficult to chart. One notable instance of a relationship which Britain has, during the past 50 years, believed to be special is hers with the United States.

special representative. (1) The title often given by the UN *Secretary-General to the official who represents him at the head of a field mission with some markedly diplomatic responsibilities, such as certain *peacekeeping operations. (2) An alternative term for a *special envoy. *See also* personal representative; roving ambassador; special mission.

sphere of influence. A region within which a powerful state claims exclusive rights of *intervention. This zone may be anything from a part of a *sovereign state, as in Persia following the Anglo-Russian agreement to divide influence over it in 1907, to a number of such states, as in Eastern Europe during the *Cold War. *See also* Brezhnev Doctrine; dependent state; Monroe Doctrine; puppet state; satellite state; vassal state.

splendid isolation. The term often used to describe Britain's pre-twentieth century policy of avoiding *alliances in time of peace.

sponsion. An American term for a commitment made by a *diplomatic agent without official authorization, and voidable if inconsistent with the agent's *instructions.

sponsor. In a *multilateral forum such as the UN *Security Council, a member who has submitted a draft resolution.

spouse, diplomatic. The partner, marital or not, of a *diplomatic agent.

staffeto. Alternatively a *staffette* or *estafette*, a courier of the imperial German postal service run by the von Taxis family from the fifteenth century until the middle of the nineteenth.

stagiaire. A young person doing a *stage* (training period or course) of practical work experience, generally with a theoretical component – an apprentice or student. The term is currently favoured for those young graduates of *EU member states who are attached to one or other of the Directorates-General of the *European Commission.

stalemate. *See* impasse.

standard of civilization. *See* international minimum standards.

standard time. *See* Greenwich Mean Time.

standing conference. One which is permanently in being in the sense that it meets from time to time rather than on just one occasion.

standstill agreement. An *agreement not to take any further action on a particular issue, or not to take any action on it prior to a specific date or during the course of a specific negotiation.

standstill ceasefire. *See* ceasefire.

stare decisis. The principle that a court must apply the legal principle reflected in a decided case to other cases of the same character. The *International Court of Justice, however, is not obliged to proceed on this basis. But its judgments naturally have a considerable persuasive character, both for itself and for states.

state. Any territorial entity which enjoys *sovereignty (sense 1), no matter how tiny or weak. So far as non-sovereign territorial entities are concerned, the term tends to be restricted to those whose size and governmental powers are judged to be significant, such as the constituent entities of a *federal state.

statecraft. The art of preserving and strengthening the *state relative to other states without serious reference to political ideals or any system of private morality; that is to say, the practical application of the doctrine of *raison d'état*. Statecraft is thus a very broad concept, including *foreign policy (for example, whether *alliance or *neutrality in a war is best for the state) as well as the appropriate deployment of instruments in its support: *diplomacy (sense 1), *war, and *propaganda. Henry *Kissinger's book published in 1994 may be called

Diplomacy but it is really about statecraft. However, the term smacks of the Old World and *power politics in general and of *Machiavelli in particular, and for these reasons is out of fashion.

State Department. Formally the 'Department of State', the United States' ministry of foreign affairs. Initially, in 1789, it was called the Department of Foreign Affairs, but within a few months its name was changed to Department of State in recognition of its acquisition of certain *domestic* duties. Although these were subsequently surrendered, the name stuck.

state funeral. *See* working funeral.

state immunity. Sometimes called 'sovereign immunity', the doctrine which deals with the immunity of foreign states from the jurisdiction of local courts and law-enforcement agencies. At one time the immunity was complete. But with the increased tendency of states to engage in commercial activity, many states have drawn a distinction between these 'private acts' and a state's 'public acts', immunity being granted only to the latter. Britain and the United States are among those who have withdrawn foreign states' immunity from suit in respect of private acts, their decisions being taken in the late 1970s.

states-system. A collectivity of states whose relations – diplomatic and commercial – are organized and continuous. Sometimes rendered 'state-system' or 'system of states', it is a term which was once common, especially in British writing. However, it has tended to lose ground to the more nebulous term, *international system. See also* international society; Westphalia, Congress of (1644–48).

state visit. A visit of a markedly ceremonial nature paid by one *head of state to another. Though usually of most importance for its symbolic significance and not, unlike the *summit, ending with an agreement or *communiqué, the state visit may provide a cover for important talks. It is normal for the head of state to be accompanied by at least one government minister (sometimes many more), such a person being known as a 'minister-in-attendance'. Except in the case of a British head of state visiting one of her Realms, a head of state would also usually have his or her *ambassador (sense 1) or *high commissioner in attendance.

The visits made abroad by heads of state are not always of a markedly ceremonial nature; furthermore, they are sometimes the guest of a *head of government rather than a head of state. As a result, other terms have evolved to describe visits of this kind though there is unfortunately little consistency of usage. The term 'official visit' is commonly used to describe visits which have one or both of these characteristics, while a meeting between heads of state devoid of ceremonial is also known sometimes as a 'working visit', though it might as well be called a bilateral summit and sometimes is. When a head of state visits another state for purely personal reasons, for example to receive medical attention of a kind not available at home, this is known as a 'private' or 'unofficial' visit. *See also* stop-over visit.

stationnaire. A small warship or *gunboat stationed by a state at a foreign port chiefly for the protection of its citizens residing there. Usually they were put at the disposal of the ambassador. The years before the First World War were the heyday of the *stationnaire*, or 'guardship' as they were also known.

status of forces agreement (SOFA). When units of a state's armed forces are stationed abroad on non-combatant duty, as at a foreign military *base, or when the UN establishes a *peacekeeping force, it is highly desirable that the legal position of such forces should be clearly established. This may be done through the conclusion of a status of forces agreement between the host state and the sending state or organization.

status quo. The existing state of affairs or things as they are now. Such a condition is, by definition, beloved of conservatives. *See also status quo ante.*

status quo ante. The previous state of affairs. *See also status quo.*

Statute of Anne. *See* Act of Anne.

step-by-step diplomacy. In *negotiations between erstwhile bitter adversaries, the approach which favours seeking agreement on relatively uncontroversial subjects before attempting to tackle the most sensitive ones. Well known to have been adopted by Henry *Kissinger in his Middle East negotiations in the early 1970s, the theory is that only by this means will the necessary trust and stability be established to make complete political resolution of a conflict ultimately possible. It resembles the theory of *functionalism which underpinned the launch of European integration in the early 1950s. The only problem with this plausible approach is that it takes a great deal of time, and time is not always available.

sticking point. In *negotiations, an issue on which one of the parties cannot *compromise or make *concessions. If there is no agreement on such an issue discussion may have to be postponed until a future occasion. It need not be but usually is a matter of detail. *See also* bottom line.

stop-over visit. A brief visit made to one state en route to a more important engagement in another. Such visits may be made by *heads of government, *ministers (sense 3), and *officials, as well as by *heads of state. *See also* state visit.

stopping the clock. In *negotiations where success seems imminent but a declared deadline has been reached, the process of stopping the clock so that the deadline is nominally retained but is, in practice, given a short extension. *See also* eleventh hour.

straw poll. *See* straw vote.

straw vote. An informal counting of opinions, as in judging the direction of the wind by casting a straw into the air. The straw poll, as it is alternatively known, is a common device employed in *consensus decision-making in *international organizations, not least for the selection of chief administrative officers.

subject of international law. An entity enjoying *international personality. *See also* object of international law.

Sublime Porte. The term widely used for the Ottoman government until the Ottoman Empire was dissolved following the First World War. It is a half English and half French rendering of *Bāb-i Ali* (strictly, 'high gate'), the original name of the gate at the end of the second court of the sultan's palace in Istanbul (today known as the Topkapi Palace). This name was later transferred to the *grand vizier's residence outside the palace; hence its association with the Ottoman government.

subsidiarity. The principle whereby the *European Union does not take action (except in the areas which fall within its exclusive competence) unless it is likely to be more effective than action taken at national, regional or local level.

Suez crisis. The 1956 crisis in which, in response to Egypt's nationalization of the Suez Canal, Britain and France, in conjunction with Israel, invaded Egypt. Their attempt to undo the nationalization, and topple President Nasser of Egypt, was dramatically unsuccessful.

summer embassy. The cooler location, adjacent to the capital of a hot country, to which an embassy sometimes moved during the summer months.

summitry. The use of meetings of *heads of state or *heads of government for diplomatic or *propaganda purposes. There are two main kinds: ad hoc summits, which are called as the occasion seems to demand, and are well illustrated by the Camp David summit on the Middle East in September 1978; and serial summits, which usually have their origin in ad hoc summits but then become part of a regular series, as with the meetings of the *European Council or the *Commonwealth

Heads of Government Meetings (CHOGMs). Summitry has very ancient origins but did not acquire this title until developed by the press following use of the word 'summit' by Winston Churchill in the course of a speech at Edinburgh in February 1950. *See also* Air Force One; communiqué; Commynes; declaration (sense 1).

superpower. The current term for what, until the end of the Second World War, used to be called a *great power, i.e. a power of the first rank in terms of reputation for military strength. Since the end of the *Cold War, and the disintegration of the Soviet Union, the United States has generally been seen as the sole superpower. *See also* major power; middle power; permanent members; Security Council.

supranationalism. The situation which exists where, on matters within its competence, an *international organization has the legal power directly to *bind natural and legal persons within the member states. It is thus as if on these matters state boundaries did not exist. This contrasts with the more usual organizational situation where, even if such a body has the power to bind its members, it only binds the state as such. The *European Union is the sole instance (as at the beginning of the twenty-first century) of a supranational organization.

suzerainty. A situation in which one *sovereign state exercises an acknowledged and significant degree of supremacy over another, often on the basis of a *treaty between them, but possibly on a political basis alone. The relationship may be marked by the payment of *tribute to the suzerain. The term went out of fashion in the earlier part of the twentieth century. *See also* dependent state; protected state (sense 1); vassal state.

SVR. The Russian Foreign Intelligence Service, a successor body to the *KGB. *See also* FSB.

T

tabled offers. In *negotiations: (1) offers which have been withdrawn (American usage); or (2) offers which have been submitted (British usage).

tacite reconduction. The continuation in force of an agreement after the period stipulated in it has elapsed, the signatories having raised no objections.

Talleyrand-Périgord, Charles-Maurice de (1754–1838). A French politician, diplomat and foreign minister. Brilliant, practical, unscrupulous, and a man capable of immense personal charm, Talleyrand was born into the high aristocracy but developed a liberal and reformist outlook. He was a politician of great influence within France from the earliest days of the revolution in 1789 until his death. He was also a minister of foreign affairs with a remarkable capacity for surviving under different regimes, and one of the most dextrous negotiators of his age.

Talleyrand managed the conduct of French diplomacy under the Directory (1797–99) and Napoleon (1799–1808), as well as under the restored Bourbon king, Louis XVIII (1814–15). Having brilliantly secured the re-entry of France into the circle of *great powers at the Congress of *Vienna and played a pivotal role in rebuilding the European equilibrium, Talleyrand ended his diplomatic career as ambassador to London (1830–34), by which time he was in his early eighties. Opportunists, among others, have condemned him for opportunism, though it is difficult to see how this squares with the risks he took in opposing Napoleon, especially after his dismissal in 1808. *See also* Metternich.

telecommunication. Any mode of communication over a long distance which requires human agency only in the sending and reception of the message which it contains and not, as with a *diplomatic courier, in its carriage. The use of smoke-signals,

257

mechanical telegraph ('semaphore'), towers, drums, and pigeons with messages tied to their legs, therefore, are instances of telecommunication just as much as *telegrams, faxes, and e-mails. Nevertheless, it is not surprising that telecommunication did not make a major impact on diplomacy until the introduction of the electric *telegraph towards the middle of the nineteenth century. *See also* airgram; International Telecommunication Union.

telegram. A printed out message sent by *telegraph. The telegram has traditionally had its own special format: a 'from ... to ...' heading (e.g. 'Outward Telegram from Ministry of Foreign Affairs "X" to Mission "Y"'; 'Inward Telegram to MFA "X" from Mission "Y"'), precise times of despatch and receipt, a number, security classification, subject heading, numbered paragraphs, and circulation list. These features have tended to contribute to the impersonality of this form of diplomatic communication. On the other hand, the basic text of a telegram may be written in a style much like that of a letter, if generally pithier, and steadily became the normal means of communication between MFAs and missions abroad from the middle of the nineteenth century until it began to give ground to electronic mail at the end of the twentieth. *See also* despatch; Greenwich Mean Time; NO DIS; saving; savingram; unofficial letter; Z.

telegraph, electric. A form of *telecommunication in which electric current is passed along a wire or cable (land or submarine), the circuit being made and broken in the transmitting device in such a fashion as to produce a code or letters in the receiver. Introduced into diplomacy towards the middle of the nineteenth century, the telegraph – by making it possible to issue new *instructions almost instantaneously – is generally believed to have made extinct the great ambassador such as Stratford *Canning, who was 'great' largely by virtue of being a law unto himself. Less carefully considered than its impact on the *influence* of the resident ambassador (which itself may have been exaggerated) have been the implications of the telegraph for the *usefulness* of this kind of envoy. In fact, it has made the resident ambassador a more flexible instrument of ministries of foreign affairs.

temporary diplomat. Someone temporarily attached to a *diplomatic service in the capacity of a *diplomatic agent.

terra nullius. Territory which is not under the jurisdiction of any state – and hence available for peaceful *annexation. To all intents and purposes the concept is now a historical curiosity. Sometimes *terra nullius* was referred to as *res nullius*.

territorial division. *See* geographical department.

territorial sea. That part of the sea adjacent to the land over which the coastal state is entitled to exercise *sovereignty (sense 2). It may not exceed 12 nautical miles in breadth. For long it was known as territorial waters.

territorial waters. *See* territorial sea.

terrorism. (1) The use or threat of violence against civilian targets for political ends, including its use by states themselves. Terrorism spreads fear more widely by appearing to operate randomly. (2) The somewhat narrower definition employed by the US *State Department: 'premeditated, politically motivated violence perpetrated against noncombatant targets by subnational groups or clandestine agents, usually intended to influence an audience.' (3) Political violence committed by those of whom one disapproves – 'one man's terrorist is another man's freedom fighter'.

As representatives of states, diplomats and *diplomatic premises became particular targets for terrorists (senses 1 and 2) in the last four decades of the twentieth century. Despite the special obligation to give them physical protection which is placed on *receiving states by the Vienna Convention on *Diplomatic Relations (1961), not all of their governments have had either the will or the capacity to provide it. *See also* compound; diplomatic protection (sense 2); hostage; Inman standards.

third party. Any party (state, international organization, non-governmental organization, or individual) not directly involved in a particular bilateral relationship. *See also* conciliation; good offices; mediation.

third room. The traditional description in the *Foreign and Commonwealth Office for the junior members in each of its *departments. It owes its origin to the fact that they usually worked in one large office while the head of the department and his chief assistant each had rooms of their own.

third secretary. In *diplomatic ranks, that which lies beneath *second secretary. In the Indian Foreign Service, third secretaries are always probationers or 'officer-trainees'. *See also* secretary of embassy/legation.

Third World. In French *tiers monde*, a term used to describe all of those states which possess neither developed capitalist ('first world') nor developed socialist ('second world') political and economic systems. The emergence of this expression, which has been attributed to its use by the French economist and geographer Alfred Sauvy in an article in 1952, coincided with the major period of decolonization in the 1950s and early 1960s. The decay or collapse of the Communist command economies, together with the emergence of huge differences in standards of living between groups within the Third World, have rendered the term largely meaningless. *See also* Least Developed Country; Newly Industrialized Country.

thirty-eighth floor. The top occupied floor of the UN headquarters building in New York, which houses the top official – the Secretary-General.

tit-for-tat expulsions. An exchange of expulsions of *diplomatic agents. This usually begins when one state declares a number of members of a *diplomatic mission *persona non grata* for having engaged in 'activities incompatible with their status', i.e. almost invariably *espionage. The state that has suffered then replies by expelling a group of diplomats from the first state who – if the size of that state's diplomatic mission permits it – are equivalent in number and rank to those who have been returned to it. This is a good example of the principle of *reciprocity.

Torcy, Jean-Baptiste Colbert, Marquis de (1665–1746). French foreign secretary in the final years of the reign of Louis XIV. Among other things, Torcy was the instigator in 1712 of the small *Académie politique*. Designed to train *secretaries of embassy who might subsequently be promoted to the highest ranks, it has since been customary to refer to this as the first 'school for ambassadors'. Its curriculum consisted chiefly of *international law,

modern diplomatic history, and languages. Though the academy began to go downhill after the departure of Torcy in 1715 and collapsed in 1721, the idea that diplomacy was a profession and that entrants should be trained had been firmly planted. *See also* Callières.

tour d'horizon. *See* exchange of views.

tour of duty. The period of time spent by a diplomat at a post abroad, today typically three years. At *hardship posts, however, it is sometimes shorter, and at the most comfortable posts sometimes longer. A period in the ministry of foreign affairs at home is also sometimes described as a 'tour'.

track one diplomacy. A *mediatory (sense 2) effort by one or more states, or by an *international organization.

track two diplomacy. Formerly known as 'citizen diplomacy', *mediation (sense 2) in an inter- or intra-state conflict conducted by any agency other than a state or an intergovernmental organization, typically by a *non-governmental organization. The term was coined in 1981 by Joseph Montville, then a US diplomat. Track two diplomacy may be pursued on its own or in partnership with *track one diplomacy, in which case it will form part of an instance of *twin-track diplomacy.

trade commissioner. (1) The title – less common since the middle of the twentieth century – often given to a *non-diplomatic agent charged with the furtherance of the sending entity's trade. The agent would be non-diplomatic either because the sending entity lacked *sovereignty (sense 1) (and therefore could not accredit *diplomatic agents), or because the task was deemed inappropriate for a diplomatic agent, or because it was conducted outside the *capital city (where, ordinarily, agents were not eligible for *diplomatic status). Such agents were frequently officials of a governmental agency other than the ministry of foreign affairs. Nowadays, trade promotion is accepted as part of a diplomat's job. When, therefore, it is conducted at a capital city, it is entrusted to the *sending state's *diplomatic mission, and the individuals in question will almost certainly enjoy diplomatic status – although they may not be members of their states' foreign service but *temporary diplomats. When the task is performed in a city other than the capital, the officers concerned are often part of a consulate, and hence have a consular title – for example, 'vice-consul (commercial)' – and *consular status. *Agents-general play a somewhat similar role to that performed by this kind of trade commissioner. *See also* satellite office. (2) A now comparatively rare term for a *commercial officer attached to a diplomatic mission. The best-known contem-porary examples are provided by the staff of the Trade Commissioner Service of Canada. *See also* Commercial Diplomatic Service; trade representative.

trade commissioner, EU. The member of the *European Commission responsible for the EU's common trade policy.

trade mission. A party of business-men visiting prospective customers overseas, usually with the assistance of their *embassy (sense 3) in the country in question. *See also* commercial diplomacy; commercial officer; economic officer; trade office.

trade office. Often previously known as a 'trade mission', one generally established by a state outside the capital city of the *receiving state, with a view to furthering the *sending state's trade or commerce. However, when such an office is employed as a disguise for work that is as political as it is economic, notably when states are not in *diplomatic relations (sense 1), it is usually located inside the capital, as in the case of the British Trade Mission (subsequently Embassy) opened in Cairo at the end of the 1950s. Sometimes such a post is called a trade promotion office, or a commercial office. *See also* representative office; satellite office; trade commissioner; trade officer; trade representative.

trade officer. A *non-diplomatic agent who serves in, and is very possibly the head of, a state's *trade office or commercial office outside the capital city of the *receiving state. Sometimes such an officer is attached to a *consular post, in which case he or she is likely to enjoy, as of right, *consular privileges and immunities. Otherwise, special arrangements may be made for the officer to be accorded certain privileges and immunities, either formally or as a matter of understood courtesy. Such arrangements are likely to bear a fairly close relationship to those for *consular officers as set out in the 1963 Vienna Convention on *Consular Relations. Today a trade officer is very likely to be a member of his or her state's foreign service. *See also* trade commissioner; trade representative.

trade representative. A catch-all term for any diplomatic, consular, or non-diplomatic agent charged with trade responsibilities. Lists of 'trade representatives' are sometimes found in *consular lists, and sometimes issued separately by the *senior member.

traditional peacekeeping. *See* peacekeeping.

transnational corporation (TNC). *See* multinational corporation.

Treaties, Vienna Convention on the Law of. *See* Law of Treaties.

treaty. An agreement whereby two or more states signify their intention to establish a new legal relationship between themselves – one which, being legal, involves the creation of *binding obligations. In almost all cases treaties are in written form, and the Vienna Convention on the *Law of Treaties confines the term to written instruments. However, it is possible to make an oral agreement which has the same status as a written one. Treaties may be concluded as between *heads of state, states, governments, *ministers (sense 3), or between any other authorized agents. A variety of terms besides that of 'treaty' may be used to describe the new instrument, such as convention, protocol, agreement, *procès-verbal*, declaration, *modus vivendi*, exchange of *notes, exchange of letters, and final act. Other than in very exceptional circumstances, a treaty may not impose obligations or confer rights on third parties without their consent. *See also* accession; adoption; declaration (sense 4); depositary; entry into force; initialling; interim agreement; ratification; reservation; signature; United Nations Treaty Series.

triangular diplomacy. The term employed by Henry A.*Kissinger to describe the relationship which he sought to create in the early 1970s between Washington, Moscow, and Peking. This meant *détente with the Soviet Union and *rapprochement with the People's Republic of China, together with a continuation of the deep Sino-Soviet rift – the third side of the triangle. As the only party to be on reasonable terms with both, Kissinger believed, with some justice, that only the United States was in a position to obtain concessions from each by the simple expedient of intimating the possibility of moving even closer to the other.

tribute. Money or more often goods delivered by a *vassal state to a *suzerain, usually at prescribed intervals. Both the Chinese and Ottoman Empires were well known for exacting tribute from the smaller states and tribes along their frontiers. Not a feature of a diplomatic relationship, which assumes sovereign equality, tribute is less important to the suzerain for its economic value than for the mark of submission which it represents. Since, however, envoys from non-tributary states who journeyed to such imperial courts to establish *diplomatic relations (sense 1) with them invariably carried gifts of their own, this naturally led to misunderstanding, especially in China. According to Chinese ceremonial, objects offered *to* the Emperor were tribute by definition; 'gifts' were objects offered *by* the Emperor. Hence the boats provided by the Chinese for Lord Macartney's ill-fated journey from the coast to Tientsin in 1793 carried banners bearing the legend: 'Envoy paying tribute to the Great Emperor'. This was just the beginning of Macartney's problems. *See also* audience; kowtow.

troika. A triumvirate, from the Russian for a sledge drawn by three horses. The word entered diplomatic currency in 1960 when the Soviet Union proposed, unsuccessfully, that the office of UN Secretary-General be shared by representatives from the East, the West and those who fell into neither of these camps – the *neutralists. *See also* troika (EU).

troika (EU). Until the changes introduced into *European Union external representation in 1999, the *troika consisted of the representatives of the state currently holding the presidency of the *Council of Ministers, together with those of the ones immediately preceding and succeeding it. Since the rotating presidency is held by a member state for only six months at a time, these three parties worked in diplomatic harness to preserve continuity of experience and enhance the political weight of EU external representation. The preceding state provided advice to the current holder, while the one which was next in line learned by apprenticeship. The *European Commission was also permanently associated with the troika, thereby providing further continuity. Following the appointment in mid-1999 of the first *High Representative for the Common Foreign and Security Policy, the troika was abolished.

truce. An imprecise term, which probably indicates a temporary cessation of armed hostilities. *See also* armistice; ceasefire.

trusteeship. The idea that a territory should be administered by a state which, for the time being, is deemed better able to look after it than its own inhabitants. During the late twentieth century this idea became deeply out of keeping with the ethos of the times. However, during the 1990s the idea was mooted in certain quarters that collapsed states might be placed under some kind of international trusteeship. Unsurprisingly, as a formal status this had no attraction whatsoever for the generality of states and so nothing came of it. But in one or two cases, notably Kosovo following the imposition, with UN *Security Council approval, of international control over the province in 1999, the practicalities of the situation began to look rather like that of *de facto* trusteeship. *See also* Trusteeship Council; trusteeship system.

Trusteeship Council. The UN organ set up to supervise the work of the states administering those territories which became part of the *trusteeship system. It was a somewhat more intrusive body than that instituted by the *mandates system. However, as all such territories have moved away from this status (most becoming *sovereign states, but some integrating into adjacent states), the Council has no remaining functions – but instead of being wound up it has been left available for use as and where it may be required.

trusteeship system. The UN system which replaced that for *mandates, providing for the supervision by the Organization's *Trusteeship Council of states administering *trust territories. A few mandates achieved *independence (sense 1) immediately after the Second World War, and one – South West Africa – could not be transferred to the new system as the mandatory power (South Africa) refused to cooperate. But the other mandatories who had been on the victorious side agreed to change their mandates into trust territories; one defeated mandatory (Japan) had her mandates passed to the United States; and the mandatory who during the War moved from the losing to the winning side (Italy) was again put in charge of Italian Somaliland. Provision was made for states administering *non-selfgoverning territories to put them under the system, but none did so. As all trust territories have now become, or joined, *sovereign states, the system is effectively defunct.

trust territories. Territories placed under the UN *trusteeship system.

twin-track diplomacy. The conduct of a *negotiation by two separate but co-ordinated means. *See also* backchannel; track two diplomacy.

two track diplomacy. *See* twin-track diplomacy.

U

ultimatum. An announcement of a party's non-negotiable demand or position, though there are variations both in form and implication:

(1) A formal announcement that failure to undertake a specified action, usually by a specified time, will result in a specified penalty, usually involving the use of force; in other words, a very precise military threat. An ultimatum of this kind was traditionally delivered by *note or memorandum and required a 'prompt, clear and categorical reply'. Perhaps because the meaning of this term is so clear and because it carries a great deal of historical baggage, it can be provocative. David Owen, speaking of the time when he was the EU *mediator in the former Yugoslavia in 1994, has reported that the Bosnian Serbs were 'very angry about the constant use of the word "ultimatum" because it was the emotive word used by the Germans before the bombing of Belgrade in 1941'. The Serbs were lucky; on more than one occasion in the Second World War an ultimatum from Hitler followed rather than preceded military action, a practice 'greatly to be deprecated', notes the most recent edition of *Satow's Guide*.

(2) An indication made by one side during a negotiation (usually at a fairly advanced stage) of the absolute minimum it is prepared to accept and/or the maximum it is willing to concede: 'this is an ultimatum – take it or leave it'.

ultimo. Of last month, as in 'Thank you for your *despatch of the 19th ultimo.' Now historical. *See also* instant.

unanimity rule. The taking of decisions in an *international organization or an international conference on the basis of unanimity, that is, on the basis of the expressed agreement of all members or participants. In these circumstances each member or participant has a *veto. It used to be the norm, and for that reason was generally applicable in the *League of Nations. But since the Second World War it has become much less common. However, it is still found in those (few) organizations where it is necessary, for their continued well-being, that in respect of at least part of their work, all the members should march in step. A prominent example is the *North Atlantic Council of NATO. *See also* consensus decision-making; constructive abstention; Council of Ministers (European); weighted voting.

under flying seal (UFS). A *despatch sent UFS was one sent from one point to another via a third, the latter being either invited or required to read it before resealing it and sending it on its way. For example, this might have been a despatch sent from a ministry of *foreign affairs to one of its embassies abroad via another one in the same region, or one from a *consular mission to the ministry of foreign affairs at home via the embassy under whose immediate authority the consular mission fell. A feature of the era before copying documents was easy and cheap, which extended into the twentieth century, sending messages UFS was an effective method of keeping informed those within the same diplomatic service with the most need for the information contained in the despatch.

unequal treaty. The term applied by the Chinese to the *treaties under which they were forced by superior military power to cede or lease land and grant sweeping *exterritorial rights to the European powers in the middle of the nineteenth century. The 'treaty system' which replaced the previous 'tributary system' for dealing with barbarians was established by the Treaty of Nanking in 1842 and the Treaties of Tientsin of 1858 but only finally accepted by the Manchu dynasty after the occupation of Peking in 1860 and the plundering and burning of the Summer Palace. The unequal treaties were not finally abolished until 1943. *See also* capitulations.

unfriendly act. Traditional *diplomatic language (sense 1) for an action likely to lead to war. More generally, any action which is deemed to be unnecessarily hostile, especially by a state with whom the aggrieved state considered itself to be in *friendly relations.

unilateral declaration. A *binding undertaking made unilaterally by a *minister (sense 3) of one sovereign state to another sovereign state. The undertaking may even be made orally.

unilateral diplomacy. *See* diplomatic representation.

unilateralism. The disposition to act alone, without concerting with allies or bowing to the opinion of a body such as the UN *Security Council. To the distress of the

*European Commission, it periodically breaks out in the *European Union.

United Nations (UN). Established in 1945 by the victorious powers in the Second World War, initially the UN had 51 member states. Subsequently the *neutral states in that war, the defeated states, and the numerous new states which emerged with the end of *colonialism and the breakdown of some federal states were also admitted, so that in December 2002 the UN had 191 members.

The UN's main initial purpose was to maintain international peace and security on the basis of the principle of *collective security, which largely fell by the wayside on account of the mutual distrust of its two major members, the Soviet Union and the United States. But, largely through its *Security Council, the UN made some useful contributions in the area of *peacekeeping; and since the end of the *Cold War has operated much more on the lines expressed in the UN *Charter.

The Charter also spoke of the need to respect the principle of *self-determination, of the desirability of cooperation on economic, social, cultural, and humanitarian matters, and of promoting respect for *human rights. In all these areas there has, over the years, been a huge expansion in the UN's work, for which the *General Assembly and the *Economic and Social Council are chiefly responsible. The *Trusteeship Council also played a part. The *pacific settlement of disputes always lies high on the UN's agenda, and in that connection the work of the *International Court of Justice must be mentioned.

The UN's headquarters is in New York, United States. But many members of its *secretariat are based at widely spread locations throughout the world, including those who service the UN's regional economic commissions and some of its programmes. The Secretary-General heads the secretariat; the current, and seventh, incumbent, is Kofi Annan, a national (sense 2) of Ghana.

See also multilateral diplomacy; specialized agencies; UN system.

United Nations family. *See* United Nations system.

United Nations High Commissioner for Human Rights. An Office established in 1993 to encourage respect for human rights through discussion with states and international organizations. The High Commissioner is also responsible for coordinating all the UN's human rights activities.

United Nations High Commissioner for Refugees (UNHCR). The Office of the UNHCR, established in 1951, is an important body within the *United Nations system. Its headquarters is in Geneva, Switzerland.

United Nations system. A term which is sometimes used to refer collectively to the UN, certain UN programmes and funds (such as the UN Children's Fund – UNICEF – and the UN Development Programme), and the *specialized agencies. This group is also sometimes known as the UN family, or the UN family organizations.

United Nations Treaty Series. The UN-published series containing the treaties registered with its *secretariat by the organization's members (who are obliged under the UN Charter so to register all their treaties). Reflecting the UN's inheritance from the *League of Nations of a commitment to *open diplomacy, the series has now become extremely large.

Uniting for Peace resolution. A resolution passed by the UN *General Assembly in 1950 in the hope that it would facilitate Assembly recommendations for the maintenance of peace in circumstances where the *Security Council was unable to act because of a *veto. At its core was the provision that in this event an emergency special session of the Assembly could be called on 24 hours notice on the vote of any seven members of the Council or on the call of a majority of UN members. It was passed in face of strong opposition from the Soviet bloc, but was never used against these states in the manner in which they feared – and the then-Western

majority in the UN hoped. It has, however, been used on a number of other types of occasion.

Universal Declaration of Human Rights. A *declaration (sense 1) of the UN *General Assembly passed in 1948 which set out the basic rights and fundamental freedoms to which all men and women everywhere in the world were deemed to be entitled. The subsequent endeavour to translate these rights into legal (and hence *binding) obligations bore fruit in two 1966 treaties: the International Covenant on Economic, Social and Cultural Rights, and the International Covenant on Civil and Political Rights, both of which *entered into force in 1976, and to both of which the majority of states are parties. Quite apart from them, however, many provisions of the Universal Declaration are widely thought to have the weight of *customary law. There is often, however, a gulf between the law and state practice, which can be very difficult to bridge. *See also* human rights.

UNO-City. A popular name for the Vienna International Centre, opened in 1979, where the *UN system has a significant presence.

unofficial letter. A British Diplomatic Service term for a letter sent by a member of a diplomatic mission to a named officer at home, or vice versa. *See also* despatch; savingram; telegram.

UpDK. *See GlavUpDK.*

UTC. The acronym for Coordinated Universal Time, the accepted term for what used to be – and often still is – called *Greenwich Mean Time. The new term emerged in 1970 from the *International Telecommunication Union, which also felt that in order to eliminate confusion a single acronym should be adopted. However, it was found impossible to agree on using either the English word order, CUT, or the French word order, TUC, and UTC was chosen as a compromise. Whether the objective of employing one acronym to remove confusion was actually achieved must be considered a moot point!

uti possidetis. The doctrine that existing territorial boundaries should be preserved. It was used in support of the claim of the incoming regimes in former colonial territories to inherit all of the territory; and subsequently in support of their denial of the right of ethnic sub-groups to secede or join a neighbouring state. Both assertions were well received. The first minimized problems for the outgoing colonial powers; and the second was thought by all the successor regimes to be very much in their interest.

V

vacant seat formula. An expedient sometimes adopted by *international organizations when more than one group claims to be the legitimate government of a member state. Instead of accepting the *credentials of one of the groups (thus rejecting the other), the organization may simply leave that state's seat temporarily vacant. This was done literally – and graphically – in the rather different circumstances which resulted from the refusal of the United States Senate to allow its country to join the *League of Nations, in the creation of which its president, Woodrow *Wilson, had played an important part. At the League Council, a seat was left vacant for the absent permanent member, and remained vacant throughout the League's life: the 'empty chair'.

valedictory despatch. A head of mission's last *despatch before leaving his or her post. Traditionally, this is a reflective summing up, which, for the brave, will contain some predictions for the future course of events in the country concerned and thoughts about how policy might accordingly be shaped towards it. *See also* farewell call.

vassal state. Somewhat akin to the modern concept of a *satellite state, a state required to pay *tribute to a *suzerain (and hence sometimes known as a tributary state). It is now a little-used term. *See also* dependent state; puppet state.

Vatican City State. The 'minuscule' *state in Rome, as it was described by Pope Paul VI at the UN in 1965, granted to the *Holy See under the *Lateran Treaties of 1929. In area the Vatican City is about one-sixth of a square mile.

Vattel, Emmerich de (1714–67). Born in Neuchâtel in Switzerland, Vattel was a diplomat but achieved his fame for his writing on *international law. In 1746 he obtained employment in the diplomatic service of the Elector of Saxony and in the following year was appointed *minister plenipotentiary at Berne. Not finding his duties taxing, it was here that he completed his major work, *Le Droit des Gens* (*The Law of Nations*). Published in 1758, this swiftly became a standard work, not least for its treatment of *diplomatic law. Indeed, it has been said that this represents the last of the great classic writings on the subject. In Vattel, *diplomatic privileges and immunities were grounded firmly in their *functional necessity for the efficient conduct of diplomacy.

Venetian diplomacy. The diplomacy of the mercantile and seafaring republic of Venice, which was originally shaped in the *Byzantine pattern but eventually developed a quite distinct tradition. Until the republic was extinguished by Napoleon in 1797, the Venetian diplomatic service, which is generally believed to have been the first organized and closely supervised diplomatic service to have been created, was regarded as the model for all Europe. Carefully selected, subject to the most austere regulations, and highly motivated to serve the republic, until the end Venetian diplomats continued to be regarded as the best informed men in the *diplomatic corps of any capital city. *See also* bailo; Barbaro; calendar; *relazione*.

venue. The place chosen for a negotiation, though Harold *Nicolson noted that 'professional diplomatists' considered it 'rather vulgar' to use this word, no doubt because of its association with sport and popular entertainment. For both practical and political reasons the choice of a venue is rarely arbitrary. Venue may be significant either by virtue of the country, the precise location within the country, or the building in question – or sometimes by virtue of all three. For example, the exploratory encounters between the United States and North Korea, which eventually led to the signing in Geneva in 1994 of the agreement between them on nuclear matters, began at an official Chinese venue: the International Club in Beijing, which is a facility belonging to the Chinese ministry of foreign affairs. The fact that China's *good offices (sense 1) had been accepted made any subsequent informal Chinese *mediation more likely and secrecy easy to obtain; Beijing itself was one of the few sites where both the United States and North Korea had major embassies; while choice of the International Club within the city (rather than one or other of the embassies) reinforced the neutrality of the setting and made Chinese support for the talks easier still.

verbatim record. *See* minutes.

veto. A vote which has the effect of killing a proposal which would otherwise have become a *resolution of the organization or a decision of the meeting in question. Depending on the *rules of procedure and the accepted practices of the body concerned, the vote may be a 'no' or simply an *abstention. *See also* Security Council.

vice-consul. *See* consular post; honorary consular officer.

vice-consulate. *See* consular post; honorary consular officer.

vice-dean. The deputy of the *dean of the *diplomatic corps. Such a person might be useful if the dean represents a government or state which is not recognized by one or more other states with ambassadors in the local diplomatic corps, though it is unusual for this to be an obstacle to the conduct of 'decanal' business.

vice-marshal of the diplomatic corps. *See* marshal of the diplomatic corps.

viceroy. A man who governs a territory in the name and by the authority of a head of state, generally a monarch; literally, a vice- or deputy-king; hence a 'vicereine' is a vice- or deputy-queen. *See also* proconsul.

Vienna, Congress of (1814–15). The *congress of the powers, dominated by *Metternich but not at the expense of *Talleyrand, which restored the *international order in Europe following the protracted convulsions of the Napoleonic Wars. For diplomacy, the *Regulation which it agreed solved at long last the serious problem of *precedence, while the restoration of the Swiss Confederation and the guarantee by the Congress of Switzerland's *permanent neutrality fortified a tradition which was subsequently to prove of considerable value to the world diplomatic system.

Vienna Conventions. *See* Consular Relations; Diplomatic Relations; Law of Treaties; Representation of States in their Relations with International Organizations of a Universal Character.

Vienna, Diplomatic Academy of. The Austrian training school for diplomats. Reopened in 1964 when Bruno *Kreisky was foreign minister, the *Diplomatische Akademie*, which is located in the consular wing of the *Theresianum* in Vienna, traces its origins to the reforms of Count *Kaunitz in the middle of the eighteenth century.

Vietnam War. The huge armed effort by the United States over almost a decade (1964–73) which tried, unsuccessfully, to prevent South Vietnam falling to the North Vietnamese-led Communist insurrection. *See also* Bunker.

vin d'honneur. A reception to mark a significant event in a diplomat's career, such as the presentation of *letters of credence to the *receiving state's head of state.

virtual diplomacy. The conduct of *diplomacy (sense 1) via electronic information and communications technologies (ICTs) and thus without face-to-face contact. Credit for the invention of this term in the late 1990s is claimed by the United States Institute of Peace. However, while ICTs are making a large difference to the ways in which some states arrange communication between their foreign ministries and their diplomatic missions, and provide them with background material, such developments do not undermine the utility of traditional diplomatic missions for the performance of *diplomatic functions. *See also* telecommunication.

virtual embassy. An *embassy (sense 1) which is so small that it may even be located in a hotel room, provided it has a computer with a modem and wire or wireless access. An obvious misnomer, as such an embassy is not intangible, but just virtually virtual. *See also* rapid reaction embassy.

visa. (1) Earlier *visé* (from *viser*, to look at), an entry in a passport providing evidence that it has been examined and found correct. (2) A special authorization (stamped or placed in a passport) to visit or to undertake paid or business activity in a state. This is frequently required but does not always guarantee entry. Arriving diplomats are not exempt from visa regulations. *See also* letter of protection (sense 1); right of transit; safe-conduct.

visiting fireman. Anyone who arrives from the outside at the scene of a difficult negotiation to reinforce or take over from those already charged with its conduct. In embassies the term is usually applied to a senior official or minister arriving from home. At the UN *Security Council it can mean more or less anybody who is not a member but is given a hearing, including representatives of *nongovernmental organizations. Since 'visiting firemen' are often more intent on fanning the flames of controversy than hosing them down, it will be understood that the phrase is commonly employed with heavy irony. *See also* special envoy.

vital interest. An interest considered so essential to the general well-being of a state that it is one in defence of which it is prepared to go to war. *See also* honour; necessity.

voeu. A recommendation, wish or view recorded at a conference to accompany a *treaty but which has no *binding force upon the signatories; in some circumstances it may be more or less a pious hope. The Assembly of the *League of Nations, which generally took decisions on the basis of the *unanimity rule (and always so in respect of important substantive matters), utilized the idea of a *voeu* by ruling that a decision which could be so described needed only a simple majority.

volte face. A complete reversal of a position, or about-turn.

W

waiver. The process whereby a state, in respect of one of its *diplomatic agents or *consular officers, sets aside the right of *diplomatic or *consular immunity which is normally enjoyed by the individual in question. This is not a frequent occurrence, and is only done after careful consideration. However, in recent years waiver appears to have been sought by a *receiving state rather more strongly than hitherto, often with success.

war. An *armed conflict which has been formally instituted by a declaration of war or the expiry of an *ultimatum. Since 1945 such announcements have gone resoundingly out of fashion, no state wishing to lay itself open to the charge of having initiated a war; associatedly, all armed action is now described as defensive in character, or as in necessary support of some universal norms, such as those relating to *human rights. *See also* Briand–Kellogg Pact; neutrality; permanent neutrality.

war crime. A breach, by an individual, of the *laws of war (or of, as this subject is now known, *international humanitarian law). Such laws used to refer only to those who participated immediately in war. But in the major war crimes trials which took place after the Second World War, the concept of war crimes was extended to cover crimes against peace, and crimes against humanity – for which the political leaders of the defeated states could be, and were, indicted. *See also* international criminal law.

warden network. The members of a *sending state's *expatriate community who have volunteered to act as points of contact across the country during a local crisis or emergency. Such networks are now common in chronically unstable or hostile regions, though their efficiency has been impaired when, for their own safety, wardens have themselves been ordered by their companies to leave the country during an emergency. *See also* emergency room; hot line.

Warsaw Pact. Concluded in 1955 (and formally titled the Eastern European Mutual Assistance Treaty), the Pact was a *Cold War *alliance between the Soviet Union and seven states in east and central Europe. It provided for a unified military command with its headquarters in Moscow. It was wound up in 1991.

way bill. *See* diplomatic courier.

weighted voting. The system adopted in certain *international organizations, notably the International Monetary Fund, the International Bank for Reconstruction and Development, and the *European Union, of allocating votes in proportion to the 'weight' of the members, usually judged by the size of their financial or other contributions to them. This has appeal for *realists but it is politically sensitive. First, it draws attention to the large material differences between states when set alongside their *equality of status. Secondly, there is usually dispute over the criteria to be employed in computing these differences, as well as in applying the criteria if and when they have been chosen. Where weighted voting is the formal rule, in practice the influence of the *consensus method is usually considerable. *See also* qualified majority voting (QMV).

West, the. (1) Often used during the *Cold War to refer to the non-Communist states of Europe and America, and more particularly to those of them who were members of *NATO, which was then an *alliance established to counter the *Eastern bloc. (2) That part of the world which is generally termed western, as contrasted (in both historical and cultural terms) with the East or the Orient.

Western European Union (WEU). The WEU dates from 1955, but has its origins in an earlier arrangement made by the Brussels Treaty of 1948. It has always had some difficulty in carving out a distinctive niche for itself, and for much of its life seemed content to take something of a back seat. During the last fifteen years it has been more proactive, with a certain measure of success. But it still remains caught, as it were, between *NATO and the *European Union.

Westphalia, Congress of (1644–48). The *congress at which an end to the Thirty Years' War was negotiated. It had *venues at two Westphalian towns: Catholic Münster, to which were assigned the *plenipotentiaries of France; and Protestant Osnabrück, 55 kilometres removed, to which were assigned those of Sweden. The representatives of the Emperor, the third of the main parties at the congress, were divided between the two towns, while the plenipotentiaries of the many other parties (including the Spanish, the Swiss, and the Dutch) gravitated to the one or the other depending on whether they were closer to France or Sweden, or on whether one of the venues had already attracted the delegation with which they wished chiefly to negotiate. The main fruits of the negotiations were the two treaties of peace signed on 24 October 1648 between the Empire and Sweden and the Empire and France. Known collectively as either the 'Treaty' or the 'Peace' of Westphalia, they are generally reckoned to have resolved the structure and codified the constitutional rules of the European *states-system as it had emerged from the unity of medieval Christendom. Thereafter, it has not been unusual to see the term 'Westphalian system' used to describe the post-1648 system of international relations, i.e. that in which states – secular, sovereign, independent, and equal – are the members, and stability is preserved by the *balance of power, *diplomacy and *international law. *See also* international society.

Westphalian system. *See* Westphalia, Congress of (1644–48).

Whitehall. The name of a street in London which, because a number of government offices front on to it, is sometimes used – particularly by those posted abroad – as a synonym for the government of Britain, or for a particular government department.

Wicquefort, Abraham de (1598–1682). An *intelligencer, *gazetteer and, like *Machiavelli, a diplomat of the second order who is remembered more for what he wrote than for his other accomplishments. Born in Holland, Wicquefort nevertheless spent most of his diplomatic career in Paris. Here he served as *resident of the Elector of Brandenburg-Prussia from 1626 until 1658, when, having fallen foul of Mazarin, he was first briefly imprisoned in the Bastille and then expelled. Invited to The Hague by John de Witt, the Grand Pensionary of Holland, Wicquefort was employed as a translator for the States General but chiefly as the Grand Pensionary's special secretary for French correspondence. In 1675 Wicquefort, who had in the previous year also secured the appointment of resident in Holland of the Duke of Brunswick-Luneburg-Celle, was accused by his enemies of selling state secrets. He was tried by the Court of Holland and, despite his plea of *diplomatic immunity, imprisoned for life on the grounds that he remained a Dutch national in the paid service of its government to which he had taken an oath of secrecy. Sent, like *Grotius before him, to the prison of Loevestein (though he escaped to Celle in 1679), he devoted his time to furious writing. Without the aid of his large library, which had been confiscated, he wrote first the *Mémoires touchant les ambassadeurs et les ministres publics*, which he signed simply 'L.M.P.' (*Le Ministre Prisonnier*), and then his massive *L'Ambassadeur et ses fonctions*. First published in the year before he died, translated into English as *The Embassador and His Functions* in 1716, and subsequently reissued many times, this became the most highly regarded manual of diplomacy of the eighteenth century. As has been remarked, Wicquefort was the *Satow of the *ancien régime*. See *also* locally engaged staff.

wife, diplomatic. *See* spouse, diplomatic.

Wilhelmstrasse. *See Auswärtiges Amt (AA).*

Wilson, President Woodrow (1856 –1924). The American President who, in January 1918, enunciated his 'Fourteen Points' for a just end to the war (which the United States had joined in 1917) against the Central Powers. Wilson included references to the need for peaceful change on the basis of *self-determination (only, however, in Europe); but most notably he called for what was soon to be termed *open diplomacy, and for 'a general association of nations' to guarantee the 'political independence and territorial integrity [of] great and small states alike'. This last soon found expression in the *League of Nations and its scheme for *collective security – but the United States did not become a member, chiefly because of the hostility of its Senate to the whole idea.

Wisma Putra. The Malaysian ministry of *foreign affairs, so-called because since 1966 it has occupied a building of this name. However, since 2001 the ministry has been operating from a new Wisma Putra complex in the recently developed administrative city of Putrajaya, 20 kilometres south of Kuala Lumpur. The old office in the federal capital has been taken over by the Institute of Diplomacy and Foreign Relations.

working copy (of credentials). The copy of an incoming *head of mission's *credentials which is furnished on arrival to the *receiving state's foreign ministry. It is sometimes called 'true copy' and is known in French as the *copie figurée* (earlier as *copie d'usage*). *See also* letters of credence; presentation of credentials.

working funeral. The funeral of a major political leader which is attended by scores of high-level delegations from abroad. It is thus an opportunity not only for diplomatic *signalling but also for confidential discussion between the mourners and the politically bereaved government, and perhaps more especially between the mourners themselves. The term has been attributed to Robert Carvel, Political Editor of the London *Evening Standard*, who introduced it in an article on the Requiem Mass for West German Chancellor, Konrad Adenauer, in April 1967.

Funerals of this kind, which are attended by high ceremony and generally styled 'state funerals', are extremely useful in diplomacy. They provide an occasion which is above reproach for *heads of state and government to break existing commitments for discussion on an urgent matter of the moment; and they provide a cloak behind which the representatives of hostile states may meet. If the deceased leader was an incumbent rather than retired, the funeral also provides what will probably be the first opportunity for foreign leaders to make contact with his or her successor.

working visit. *See* state visit.

world public opinion. *See* General Assembly.

World Trade Organization (WTO). This international organization was established in 1994 as the successor body to the General Agreement on Tariffs and Trade (GATT). It is intended to continue and strengthen GATT's work. Its headquarters is in Geneva, Switzerland. It is not part of the *United Nations system, but has cooperating arrangements and practices with the UN.

Wotton, Sir Henry (1568–1639). The English diplomat and poet who has gone down in diplomatic legend as the author of the epigram, often misquoted, that 'An Ambassador is an honest man, sent to lie abroad for the good of his country'. Wotton (pronounced 'Wootton') was an amiable but impecunious dilettante and literary amateur. He did not find stable employment until knighted on the accession of James I and sent to Venice as *resident ambassador. On his way out, in 1604, he stayed in Augsburg. Having already some reputation in the town, he was invited by a resident to write some *bon mot* in a notebook kept for the purpose, and the famous quotation was the result. It was intended, of course, as a pun on the word 'lie', which in this context could mean either 'sojourn abroad' or 'tell lies abroad'. (It is not known whether Wotton also meant it to refer to having sexual relations.) Unfortunately for Sir Henry, while he appears to have conceived the saying in English, he wrote it out in Latin: '*Legatus est vir bonus peregrè missus ad mentiendum Reipublicæ causâ.*' According to his friend Isaak Walton, 'the word lie (being the hinge upon which the conceit was to turn) was not so expressed in Latin [*mentiendum*], as would admit (in the hands of an enemy especially) so fair a construction as Sir Henry thought in English'. This was his undoing, for the notebook eventually fell into the hands of a Catholic controversialist who used it in a polemic against James I published in 1611, presenting it as evidence that the king had sent a confessed liar to represent him abroad. James never entirely forgave Wotton the indiscretion which provided such ammunition to his enemies. The hopes cherished by the diplomat in 1612 of being the King's secretary were accordingly dashed, and Wotton was doomed to remain in Venice (with interludes elsewhere) until 1624. In all, he spent nearly twenty years as either resident ambassador or *ambassador in ordinary in Venice, and ended his career as provost of Eton College.

Wriston Report (1954). *See* Foreign Service, US.

Y

Yalta formula. The provisions which find expression in Article 27 of the UN *Charter on the voting procedure of the *Security Council, including (therefore) the *veto; so called because it was agreed at the Soviet Crimean resort of Yalta at a summit meeting of the Big Three (the USA, USSR, and Britain) in February 1945.

Yom Kippur War. The Israeli term for the *October War (1973).

Z

Z. The abbreviated telegraphic indication of *Greenwich Mean Time.

zone of separation. *See* buffer zone.

A Guide to the Key Articles of the Vienna Convention

The Vienna Convention on Diplomatic Relations (1961)

The States Parties to the present Convention,

Recalling that peoples of all nations from ancient times have recognized the status of diplomatic agents,

Having in mind the purposes and principles of the Charter of the United Nations concerning the sovereign equality of States, the maintenance of international peace and security, and the promotion of friendly relations among nations,

Believing that an international convention on diplomatic intercourse, privileges and immunities would contribute to the development of friendly relations among nations, irrespective of their differing constitutional and social systems,

Realizing that the purpose of such privileges and immunities is not to benefit individuals but to ensure the efficient performance of the functions of diplomatic missions as representing States,

Affirming that the rules of customary international law should continue to govern questions not expressly regulated by the provisions of the present Convention,

Have agreed as follows:

Article 1

For the purpose of the present Convention, the following expressions shall have the meanings hereunder assigned to them:

(a) the 'head of the mission' is the person charged by the sending State with the duty of acting in that capacity;

(b) the 'members of the mission' are the head of the mission and the members of the staff of the mission;

(c) the 'members of the staff of the mission' are the members of the diplomatic staff, of the administrative and technical staff and of the service staff of the mission;

(d) the 'members of the diplomatic staff' are the members of the staff of the mission having diplomatic rank;

(e) a 'diplomatic agent' is the head of the mission or a member of the diplomatic staff of the mission;

(f) the 'members of the administrative and technical staff' are the members of the staff of the mission employed in the administrative and technical service of the mission;

(g) the 'members of the service staff' are the members of the staff of the mission in the domestic service of the mission;

(h) a 'private servant' is a person who is in the domestic service of a member of the mission and who is not an employee of the sending State;

(i) the 'premises of the mission' are the buildings or parts of buildings and the land ancillary thereto, irrespective of ownership, used for the purposes of the mission including the residence of the head of the mission.

Article 2

The establishment of diplomatic relations between States, and of permanent diplomatic missions, takes place by mutual consent.

Article 3

1. The functions of a diplomatic mission consist *inter alia* in:

(a) representing the sending State in the receiving State;

(b) protecting in the receiving State the interests of the sending State and of its nationals, within the limits permitted by international law;

(c) negotiating with the Government of the receiving State;

(d) ascertaining by all lawful means conditions and developments in the receiving State, and reporting thereon to the Government of the sending State;

(e) promoting friendly relations between the sending State and the receiving State, and developing their economic, cultural and scientific relations.

2. Nothing in the present Convention shall be construed as preventing the performance of consular functions by a diplomatic mission.

Article 4

1. The sending State must make certain that the *agrément* of the receiving State has been given for the person it proposes to accredit as head of the mission to that State.

2. The receiving State is not obliged to give reasons to the sending State for a refusal of *agrément*.

Article 5

1. The sending State may, after it has given due notification to the receiving State concerned, accredit a head of mission or assign any member of the diplomatic staff, as the case may be, to more than one State, unless there is express objection by any of the receiving States.

2. If the sending State accredits a head of mission to one or more other States it may establish a diplomatic mission headed by a chargé d'affaires ad interim in each State where the head of mission has not his permanent seat.

3. A head of mission or any member of the diplomatic staff of the mission may act as representative of the sending State to any international organization.

Article 6

Two or more States may accredit the same person as head of mission to another State, unless objection is offered by the receiving State.

Article 7

Subject to the provisions of Articles 5, 8, 9 and 11, the sending State may freely appoint the members of the staff of the mission. In the case of military, naval or air attachés, the receiving State may require their names to be submitted beforehand, for its approval.

Article 8

1. Members of the diplomatic staff of the mission should in principle be of the nationality of the sending State.

2. Members of the diplomatic staff of the mission may not be appointed from among persons having the nationality of the receiving State, except with the consent of that State which may be withdrawn at any time.

3. The receiving State may reserve the same right with regard to nationals of a third State who are not also nationals of the sending State.

Article 9

1. The receiving State may at any time and without having to explain its decision, notify the sending State that the head of the mission or any member of the diplomatic staff of the mission is *persona non grata* or that any other member of the staff of the mission is not acceptable. In any such case, the sending State shall, as appropriate, either recall the person concerned or terminate his functions with the mission. A person may be declared *non grata* or not acceptable before arriving in the territory of the receiving State.

2. If the sending State refuses or fails within a reasonable period to carry out its obligations under paragraph 1 of this Article, the receiving State may refuse to recognize the person concerned as a member of the mission.

Article 10

1. The Ministry for Foreign Affairs of the receiving State, or such other ministry as may be agreed, shall be notified of:
(a) the appointment of members of the mission, their arrival and their final departure or the termination of their functions with the mission;
(b) the arrival and final departure of a person belonging to the family of a member of the mission and, where appropriate, the fact that a person becomes or ceases to be a member of the family of a member of the mission;
(c) the arrival and final departure of private servants in the employ of persons referred to in sub-paragraph (a) of this paragraph and, where appropriate, the fact that they are leaving the employ of such persons;
(d) the engagement and discharge of persons resident in the receiving State as members of the mission or private servants entitled to privileges and immunities.
2. Where possible, prior notification of arrival and final departure shall also be given.

Article 11

1. In the absence of specific agreement as to the size of the mission, the receiving State may require that the size of a mission be kept within limits considered by it to be reasonable and normal, having regard to circumstances and conditions in the receiving State and to the needs of the particular mission.
2. The receiving State may equally, within similar bounds and on a non-discriminatory basis, refuse to accept officials of a particular category.

Article 12

The sending State may not, without the prior express consent of the receiving State, establish offices forming part of the mission in localities other than those in which the mission itself is established.

Article 13

1. The head of the mission is considered as having taken up his functions in the receiving State either when he has presented his credentials or when he has notified his arrival and a true copy of his credentials has been presented to the Ministry for Foreign Affairs of the receiving State, or such other ministry as may be agreed, in accordance with the practice prevailing in the receiving State which shall be applied in a uniform manner.
2. The order of presentation of credentials or of a true copy thereof will be determined by the date and time of the arrival of the head of the mission.

Article 14

1. Heads of mission are divided into three classes, namely:
(a) that of ambassadors or nuncios accredited to Heads of State, and other heads of mission of equivalent rank;
(b) that of envoys, ministers and internuncios accredited to Heads of State;
(c) that of chargés d'affaires accredited to Ministers of Foreign Affairs.
2. Except as concerns precedence and etiquette, there shall be no differentiation between heads of mission by reason of their class.

Article 15

The class to which the heads of their missions are to be assigned shall be agreed between States.

Article 16

1. Heads of mission shall take precedence in their respective classes in the order of the date and time of taking up their functions in accordance with Article 13.

2. Alterations in the credentials of a head of mission not involving any change of class shall not affect his precedence.

3. This article is without prejudice to any practice accepted by the receiving State regarding the precedence of the representative of the Holy See.

Article 17

The precedence of the members of the diplomatic staff of the mission shall be notified by the head of the mission to the Ministry for Foreign Affairs or such other ministry as may be agreed.

Article 18

The procedure to be observed in each State for the reception of heads of mission shall be uniform in respect of each class.

Article 19

1. If the post of head of the mission is vacant, or if the head of the mission is unable to perform his functions, a chargé d'affaires ad interim shall act provisionally as head of the mission. The name of the chargé d'affaires ad interim shall be notified, either by the head of the mission or, in case he is unable to do so, by the Ministry for Foreign Affairs of the sending State to the Ministry for Foreign Affairs of the receiving State or such other ministry as may be agreed.

2. In cases where no member of the diplomatic staff of the mission is present in the receiving State, a member of the administrative and technical staff may, with the consent of the receiving State, be designated by the sending State to be in charge of the current administrative affairs of the mission.

Article 20

The mission and its head shall have the right to use the flag and emblem of the sending State on the premises of the mission, including the residence of the head of the mission, and on his means of transport.

Article 21

1. The receiving State shall either facilitate the acquisition on its territory, in accordance with its laws, by the sending State of premises necessary for its mission or assist the latter in obtaining accommodation in some other way.

2. It shall also, where necessary, assist missions in obtaining suitable accommodation for their members.

Article 22

1. The premises of the mission shall be inviolable. The agents of the receiving State may not enter them, except with the consent of the head of the mission.

2. The receiving State is under a special duty to take all appropriate steps to protect the premises of the mission against any intrusion or damage and to prevent any disturbance of the peace of the mission or impairment of its dignity.

3. The premises of the mission, their furnishings and other property thereon and the means of transport of the mission shall be immune from search, requisition, attachment or execution.

Article 23

1. The sending State and the head of the mission shall be exempt from all national, regional or municipal dues and taxes in respect of the premises of the mission, whether owned or leased, other than such as represent payment for specific services rendered.

2. The exemption from taxation referred to in this Article shall not apply to such dues and taxes payable under the law of the receiving State by persons contracting with the sending State or the head of the mission.

Article 24

The archives and documents of the mission shall be inviolable at any time and wherever they may be.

Article 25

The receiving State shall accord full facilities for the performance of the functions of the mission.

Article 26

Subject to its laws and regulations concerning zones entry into which is prohibited or regulated for reasons of national security, the receiving State shall ensure to all members of the mission freedom of movement and travel in its territory.

Article 27

1. The receiving State shall permit and protect free communication on the part of the mission for all official purposes. In communicating with the Government and the other missions and consulates of the sending State, wherever situated, the mission may employ all appropriate means, including diplomatic couriers and messages in code or cipher. However, the mission may install and use a wireless transmitter only with the consent of the receiving State.

2. The official correspondence of the mission shall be inviolable. Official correspondence means all correspondence relating to the mission and its functions.

3. The diplomatic bag shall not be opened or detained.

4. The packages constituting the diplomatic bag must bear visible external marks of their character and may contain only diplomatic documents or articles intended for official use.

5. The diplomatic courier, who shall be provided with an official document indicating his status and the number of packages constituting the diplomatic bag, shall be protected by the receiving State in the performance of his functions. He shall enjoy personal inviolability and shall not be liable to any form of arrest or detention.

6. The sending State or the mission may designate diplomatic couriers *ad hoc*. In such cases the provisions of paragraph 5 of this Article shall also apply, except that the immunities therein mentioned shall cease to apply when such a courier has delivered to the consignee the diplomatic bag in his charge.

7. A diplomatic bag may be entrusted to the captain of a commercial aircraft scheduled to land at an authorized port of entry. He shall be provided with an official docu-

ment indicating the number of packages constituting the bag but he shall not be considered to be a diplomatic courier. The mission may send one of its members to take possession of the diplomatic bag directly and freely from the captain of the aircraft.

Article 28

The fees and charges levied by the mission in the course of its official duties shall be exempt from all dues and taxes.

Article 29

The person of a diplomatic agent shall be inviolable. He shall not be liable to any form of arrest or detention. The receiving State shall treat him with due respect and shall take all appropriate steps to prevent any attack on his person, freedom or dignity.

Article 30

1. The private residence of a diplomatic agent shall enjoy the same inviolability and protection as the premises of the mission.

2. His papers, correspondence and, except as provided in paragraph 3 of Article 31, his property, shall likewise enjoy inviolability.

Article 31

1. A diplomatic agent shall enjoy immunity from the criminal jurisdiction of the receiving State. He shall also enjoy immunity from its civil and administrative jurisdiction, except in the case of:
(a) a real action relating to private immovable property situated in the territory of the receiving State, unless he holds it on behalf of the sending State for the purposes of the mission;
(b) an action relating to succession in which the diplomatic agent is involved as executor, administrator, heir or legatee as a private person and not on behalf of the sending State;
(c) an action relating to any professional or commercial activity exercised by the diplomatic agent in the receiving State outside his official functions.

2. A diplomatic agent is not obliged to give evidence as a witness.

3. No measures of execution may be taken in respect of a diplomatic agent except in the cases coming under sub-paragraphs (a), (b) and (c) of paragraph 1 of this Article, and provided that the measures concerned can be taken without infringing the inviolability of his person or of his residence.

4. The immunity of a diplomatic agent from the jurisdiction of the receiving State does not exempt him from the jurisdiction of the sending State.

Article 32

1. The immunity from jurisdiction of diplomatic agents and of persons enjoying immunity under Article 37 may be waived by the sending State.

2. Waiver must always be express.

3. The initiation of proceedings by a diplomatic agent or by a person enjoying immunity from jurisdiction under Article 37 shall preclude him from invoking immunity from jurisdiction in respect of any counter-claim directly connected with the principal claim.

4. Waiver of immunity from jurisdiction in respect of civil or administrative proceedings shall not be held to imply waiver of immunity in respect of the execution of the judgement, for which a separate waiver shall be necessary.

Article 33

1. Subject to the provisions of paragraph 3 of this Article, a diplomatic agent shall with respect to services rendered for the sending State be exempt from social security provisions which may be in force in the receiving State.

2. The exemption provided for in paragraph 1 of this Article shall also apply to private servants who are in the sole employ of a diplomatic agent, on condition:

(a) that they are not nationals of or permanently resident in the receiving State; and

(b) that they are covered by the social security provisions which may be in force in the sending State or a third State.

3. A diplomatic agent who employs persons to whom the exemption provided for in paragraph 2 of this Article does not apply shall observe the obligations which the social security provisions of the receiving State impose upon employers.

4. The exemption provided for in paragraphs 1 and 2 of this Article shall not preclude voluntary participation in the social security system of the receiving State provided that such participation is permitted by that State.

5. The provisions of this Article shall not affect bilateral or multilateral agreements concerning social security concluded previously and shall not prevent the conclusion of such agreements in the future.

Article 34

A diplomatic agent shall be exempt from all dues and taxes, personal or real, national, regional or municipal, except:

(a) indirect taxes of a kind which are normally incorporated in the price of the goods or services;

(b) dues and taxes on private immovable property situated in the territory of the receiving State, unless he holds it on behalf of the sending State for the purpose of the mission;

(c) estate, succession or inheritance duties levied by the receiving State, subject to the provisions of paragraph 4 of Article 39;

(d) dues and taxes on private income having its source in the receiving State and capital taxes on investments made in commercial undertakings in the receiving State;

(e) charges levied for specific services rendered;

(f) registration, court or record fees, mortgage dues and stamp duty, with respect to immovable property, subject to the provisions of Article 23.

Article 35

The receiving State shall exempt diplomatic agents from all personal services, from all public service of any kind whatsoever, and from military obligations such as those connected with requisitioning, military contributions and billeting.

Article 36

1. The receiving State shall, in accordance with such laws and regulations as it may adopt, permit entry of and grant exemption from all customs duties, taxes, and related charges other than charges for storage, cartage and similar services, on:

(a) articles for the official use of the mission;

(b) articles for the personal use of a diplomatic agent or members of his family forming part of his household, including articles intended for his establishment.

2. The personal baggage of a diplomatic agent shall be exempt from inspection, unless there are serious grounds for presuming that it contains articles not covered by the exemptions mentioned in paragraph 1 of this Article, or articles the import or export of which is prohibited by the law or controlled by the quarantine regulations of

the receiving State. Such inspection shall be conducted only in the presence of the diplomatic agent or of his authorized representative.

Article 37

1. The members of the family of a diplomatic agent forming part of his household staff, if they are not nationals of the receiving State, enjoy the privileges and immunities specified in Articles 29 to 36.

2. Members of the administrative and technical staff of the mission, together with members of their families forming part of their respective households, shall, if they are not nationals of or permanently resident in the receiving State, enjoy the privileges and immunities specified in Articles 29 to 35, except that the immunity from civil and administrative jurisdiction of the receiving State specified in paragraph 1 of Article 31 shall not extend to acts performed outside the course of their duties. They shall also enjoy the privileges specified in Article 31, paragraph 1, in respect of articles imported at the time of first installation.

3. Members of the service staff of the mission who are not nationals of or permanently resident in the receiving State shall enjoy immunity in respect of acts performed in the course of their duties, exemption from dues and taxes on the emoluments they receive by reason of their employment and the exemption contained in Article 33.

4. Private servants of members of the mission shall, if they are not nationals of or permanently resident in the receiving State, be exempt from dues and taxes on the emoluments they receive by reason of their employment. In other respects, they may enjoy privileges and immunities only to the extent admitted by the receiving State. However, the receiving State must exercise its jurisdiction over those persons in such manner as not to interfere unduly with the performance of the functions of the mission.

Article 38

1. Except insofar as additional privileges and immunities may be granted by the receiving State, a diplomatic agent who is a national of or permanently resident in that State shall enjoy only immunity from jurisdiction, and inviolability, in respect of official acts performed in the exercise of his functions.

2. Other members of the staff of the mission and private servants who are nationals of or permanently resident in the receiving State shall enjoy privileges and immunities only to the extent admitted by the receiving State. However, the receiving State must exercise its jurisdiction over those persons in such a manner as not to interfere unduly with the performance of the functions of the mission.

Article 39

1. Every person entitled to privileges and immunities shall enjoy them from the moment he enters the territory of the receiving State on proceeding to take up his post or, if already in its territory, from the moment when his appointment is notified to the Ministry for Foreign Affairs or such other ministry as may be agreed.

2. When the functions of a person enjoying privileges and immunities have come to an end, such privileges and immunities shall normally cease at the moment when he leaves the country, or on expiry of a reasonable period in which to do so, but shall subsist until that time, even in case of armed conflict. However, with respect to acts performed by such a person in the exercise of his functions as a member of the mission, immunity shall continue to subsist.

3. In case of the death of a member of the mission, the members of his family shall continue to enjoy the privileges and immunities to which they are entitled until the expiry of a reasonable period in which to leave the country.

4. In the event of the death of a member of the mission not a national of or permanently resident in the receiving State or a member of his family forming part of his household, the receiving State shall permit the withdrawal of the movable property of the deceased, with the exception of any property acquired in the country the export of which was prohibited at the time of his death. Estate, succession and inheritance duties shall not be levied on movable property the presence of which in the receiving State was due solely to the presence there of the deceased as a member of the mission or as a member of the family of a member of the mission.

Article 40

1. If a diplomatic agent passes through or is in the territory of a third State, which has granted him a passport visa if such visa was necessary, while proceeding to take up or return to his post, or when returning to his own country, the third State shall accord him inviolability and such other immunities as may be required to ensure his transit or return. The same shall apply in the case of any members of his family enjoying privileges or immunities who are accompanying the diplomatic agent, or travelling separately to join him or return to their country.

2. In circumstances similar to those specified in paragraph 1 of this Article, third States shall not hinder the passage of members of the administrative and technical or service staff of a mission, and of members of their families, through their territories.

3. Third States shall accord to official correspondence and other official communications in transit, including messages in code or cipher, the same freedom and protection as is accorded by the receiving State. They shall accord to diplomatic couriers, who have been granted a passport visa if such visa was necessary, and diplomatic bags in transit the same inviolability and protection as the receiving State is bound to accord.

4. The obligations of third States under paragraphs 1, 2 and 3 of this Article shall also apply to the persons mentioned respectively in those paragraphs, and to official communications and diplomatic bags, whose presence in the territory of the third State is due to *force majeur*.

Article 41

1. Without prejudice to their privileges and immunities, it is the duty of all persons enjoying such privileges and immunities to respect the laws and regulations of the receiving State. They also have a duty not to interfere in the internal affairs of that State.

2. All official business with the receiving State entrusted to the mission by the sending State shall be conducted with or through the Ministry for Foreign Affairs of the receiving State or such other ministry as may be agreed.

3. The premises of the mission must not be used in any manner incompatible with the functions of the mission as laid down in the present Convention or by other rules of general international law or by any special agreements in force between the sending and the receiving State.

Article 42

A diplomatic agent shall not in the receiving State practise for personal profit any professional or commercial activity.

Article 43

The function of a diplomatic agent comes to an end, *inter alia*:
(a) on notification by the sending State to the receiving State that the function of the diplomatic agent has come to an end;

(b) on notification by the receiving State to the sending State that, in accordance with paragraph 2 of Article 9, it refuses to recognize the diplomatic agent as a member of the mission.

Article 44

The receiving State must, even in case of armed conflict, grant facilities in order to enable persons enjoying privileges and immunities, other than nationals of the receiving State, and members of the families of such persons irrespective of their nationality, to leave at the earliest possible moment. It must, in particular, in case of need, place at their disposal the necessary means of transport for themselves and their property.

Article 45

If diplomatic relations are broken off between two States, or if a mission is permanently or temporarily recalled:
(a) the receiving State must, even in case of armed conflict, respect and protect the premises of the mission, together with its property and archives;
(b) the sending State may entrust the custody of the premises of the mission, together with its property and archives, to a third State acceptable to the receiving State;
(c) the sending State may entrust the protection of its interests and those of its nationals to a third State acceptable to the receiving State.

Article 46

A sending State may with the prior consent of a receiving State, and at the request of a third State not represented in the receiving State, undertake the temporary protection of the interests of the third State and of its nationals.

Article 47

1. In the application of the provisions of the present Convention, the receiving State shall not discriminate as between States.
2. However, discrimination shall not be regarded as taking place:
(a) where the receiving State applies any of the provisions of the present Convention restrictively because of a restrictive application of that provision to its mission in the sending State;
(b) where by custom or agreement States extend to each other more favourable treatment than is required by the provisions of the present Convention.

Article 48

The present Convention shall be open for signature by all States Members of the United Nations or of any of the specialized agencies or Parties to the Statute of the International Court of Justice, and by any other State invited by the General Assembly of the United Nations to become a Party to the Convention, as follows: until 31 October 1961 at the Federal Ministry for Foreign Affairs of Austria and subsequently, until 31 March 1962, at the United Nations Headquarters in New York.

Article 49

The present Convention is subject to ratification. The instruments of ratification shall be deposited with the Secretary-General of the United Nations.

Article 50

The present Convention shall remain open for accession by any State belonging to any of the four categories mentioned in Article 48. The instruments of accession shall be deposited with the Secretary-General of the United Nations.

Article 51

1. The present Convention shall enter into force on the thirtieth day following the date of deposit of the twenty-second instrument of ratification or accession with the Secretary-General of the United Nations.

2. For each State ratifying or acceding to the Convention after the deposit of the twenty-second instrument of ratification or accession, the Convention shall enter into force on the thirtieth day after deposit by such State of its instrument of ratification or accession.

Article 52

The Secretary-General of the United Nations shall inform all States belonging to any of the four categories mentioned in Article 48:

(a) of signatures to the present Convention and of the deposit of instruments of ratification or accession, in accordance with Articles 48, 49 and 50;

(b) of the date on which the present Convention will enter into force, in accordance with Article 51.

Article 53

The original of the present Convention, of which the Chinese, English, French, Russian and Spanish texts are equally authentic, shall be deposited with the Secretary-General of the United Nations, who shall send certified copies thereof to all States belonging to any of the four categories mentioned in Article 48.

IN WITNESS WHEREOF the undersigned Plenipotentiaries, being duly authorized thereto by their respective Governments, have signed the present Convention.

DONE at Vienna, this eighteenth day of April one thousand nine hundred and sixty-one.

Bibliography

In addition to standard reference works such as the *Dictionary of National Biography, American National Biography, Biographie Universelle – Ancienne et Moderne, Whitaker's Almanack,* and *The Statesman's Yearbook,* together with the diplomatic lists and foreign service lists of a number of states, the following were especially useful:

Adair, E. R., *The Exterritoriality of Ambassadors in the Sixteenth and Seventeenth Centuries* (Longman: London, 1929).

Adcock, Sir Frank, and D. J. Mosley, *Diplomacy in Ancient Greece* (Thames & Hudson: London, 1975).

Bailey, Sydney D. and Sam Daws, *The Procedure of the UN Security Council,* 3rd edn (Clarendon Press: Oxford, 1998).

Bainbridge, Timothy, *The Penguin Companion to European Union,* 2nd edn (Penguin Books: London, 1998).

Barston, R. P., *Modern Diplomacy,* 2nd edn (Longman: London, 1997).

Busk, Sir Douglas, *The Craft of Diplomacy: How to run a diplomatic service* (Praeger: New York, 1967).

Bynkershoek, Cornelius van, *De Foro Legatorum: The jurisdiction over ambassadors in both civil and criminal cases,* first publ. 1721, repr. (Oceana: New York, 1964).

Cable, James, *Gunboat Diplomacy, 1919–1979: Political applications of limited naval force,* 2nd edn (Macmillan – now Palgrave Macmillan: London, 1981).

Dembinski, Ludwig, *The Modern Law of Diplomacy. External Missions of States and International Organizations* (Nijhoff: Dordrecht, 1988, for the United Nations Institute for Training and Research).

Denza, Eileen, *Diplomatic Law: Commentary on the Vienna Convention on Diplomatic Relations,* 2nd edn (Clarendon Press: Oxford, 1998).

Detmold, Christian E., *The Historical, Political, and Diplomatic Writings of Niccolo Machiavelli* (James R. Osgood: Boston, 1882), vols. III and IV ('The Missions').

Gentili, Alberico, *De Legationibus Libri Tres,* first publ. 1585, repr. (Oceana: New York, 1964).

Goldstein, Erik, 'The Politics of the State Visit', *DSP Discussion Paper,* no. 26, Feb. 1997.

Gore-Booth, Lord, *Satow's Guide to Diplomatic Practice,* 5th edn (Longman: London, 1979).

Grenville, J. A. S. and B. Wasserstein, *The Major International Treaties Since 1945: A History and Guide with Texts* (Methuen: London and New York, 1987).

Hamilton, Keith and Richard Langhorne, *The Practice of Diplomacy: Its evolution, theory and administration* (Routledge: London, 1995).

Horn, D. B., *The British Diplomatic Service, 1689–1789* (Clarendon Press: Oxford, 1961).

Jennings, Sir Robert and Sir Arthur Watts (eds), *Oppenheim's International Law,* 9th edn (Longman: London, 1992).

Jones, Raymond A., *The British Diplomatic Service, 1815–1914* (Colin Smythe: Gerrards Cross, 1983).

Lachs, Phyllis S., *The Diplomatic Corps under Charles II and James II* (Rutgers University Press: New Brunswick, New Jersey, 1965).

Lee, Luke T., *Consular Law and Practice,* 2nd edn (Clarendon Press: Oxford, 1991).

Lloyd, Lorna, 'What's in a name? The curious tale of the office of high commissioner', *Diplomacy and Statecraft*, vol. 11, no. 1 (Mar. 2000), pp. 47–77.

Loeffler, Jane C., *The Architecture of Diplomacy: Building America's embassies* (Princeton Architectural Press: New York, 1998).

Mattingly, Garrett, *Renaissance Diplomacy* (Penguin: Harmondsworth, 1965).

McClanahan, Grant V., *Diplomatic Immunity. Principles, practices, problems* (Hurst: London, 1989, for the Institute for the Study of Diplomacy).

Newsom, David D. (ed.), *Diplomacy under a Foreign Flag* (Hurst: London, 1990; St. Martin's Press – now Palgrave Macmillan: New York, 1990, for the Institute for the Study of Diplomacy).

Nicolson, Harold, *Diplomacy*, 3rd edn (Oxford University Press: London, 1969).

Platt, D. C. M., *The Cinderella Service: British Consuls since 1825* (Longman: London, 1971).

Satow, Sir Ernest, *A Guide to Diplomatic Practice*, 2nd and revised edn (Longmans, Green: London, 1922).

Scruton, Roger, *A Dictionary of Political Thought*, 2nd edn (Macmillan – now Palgrave Macmillan: Basingstoke, 1996).

Sen, B., *A Diplomat's Handbook of International Law and Practice*, 2nd edn (Nijhoff: The Hague, 1979).

Shaw, Malcolm N., *International Law*, 4th edn (Grotius Publications: Cambridge,1997).

Shearer, I. A., *Starke's International Law*, 11th edn (Butterworths: London, 1994).

Steiner, Zara (ed.), *The Times Survey of Foreign Ministries of the World* (Times Books: London, 1982).

Thayer, Charles W., *Diplomat* (Michael Joseph: London, 1960).

Vattel, Emmerich de, *Le Droit des Gens*, first publ. 1758, repr. (Oceana: New York, 1964).

Wicquefort, Abraham de, *The Embassador and His Functions*, first publ. 1681, trsl. by John Digby in 1716, repr. (Centre for the Study of Diplomacy, Leicester University: Leicester, 1997).

Wolfe, Robert (ed.), *Diplomatic Missions. The Ambassador in Canadian Foreign Policy* (School of Policy Studies, Canadian Centre for Foreign Policy Development: Queen's University, Kingston, Ontario, 1998).

Wood, John R. and Jean Serres, *Diplomatic Ceremonial and Protocol: Principles, procedures and practices* (Macmillan: London, 1970).

Young, E., 'The development of the law of diplomatic relations', *The British Yearbook of International Law 1964*, vol. 40 (Oxford University Press: London and New York, 1966), pp. 141–82.

Zartman, I. William and Maureen R. Berman, *The Practical Negotiator* (Yale University Press: New Haven, 1982).

The authors have also drawn on the following previous works of their own:

Berridge, G. R., *Talking to the Enemy: How states without 'diplomatic relations' communicate* (Macmillan – now Palgrave Macmillan: Basingstoke, 1994).

—— *Diplomacy: Theory and Practice*, 2nd edn (Palgrave – now Palgrave Macmillan: Basingstoke, 2002).

James, Alan, 'Diplomacy and International Society', *International Relations*, vol. 6, no. 6 (Nov. 1980), pp. 931–48.

—— *Sovereign Statehood: The Basis of International Society* (Allen & Unwin: London, 1986).

—— 'Diplomatic relations and contacts', *The British Yearbook of International Law 1991*, vol. 62 (Clarendon Press: Oxford, 1992), pp. 347–87.